Organic,

I N C.

SAMUEL FROMARTZ

Organic,
INC.

Natural Foods
and How They Grew

HARCOURT, INC.

Orlando   Austin   New York   San Diego   Toronto   London

www.HarcourtBooks.com

Library of Congress Cataloging-in-Publication Data
Fromartz, Samuel.
Organic, inc.: natural foods and how they grew/Samuel Fromartz.—1st ed.
p.   cm.
Includes bibliographical references.
1. Natural foods industry.   2. Natural foods—Marketing.
3. Farm produce—Marketing.   I. Title.
HD9000.5.F765   2006
338.1'71584—dc22   2005031533
ISBN-13: 978-0-15-101130-8   ISBN-10: 0-15-101130-3

Text set in Adobe Caslon
Designed by Linda Lockowitz

Printed in the United States of America

First edition
A C E G I K J H F D B

To my wife
Ellen Chafee

Contents

Introduction

On January 26, 2005, a three-judge panel of the United States Court of Appeals for the First Circuit in Boston handed down a ruling in a case brought by a small organic blueberry farmer from Maine. Although unreported in the mainstream press, it sent shock waves through the $11 billion organic food industry, which had been growing without interruption for two decades or more. The ruling, it was feared, threatened to destabilize the entire sector by removing the ORGANIC label from a host of packaged goods or forcing the products to be reformulated. The label, which had taken effect a little over two years earlier, lay at the heart of consumer trust in organic food.

The farmer, Arthur Harvey, who was seventy-two, had waged the suit on his own, fed up with what the organic food industry had become—with its mainstream processed and packaged goods clogging the arteries of supermarkets; with what he saw as the abusive actions of the U.S. Department of Agriculture, which oversaw the program; with the entire regulatory mess that seemed to miss the point that organic food was supposed to be pure, wholesome, natural, and small-scale, a true alternative to conventional food. Somewhere along the way, organic food had gone hell-bent for growth, taking a turn away from the ideals that had given birth to the movement.

But rather than get angry about this state of affairs, Harvey had holed up on his farm in Hartford, Maine, and decided to get even. He knew the entire body of organic regulations, since as an organic certifier it was his responsibility to make sure other farmers abided by them, however objectionable he found them. He read through all 554 pages, comparing the rules with the underlying law that governs organic practices, the Organic Foods Production Act of 1990. He found inconsistencies that were strong enough, he thought, to sue the then secretary of agriculture Ann Veneman. Harvey had several complaints, but the most potent focused on the nonorganic synthetic ingredients that the regulations allowed in the processing of organic food, to ease manufacturing. He also objected to the way the rules reduced a 100 percent organic feed requirement when transitioning a cow to organic milk production. These lax practices, he thought, contravened the underlying law and cheapened the purity of organic food.

Harvey's lawyer told him the fight would cost $250,000—far more money than Harvey had. The $50,000 estimated by an environmental lawyer he contacted next was still too high. But Harvey wasn't dissuaded. "Since I was trained by the Maine Municipal Association to do my work on the planning board in my town, I knew enough about regulations to see what was wrong with the organic rule," he said. So he pursued the case on his own for $10,000, filing suit in October 2002, just days after the national organic regulations took effect with great fanfare.

It was not the first time Harvey had gone up against the federal government. As a tax resister opposed to military spending, "especially nuclear weapons, and the export of arms and military forces to many places around the world," Harvey had refused to file or pay federal income taxes since 1959. His wife, Elizabeth Gravalos, hadn't paid federal taxes since the

1970s. Instead, they donated time and money to social service and environmental organizations. The IRS had come knocking at their door a couple of times, then seized the family's property in 1996 and demanded $62,000 in back taxes and penalties—about three times the annual income of the farm. When they did not pay, the IRS took the rare step of auctioning off the property at a town office across the street from their house, with protesters outside. They initially lost the blueberry field to a bidder, though luckily no one bid on the house, perhaps because it had only rudimentary plumbing and no electricity. Eventually, Gravalos's mother bought the house, and the couple's daughter successfully bid on another parcel of the land, which she later swapped for the blueberry field. They were back in business.

Harvey, an affable and intelligent man with a wiry physique, perhaps owing to his vegetarian diet, said the lesson he learned from that fight was not to stop being a tax resister, but to avoid owning property in his own name that could be seized by the government. "We own a couple of cars, so I guess they could go after those, but they aren't worth much," he told me.

Now Harvey had taken on a battle with higher stakes, to return the organic food industry to its roots, away from crass commercialism, away from industry, away from all the compromises that two decades of growth had wrought. Whether Harvey would actually achieve that goal through the court system was an open question. But once the federal appeals court in Boston ruled in his favor on that cold day in January 2005, finding that the USDA regulations did contravene the underlying organic law, the industry perked up. Many were incensed, including those fighting on another front—to win over consumers so that more people would buy organic food, expanding the market and allowing more farmland to be converted to chemical-free organic food production. This camp was growing the industry with everything from organic candy to frozen TV dinners, along with dairy, fruits, vegetables, and meat. Craig Weakley, a longtime industry participant who was director of organic agriculture at Small Planet Foods, an organic food company owned by General Mills, said standards for organic food "were not broken, but unfortunately, someone decided to fix them and was able to convince three judges."

As Katherine DiMatteo, executive director of the Organic Trade Association, said at the time: "If this goes through, in the worst-case scenario, it could devastate the industry."

What was this battle about, and why did a small farmer feel compelled to take on a multibillion-dollar industry? How had organic food evolved to the point that an internal battle might rip it apart?

Questions like these had been on my mind for two years, as I traveled around the country, visiting organic farms, talking to people who had built this movement and industry, hearing their stories and learning what drove them to grow, make, and sell organic food.

I had a couple of strong motivations. I was a longtime business reporter, often gravitating toward the start-up arena, writing about people who were either naive or strong-headed enough to build new companies. I was particularly interested in people who sought to manifest their values in their businesses, who used business to extend a larger ethical or social mission. The intersection of idealism and business was not an easy place to stand, since one usually trumped the other, leading to a downward spiral of disillusionment or compromise. But I found a few who kept at it for the long haul, who managed to reach,

if not success, at least enough of a balance of idealism and prag-
matism to keep them going.

I wondered how this dynamic played out in the organic
food industry, springing as it did from a range of motives and
movements: back-to-the-land simplicity, agrarianism, anti-
industrialism, environmentalism, nutritional and health concerns,
and, of course, the love of fresh, whole, natural food. The foundation of the industry had been laid by strong-minded and
often eccentric idealists who took their ideas extremely seriously
and tried to realize them on the farm and within business, to
bring them into the world in a way that resonated with four
centuries of utopian pursuits in America. Harvey was just one
of the more volatile examples. There were many others like him
on this landscape, even among the entrepreneurs who loathed
him for what he was doing to the organic market. It took a
while to parse the specifics of Harvey's complaint and his adversaries' positions, to understand what it all meant—a book
really to put him in context, which is why I won't return to him
until the latter stages of this story.

My curiosity, though, was also selfish, fed by my appetite. I
had been aware of organic food since at least the early 1990s—
a sister was a devotee—but I didn't plunge in for another few
years. The turning point came not because of a health scare, or
some article about pesticides, or yet another nutrition study, or
because I started gardening, or suddenly became passionate
about the demise of family farms, or any of the other myriad
factors that lead consumers to buy organic food. It came because
I had moved from my hometown of Brooklyn to Washington,
D.C., for a new job and to move in with my future wife, Ellen.
Settled in our town house on Capitol Hill, I soon became
part of a small but noticeable wave of men with a bookshelf full

of cookbooks and multiple subscriptions to food magazines. Ellen had a hellish commute to work and didn't care much for cooking, so the kitchen became my domain. I was always on the lookout for the next best recipe, grilling salmon in the garden in the middle of winter, tossing dry rubs on pork loin, slow-braising short ribs in the oven, trying my hand at Moghlai Saag and Ma Po Tofu, making pizzas, pastas, and muffins on the weekend and sautéing any kind of green.

Soon I was baking bread, with various concoctions of sourdough starter taking up residence on top of the refrigerator, or in the oven where they could grow in the faint heat of the pilot light. Ellen called them my "experiments" and railed about flour on the floor, in drawers, and in cabinets. I bought books by artisan bakers, traded recipes and tips with other enthusiastic amateur cooks, sneering at the mention of a bread machine.

Generally, though, I sought fresh and flavorful foods, which could be prepared quickly, barbeque and Indian food being exceptions. But while I wasn't slaving over multicourse gourmet meals every night, cooking was more than a hobby. It had assumed a central place in my life. When I was single in New York, with a work schedule that regularly stretched into the evening, I'd eaten a lot of takeout and restaurant food and limited my cooking mostly to the weekend, much as I enjoyed it. Now, in a more domestic setting, with a paltry choice of decent places to dine nearby, I lost my appetite for eating out. "I could make this better at home!" I'd say, when faced with a subpar restaurant meal.

It was inevitable that this outlook would one day bring me to Whole Foods Market, already a fast-growing mecca for foodies in Washington. The first thing that grabbed me—just as it was designed to do—was the veritable garden of fresh fruits and vegetables that greeted me as I walked into the store. Containers of beautiful strawberries were piled next to raspberries from South America. Deep-red hothouse tomatoes from Holland, cherry tomatoes from Maryland, grape tomatoes from Baja, heirloom tomatoes from Pennsylvania. There was Lacinata kale, red and green Swiss chard, bok choy and baby bok choy, Napa cabbage, baby Asian greens, daikon radish, broccoli rabe, red-leaf, green-leaf, and romaine lettuce along with bulk spring mix. Organic peaches were available in the summer, apples and pears year-round. Not all of the produce was organic, but much of it was, and I began buying it, figuring the lack of pesticides was a bonus for freshness and taste. Then I would move around the perimeter of the store, trying my best not to dump fresh seafood and meat and dairy on top of the produce. It would have made more sense to pick up the veggies last, so that they would be on top, but the hard facts of consumer enticement had dictated the layout of the store: the gorgeous array of fresh fruits and vegetable were the gateway to this consumer paradise. They had certainly hooked me. Without kids, I didn't think much about cost. Quality was all.

In New York, you have to understand, I didn't do supermarkets because they were impossible, nasty, and crowded. I relied on old-fashioned neighborhood and specialty stores like the Staubitz butcher shop on Court Street in Brooklyn, and Sahadi's on Atlantic Avenue, where I stocked up on spices, dried fruit, hummus, thick Middle Eastern yogurt, and olive oil. In Greenwich Village, there was Murray's Cheese Shop, where the long wait was exceeded only by the number of exotic cheeses in stock, and Faicco's Pork Store across the street, with unequaled Italian sausage. You got fresh pasta at Rafetto's on Houston Street and fresh mozzarella scooped by hand from the vat in the back of Joe's Dairy on Sullivan Street. Then I would bike down to Chinatown for bargain seafood and vegetables or visit Russ

& Daughters on the Lower East Side for smoked salmon and pickled herring, as my elderly father kibitzed with the staff.

But in Washington, I discovered that Whole Foods had brought many of these specialty foods into one convenient, upscale setting. Even the lighting was spectacular—it was designed, a marketing consultant told me, to make people look better, feel better, and thus want to buy more. The quality of the goods themselves wasn't always up to the stuff I bought in New York, but it was high, the produce especially.

I began to notice something else, too. The store was getting more and more crowded and competition for parking had become fierce. Soon, Whole Foods offered valet parking—at a supermarket!—but it was free, so I took advantage of it. My business instincts kicked in, no doubt influenced by the awareness of how much money we were spending at Whole Foods each week—and by implication, how much others must be spending, too.

I decided to get a piece of the action. Following the dictum of stock market guru Peter Lynch, who quaintly advised investing in what you knew, in companies you liked, I bought Whole Foods stock. This time, at least, it worked. Moreover, owning the stock justified whatever superfluous purchases struck my fancy—French soaps, organic orange juice, a pricey T-bone, sushi-quality tuna, Venezuelan chocolate, Italian ricotta. If they swelled Whole Foods' bottom line, they also swelled mine.

The more I spent at the store, the more I made on the stock, give or take a few swoons along the way, such as the company's ill-advised launch of a natural-food dot-com. Luckily, though, it always returned to what it knew best—selling good food in a pleasant atmosphere. And it grew steadily, even as the economy dipped into a brief recession. Overall, I earned a return in excess of 130 percent by the time I sold the stock, over a period ending in mid-2002, when I began this book project (thus cutting my sole financial connection to the organic food industry). Ellen and I had, in effect, eaten for free at Whole Foods for two and a half years. Had I continued to own the stock, it would now be up more than sixfold.

Who would have thought that a natural-food supermarket could have offered a financial refuge from the dot-com bust? But it had. Sales of organic food had shot up about 20 percent per year since 1990, reaching $11 billion by 2003, and had garnered outsized attention in the $460 billion supermarket industry. Whole Foods had grown in lockstep with the organic sector, which was no mean feat. Greater sales meant greater profits. With 172 stores in the United States, Canada, and Britain, where it had purchased the Fresh & Wild chain, it had become a growth company boasting $4 billion in sales in a stagnant industry littered with casualties, thanks to Wal-Mart's strategy of "everyday low prices." Whole Foods managed to sidestep that fray by focusing on, well, people like me. And it had done so without many noticeable marketing expenditures, like the insert ads or double coupons that supermarkets routinely offer to keep customers shopping.

Something besides advertising was driving this market and Whole Foods had tapped into it. It was the alternative supermarket not just for foodies but for the health conscious, for mothers concerned about what their kids were eating, for anyone who was uneasy about the conventional food system and all of its familiar brands. The trend wasn't lost on mainstream industry, which reacted by creating organic food aisles (or ghettos) in their stores or by buying up organic food companies for market share.

But my odyssey wasn't over. I began to shop at farmers' markets, which had proliferated in the 1990s, spurred by chefs, the food media, and the obvious quality they offered. I had shopped at them sporadically over the years in New York, but it wasn't until I came to Washington and began cooking in earnest that I became a devotee. I often visited Eastern Market, the oldest market in the city, near our home. Then I began to frequent the Dupont Circle FreshFarm Market, which was "producers only"— only growers could sell there, not vendors who pick up produce at wholesale markets.

The bounty was unmatched, even by the hyperaggressive standards of Whole Foods. And it was fun. I began to experiment with grass-fed beef, heirloom pork, eggs from pastured poultry, along with the usual seasonal vegetables and fruit. I looked forward to the market each weekend, got to know a few of the farmers, and slowly began to insinuate myself into their world. If the farmers weren't too busy, I could ask about their farms and their growing practices.

Whole Foods, it seemed, had figured out how to change the staid model of supermarkets, borrowing from the arena of specialty food stores and by heightening the customer experience. But the farmers' markets had done something similar, renewing a traditional model of direct produce sales and becoming the local alternative to the distant, anonymous farm, bringing the farmer into focus for the consumer.

Often I would load up with fresh produce at the farmers' market and then make a run to Whole Foods—which by then had opened a huge store on P Street in Washington—before heading home. The quality of the goods was a link between the two, but I wondered whether there was any implicit contradiction. Did Whole Foods represent a threat to the farmers' survival, or had the chain and its ilk ramped up the market for the

local farmers by converting new customers, as they had done
with me?

This was my starting point, what got me interested in organic
food. I am not an agrarian writing about the deep meaning of
the land, nor a gardener focused on the best organic methods,
nor a nutritionist in pursuit of the ideal diet, nor an environmental advocate preoccupied with ecology. I am a consumer
who began to buy organic food, and then wanted to understand
why. I sought to parse the myths from the realities and meet the
people who were feeding me.

Along the way, I did learn about Jeffersonian agrarianism,
organic methods and regulations, ecology, pesticides and horticulture, vegetarianism, spiritual food impulses, composting, food
safety, and the diet of an ethnographic group of people who live
in northern Pakistan, but only to inform the larger cause.
Mostly, I spent time with people who created the organic market: a farmer who gave birth to a local food network in Washington, D.C.; a Californian who is credited with revolutionizing
organic strawberry-growing methods; a New York City–born
couple who became the largest organic produce sellers in the nation, if not the world; a Boulder-based guru of soy milk who
created the largest organic packaged foods brand. My background as a business reporter gave me the skills to see how these
people worked and what made the industry click into high gear.
In this way, the two sides of my life—work and home, writing
and cooking—came together in a way I never really expected.

This endeavor was a moving target. As I became a more informed consumer, my choices about what foods to buy, and
where to buy them, evolved. In the same way, the organic food
industry was evolving, too, altered by the consumers and producers coming into the fold, the choices of what products to

make and how to make them, and simple market economics. Whole Foods grew up, as did a host of other companies that had started out as small farms and artisan ventures. Some participants left, clearly disillusioned. The success I participated in as a Whole Foods shareholder was heightening a tension with the founding ideals of the movement. This in no small way reflected the people involved, some of whom tempered the counterculture idealism of their youth and took jobs to alter the food economy in consumer-friendly ways. Such compromises rang hollow with the purists, however.

This, of course, is the nature of evolution, which dilutes the original gene pool to maintain survival. For some, like Arthur Harvey, too much of the founding essence had been compromised, sold out. But for an industry accounting for little more than 2 percent of food sales, 0.3 percent of crop- and pastureland, 2 percent of vegetable acreage, and less than 1 percent of all farms, Harvey's opponents thought the movement was just beginning.

Organic,
I N C .

1. Humus Worshippers

The Origins of Organic Food

*The birthright of all living things is health. This law is true
for soil, plant, animal and man: the health of these four is one
connected chain. Any weakness or defect in the health of any
earlier link in the chain is carried on to the next and succeeding
links, until it reaches the last, namely, man.*
—SIR ALBERT HOWARD, 1945

In 1998, Chensheng Lu, a researcher at the Department of
Health at the University of Washington, began testing children
in the Seattle area to see whether he could detect pesticide
residues in their urine. He was looking for signs of organophosphates, a class of chemicals closely related to nerve agents developed during World War II, which subsequently came into
widespread use as pesticides in a far less potent form, eventually
accounting for half of all insecticide use in the United States.
The chemicals inactivate enzymes crucial to the nervous and
hormonal system, which, at high enough levels of exposure, can
lead to symptoms as various as mild anxiety or respiratory paralysis. Long-term exposure increases the risk of neurobehavioral
damage, cancer, and reproductive disorders.

Lu and his colleagues thought that children living near
farms would have the highest levels of pesticide residues, since

they were subject to drift from nearby fields. But the 110 two- to five-year-olds he studied in the Seattle metropolitan area turned out to have higher levels of pesticide metabolites (the markers produced when the body metabolizes the chemicals). This suggested that food residues or home pesticide use, not drift, were the primary path for exposure.

The study also had a curious anomaly: One child out of the hundreds they had studied had no signs of any pesticide metabolites.

"It was kind of surprising," said Lu, who now directs the Pesticide Exposure and Risk Laboratory at Emory University's Rollins School of Public Health in Atlanta. When the researchers interviewed the parents, they learned the family ate organic food almost exclusively.

This provided the first hint of scientific evidence that an organic food diet reduced pesticide exposure in children. Another study looked at pesticide residue data from 94,000 food samples from 1994–1999 and found organic food had about two-thirds less residues than conventional food. This showed that organic consumers were getting what they paid for—lower pesticides in food—but the study looked only at what was in the overall food supply, not what people ate. By identifying metabolites in the urine—through a technique known as biomonitoring—the researchers had evidence of pesticides children had actually consumed.

Cynthia Curl, another scientist then at the University of Washington, followed up on Lu's finding and published the results in March 2003. She showed that a group of children who ate mostly organic food had one-sixth the pesticide metabolites of those who ate nonorganic food, but the study could not identify the pesticides, or determine their risk, since many different ones produced the same markers. The study only concluded that eating organic food reduced the children's risk of exposure to harmful pesticides from an "uncertain" level to a "negligible" one.

Lu, with funding from the Environmental Protection Agency, has since buttressed this conclusion. When a research team he led substituted organic foods for a conventional diet in children for five days, they could find no evidence of pesticide metabolites in their urine. When they reintroduced conventional foods, the metabolites returned. The paper concluded that an organic food diet provided "a protective mechanism" against pesticide exposure in a manner that "is dramatic and immediate."

Although the potential risks incurred by pesticide exposures over a lifetime are unknown, people who choose to eat organic for this reason have, in effect, decided to opt out of an ongoing social experiment into whether pesticides are safe. Given the number of pesticides that were once freely used but have since been removed from the market for health reasons, this is not a wild or unreasonable choice. For children the reasoning seems even clearer.

Chemicals are up to ten times more toxic in the developing bodies of infants and children than in adults, according to a 1993 report by the National Academy of Sciences (NAS), a nonpartisan, government-funded research body. At ages one to five, children also eat three to four times more food per pound of body weight than adults, and their diet is far more concentrated (infants consume seventeen times more apple juice than the U.S. average, for example). So not only are children subject to a higher dose of pesticides, but the chemicals also have a greater impact on their bodies. That conclusion, reached in the NAS study, led to an overhaul of U.S. pesticide laws in 1996, charging the EPA to consider the impact of pesticides on children, a reevaluation process that is still going on.

"If you can reduce some risk from some usage or pathway, you actually reduce your overall risk," Lu said. "And it just so happens, for kids, the majority of exposure comes from dietary intake. So the benefit can be quite overwhelming."

The curious thing about this conclusion was that the people who were buying organic food—largely women, who make most household purchasing decisions, and especially mothers—already assumed it was true. It was common sense. If you ate food from organic farms that shunned toxic pesticides, less residue would end up in your body. You might not know what substance you were avoiding, or what the actual risk was, but that didn't really matter. Why consume pesticides at all if they added no nutritional value and might be detrimental to health? And why not support a farmer who had figured out how to produce food without them? This wasn't a giant leap of faith but a conclusion consumers could easily reach, even if it required them to pay more for food.

Food scares have simply reinforced this conclusion, since they feed on consumer unease with the conventional food system. This became apparent in 1989, when CBS's *60 Minutes* aired a report about Alar, a pesticide that the government kept on the market even though it was a probable human carcinogen. Sprayed on apples, the pesticide was converted into a potential carcinogen when apples were heat-processed into juice and applesauce, products largely consumed by children. In the spotlight, the EPA banned the substance, saying that "long-term exposure to Alar poses unacceptable risks to public health." The entire episode created, as *Newsweek* put it, "A Panic For Organic," which was a mixed blessing for the young industry, since stores soon faced shortages of organic food and fraudulent items appeared, leading Congress to pass national organic food regulations in 1990.

More recent scares, surrounding meat, have had a similar effect, notably in Europe. Mad cow disease (bovine spongiform encephalopathy) arose in 1986, it is believed, from animal by-products that were once routinely fed to livestock. By the mid-nineties, the British government acknowledged that people who had eaten the meat of infected animals were dying from a new variant of Creutzfeldt-Jakob disease, which began with depression or anxiety and progressed to a crippling of the brain and death. More than 150 people died and cattle herds across Europe had to be destroyed. In late 2003, the first case of mad cow appeared in the United States, several years after cattle feed rules were revamped. No human deaths were attributed to the disease, nor did meat sales suffer, but organic meat sales jumped 78 percent. While the risk of tainted meat may be infinitesimally small, that didn't really address the main fear. Why had the conventional food industry taken these risks, anyway, when the natural diet of cattle was grass, not other animals?

Yet while a third of American women and a quarter of all men believe that pesticides, hormones, and antibiotics in food production pose a "high risk" to health, the growth of the organic food industry cannot be entirely attributed to food scares, which make headlines and then fade away. Nor can its rise be explained by fears about pesticides, although they, too, play a central role. Buying and consuming organic food has come to be viewed not only as a means of avoiding harm but as a benefit in itself, a personal way of aligning nutrition, health, and social and environmental well-being. A mother might buy organic apple juice for her child because she views it as healthier; a twenty-something single making a meal with friends might choose organic lettuce mix because she thinks it's better for the environment; a couple planning to celebrate a special occasion with a fancy dinner at a restaurant might seek a chef who relies upon organic food grown by small farmers and harvested at its peak. Where food comes from, who grows and processes it, and what happens to people and the environment along the way can bestow attributes that make it extra appealing. "Consumers don't just taste food, they experience it, and knowing a product came from a food system that treats farmers well may well enhance its flavor," researchers at Tufts University in Boston write.

While critics often portray organic farming as a preindustrial anachronism practiced by aging hippies, romantics, Luddites, and quacks who are incapable of feeding the world, this characterization never seems to get very far with consumers because it misses the central premise. Organic food exists because, like any industry, it fulfills a need, in this case arising from lapses in the perceived quality and safety of conventional food production, and from the desire for an alternative predicated upon personal and environmental health. This demand has not been manufactured (nor could it be—total U.S. sales of organic food in 2003 amounted to only a third of the $29 billion that conventional food firms shelled out for advertising that year). Demand has arisen because an alternative to the status quo implicitly made sense.

But the perception of organic food as environmentally sound and "healthier" didn't appear out of thin air. Organic food was invented in the early twentieth century, not out of a blind yearning for an agrarian past, but as a reaction to new agricultural methods and materials whose purpose was to raise output and yield. The organic pioneers wanted to go forward, but on the premise that human, animal, and environmental health were not worth sacrificing for greater production.

Although strains of an alternative movement arose even further back, it was the British organic movement of the 1920s–

1940s, which took shape as industrial methods reached the countryside, that first articulated the concerns about food production that would emerge decades later, with greater urgency. The organic pioneers came up not only with the methods but also with an alternative conception of what farming should be.

Among the most influential figures was Sir Albert Howard, a British agricultural scientist still revered in organic circles today. In India, where Howard developed new breeds of tobacco, linseed, and wheat, he was intrigued by the methods of local peasants, who grew a surplus of crops by relying on compost; he also noticed that oxen developed a high degree of disease immunity when fed from crops grown in rich composted soil. He sought the scientific basis for these observations, theorizing that the end result of a sound farming system was health. Healthy soil meant more vigorous plants, healthier animals, and more nutritious food. As British historian Philip Conford has noted, the founders came to view the organic method as a kind of "preventive medicine," with health seen as the "harmonious functioning" of a whole system.

The organic school was also reacting against the new trend of boosting crop yields through chemical fertilizers advocated by German chemist Justus von Liebig. Von Liebig had argued in 1840 that chemicals could replace manure, since it was the minerals in manure that were the source of fertility. "Organic matters, however useful they are in manures, may be dispensed with; art is capable of providing a substitute for them," Liebig said. If nitrogen, potassium, and phosphorous were fed to a plant in the proper amounts, even on depleted soils, the plant would grow. The point was to feed the plant, rather than to nurture complex biological activity within the soil.

This approach implied an entirely new type of farming system. In the pre-chemical age, a farmer could ensure soil fertility only by spreading organic matter, such as manure, fish, or bird guano, or planting a leguminous crop that could add nitrogen to the soil, or growing a cover crop that would then be plowed into the soil. In addition to adding nutrients to the soil, these methods would enhance water retention and stave off soil erosion. Thomas Jefferson, who encountered weak soils at Monticello, his hilltop Virginia estate, became a big proponent. "We will try this winter to cover our garden with a heavy coating of manure," he wrote to his daughter in 1793. "When earth is rich it bids defiance to droughts, yields in abundance, and of the best quality." But Jefferson was the exception in his time and place, when the predominant method of guaranteeing successive cash crops of tobacco or corn was to abandon exhausted fields and clear fresh land by burning virgin forest. In America, this approach had propelled the westward settlement of the continent.

The advent of synthetic fertilizers in the twentieth century provided a way to grow the same crops year after year on the same soil, with less labor. Farmers still spread manure, but they began to rely primarily upon synthetic fertilizers, ensuring more intensive production on a fixed quantity of land.

Howard opposed chemical fertilizers because he thought they represented a highly mechanistic approach to soil fertility that never added up to a complete whole. Like other organic pioneers, many of whom were also agronomists, chemists, and doctors, he wasn't antiscientific or antiprogressive; he simply sought to work within natural systems. He got his chance in 1924, when he became director of the Institute of Plant Industry, a British research hub in the Indian state of Indore, and came up with a way of creating compost in quantity.

The so-called Indore method, Howard's legacy, would be familiar to any backyard or commercial compost maker today.

Each day at the institute, workers bedded the animal stalls with vegetative waste, wood shavings, and sawdust. The next day, the bedding, now filled with animal "residues," was removed to the compost pile. Every three months, the earth beneath the animals was broken up and added to the pile, as an "activator" to help break down the organic waste. Once the material had amassed into a windrow about thirty feet long, fifteen feet wide, and three feet deep, water was added to maintain the consistency of a "pressed-out sponge" and crowbars were plunged in at regular intervals to keep oxygen circulating, feeding bacteria and fostering decomposition. The piles were turned every few weeks to stimulate biological activity that processes organic matter and kills off pathogens. Turned into the soil, the finished compost adds nitrogen, increases the flow of oxygen, improves tilth, or texture, retains water, and supports bacteria and fungi, aiding plant growth. Unlike chemical fertilizers, compost decomposes slowly, so excess nutrients are less likely to drain out into groundwater or streams.

Howard postulated that composted soil improved plant health. "The maintenance of soil fertility is the real basis of health and of resistance to disease," he wrote in *An Agricultural Testament*, published in 1940. In contrast, the Liebig method of chemical fertilizers "is based on a complete misconception of plant nutrition. It is superficial and fundamentally unsound . . . Artificial manures lead inevitably to artificial nutrition, artificial food, artificial animals, and finally to artificial men and women." Compost's positive attributes would cascade down the food chain. He cited several examples in his work, including a school in New Zealand that replaced chemical fertilizers with compost in its vegetable plots. "Formerly, in the days when artificials (chemical fertilizers) were used, colds, measles and scarlet fever used to run through the school. Now they tend to be confined to the single case brought in from outside," he wrote. He also asserted that organic vegetables tasted better because of the quality of soil. Chemical fertilizers produced vegetables that were "tough, leathery and fibrous: they also lack taste," he said.

The ideal Howard sought was nature itself, where animals roamed the forest and spread manure, and plants grew and died amid a diverse ecology. In nature, all the biological elements worked in concert. The core of the system lay on the forest floor, where decaying leaves, bark, stems and flowers, animal droppings, grasses, rodents, fungi—all of it, every remnant of a once-growing organism—combined with soil to make nature's fertilizer. Fed by rain and air, billions of invisible microbes feasted on this organic matter and broke it down. The result, humus, was the fertility source for all plants, which in turn were the sustenance for all animal life. The forest's "closed nutrient cycle"—as ecologists now call it—thrived in a cycle of death and regeneration.

Howard was influenced by the Eastern spiritual concept of the mandala, in which any sphere of life (or death) is connected with all others. "Such are the essential facts in the wheel of life. Growth on one side: decay on the other," he wrote. "The only man-made systems of agriculture—those to be found in the East—which have stood the test of time have faithfully copied this rule in Nature." He thought modern agriculture had ignored this balance, coaxing more nutrients from the soil than it could return, and thereby depleting fertility. As a result, farming had become "unbalanced," the two halves of the wheel of life unhinged. "All over the world our capital is being squandered," he wrote. "The restoration and maintenance of soil fertility has become a universal problem."

Howard was not isolated in this concern, nor in the naturalistic alternative approach he proposed to remedy it. In Germany, Rudolph Steiner founded biodynamic farming, which sprang from his mystical view of nature and the age-old methods of European peasants. Civilization, he wrote in the 1920s, had lost "its knowledge of what it takes to continue to care for the natural world. The most important things are no longer known." Biodynamic farmers, like organic ones, avoided chemicals, but they also tried "to improve the health and vitality of soil" by working with "the health-bearing forces of nature," as one group described it. If the soil was healthy, "seeds will bring forth plants which are true to their own unique nature and have more life-giving vitality to offer animals and humans."

The movement endured, and like their founders, biodynamic farmers today look to lunar and planetary calendars for auspicious times for planting. They rely on preparations made from, among other things, manure stuffed into cows' horns, and dandelions placed inside cows' entrails, buried over the winter, dug up in the spring and diluted, and sprayed on fields or compost to stimulate biological activity and harness "astral energies." One organic farmer I met in California admitted he did not buy the cosmology, but he swore by the quality of the compost (since organic farmers are, if nothing else, pragmatic). A biodynamic farmer I buy from at the FreshFarm market, Swiss-born Heinz Thomet of Next Step Produce, has some of the best organic vegetables I have sampled but says he doesn't always have time to follow proper biodynamic preparations or adhere strictly to the planting calendar. He and others I spoke with suggested that a big dose of the cosmology really amounts to observation, to being attuned to and working with ecological systems. "It's really about good farming," he said. Organic farming has thrived in large part on highly practical methods that originated with spiritual and idealistic motivations.

As for Howard, by the time he left India in 1931, the Indore institute was producing a thousand tons of compost annually, and the surrounding fields stood out like a "green jewel" in the countryside. With the publication of Howard's work, the Indore method quickly spread. One British farmer adopted it on a three-hundred-acre estate and in 1939 began selling organic vegetables in London. The method was adapted to coffee plantations outside Nairobi, to hemp and orange groves in Rhodesia, and to sugarcane plantations in South Africa, which by 1949 were collectively making a half-million cubic yards of compost annually. In Malaysia, a health officer who heard Howard's lectures built several municipal composting systems. Coconut and rubber plantations adopted the methods in Asia. In Central America, Howard's work was translated into Spanish and applied to coffee plantations. Although the organic movement had a strong affinity with agrarianism and small-scale farming, the method as Howard conceived it was not limited by scale. It couldn't be, if the aim was to be the alternative to chemically intensive farming.

So even before World War II, food, health, and soil had been linked in a foundational concept that guided the emerging organic food movement, a holy trinity that lives on in the Whole Foods tagline: "Whole Food, Whole People, Whole Planet." But not just any food—the *right* kind of foods, processed minimally and without additives, and preferably purchased close to their source. As in farming, the best food would be "natural," too.

A prominent British physician and authority on nutrition, Major General Robert McCarrison, made this link explicitly for the organic movement early in his career. Like Howard, he traveled to India, in 1907, to the region Conford refers to as a Shangri-la for the early organic movement, the mountainous realm where the Hindu Kush, Karakoram, and Himalayan ranges meet in what is now northern Pakistan, near the borders of China and Afghanistan.

During the seven years McCarrison worked among the native population there, the Hunza, he claimed to have found no one with heart disease, cancer, appendicitis, peptic ulcer, diabetes, or multiple sclerosis. They owed their long and healthful lives, McCarrison said, to exercise, low alcohol consumption, and a simple, complete diet that consisted of whole wheat flour, from which they made chapati bread, dal made of lentils and other legumes, fresh vegetables and fruit, dairy products, and little meat. They farmed narrow terrace plots fed by ancient aqueducts that channeled glacial waters to their fields; gathered animal manure, vegetative waste, and night soil and "spread out the compost evenly like butter upon bread"; and produced crops that seemed remarkably free of disease. "They follow, in a word, the garden culture of the immemorial East," he said.

McCarrison juxtaposed photographs of the Hunza, who as colonial porters had earned a reputation among the British for their "superior physique" and exceptional stamina, with people he termed the "poorer races" of India to show how superior the mountain tribe appeared. But unlike popular eugenicists of the day, who attributed this supposed racial superiority to breeding, McCarrison thought the differences were due to nutrition. The average Bengali or Madrassi subsisted on polished rice, robbed of what nutritious value the crop had; they consumed few milk products, no meat, and little fresh fruit or vegetables. "As the quality of the diet diminishes with respect to proteins, fats, minerals and vitamins, so do physical efficiency and health; a rule which applies with equal force to the European as to the Indian," he wrote.

McCarrison decided to compare this natural diet with foods the modern British ate, by feeding both to rats. One group was fed the diet of Sikhs, which was similar to that of the Hunza, and the other, a diet of the "poorer classes in Britain," which consisted of white bread, margarine, sweetened tea with milk, boiled cabbage and potatoes, and tinned meat and jam "of the cheaper sorts." On the Sikh diet, the rats "lived happily together," increased in weight and flourished, while those on the modern English diet became "stunted" and lived "unhappily together." Like a bunch of soccer hooligans, the latter bit the attendants and then began to kill and eat the weaker members of the group. On a postmortem exam after the six-month experiment ended, McCarrison found a higher incidence of lung and gastrointestinal disease among the rats on the British diet. "We do in fact, find that these two classes of ailment are amongst the most frequent of the maladies afflicting the poorer class Britisher," he said.

Just as chemical farming sapped soil fertility, the foods produced by the industrial system diminished health. Lost in the rush to modernity were all the nutrients found in whole foods grown in heavily composted soil. The arguments advanced by Howard and McCarrison spread in the interwar years in magazines and through Britain's first health-food restaurants, laying a foundation for today's alternative food movement. Unquestionably they and other organic pioneers romanticized the East, in their celebration of the noble, ageless Hunza peasants. "They are a people perhaps as ancient as the Incas but who unlike the Incas, have survived, and in their survival have preserved their ancient lore, and in the preservation of that lore have preserved the wholeness of their health and that of their crops and livestock," said Lady Eve Balfour, author of *The Living Soil* and the first president of the Soil Association, Britain's leading organic institution, founded in 1946. Such mythical views of the East were part of a "continuing European romance in which the West perceives some lack within itself and fantasizes that the answer, through a process of projection, is to be found somewhere in the East," observes contemporary scholar of Tibetan Buddhism Donald Lopez.

Yet McCarrison was clearly on to something, for the northern Indian diet he describes is not dissimilar to what doctors and nutritionists recommend today to combat heart disease, diabetes, and obesity. A diet of whole grains, fresh vegetables, fruit, and legumes, with modest consumption of meat and alcohol, would be low in cholesterol and high in complex carbohydrates. The only quibble might be over how much whole-fat dairy one should consume. The diet also seems similar in principle to that popularized by Miami cardiologist Arthur Agatston, whose South Beach diet was all the rage while I was reading up on McCarrison. Agatston came upon his diet to combat heart disease among his patients, then turned it into a bestseller when they lost weight on it. After an initial low-carb phase, the South Beach diet focuses on whole grains, vegetables and fruit, low-fat dairy and eggs, lean meat, fish, and little alcohol. "Bad" carbohydrates, like sugar and white bread, are frowned upon. Agatston and others see a diet high in refined foods as the engine of a boom-bust cycle of satiation and hunger that leads to weight gain. The body easily digests these foods, spiking blood sugar levels and pushing the pancreas into overdrive to produce insulin and channel the excess sugar to muscles, organs, or fat. By working so hard, the insulin eventually depletes blood sugar, causing energy to flag and hunger to arise, leading to a new cycle of consumption and depletion. Proteins, fats, fiber, acidic foods and complex carbohydrates like vegetables, on the other hand, are digested more slowly, allowing the pancreas to go about its work in a more reasonable way, keeping blood sugar steady and better controlling hunger cravings. But like any diet, Agatston also restricted calories, which is the key to weight loss along with exercise.

A diet of high-fiber foods—vegetables, legumes, nuts, and whole-grain foods—can have other benefits, too. A Harvard University study of forty-three thousand health professionals found a 41 percent lower risk of heart attack on a high-fiber diet. Another study, of nearly twenty-two thousand Finnish men, found that those who ate high fiber each day had a 31 percent lower risk of heart disease. A study of more than forty thousand Iowa women also found a lower risk of heart disease among those who ate whole grains. The diet is also associated with lower rates of diabetes.

The South Beach diet didn't offer up anything that nutritionists were not already saying, but thanks to its association with buff South Beach models, it took off, becoming the latest spin on a nutritional approach that echoed back to McCarrison's findings about the Hunza.

The organic pioneers also found objects of veneration closer to home, in the small farmers, artisan craftsman, and rural village life then fading from the English countryside under pressure of modernization. Reinvigorating the small farmer by ensuring a "just price" for food could save the farm and civilization itself from the path of self-destruction brought on by agribusiness, chemical methods, money-lending, and middlemen—an argument reprised in the 1970s by agrarian essayist Wendell Berry. In Britain's interwar years, these ideas fit neatly into a Christian concept of a Natural Order, in which the farmer and organic methods embodied God's work.

In the wrong hands, however, the idea became perverse. In the 1930s, for example, a virulent fascist right conceived of a natural order overseen by a superior white race, whose land-based wealth avoided the corruptions of industry. Conford notes that in one publication, a glowing review of *Mein Kampf* appeared next to articles on the virtues of organic animal husbandry. British protofascists thought agrarian life could revitalize the urban-bound Englishman, and prevent the nation from being overrun by "the unfit and the alien and from the lowest types." Others talked about the organic ideal as a return to a Golden Age of yeomen and craftsmen that had been destroyed by capitalism, socialism, and Jews. This was by no means the only strain in the organic movement of the time, but it was a central one. A natural order, as an alternative to the industrializing world, metastasized into concepts of racial superiority.

Today's organic movement appears to be more closely associated with blue states and liberal baby-boomer enclaves, but it, too, has its radical right fringe. Joe Smillie, a longtime organic farm certifier with Quality Assurance International, told me he had visited right-wing militants in Montana to certify their organic grain farms. One farmer even took him to his basement to show him his arsenal of weapons. Terry Nichols, convicted in the 1995 Oklahoma City bombing, once farmed organically. His brother James, who appears in Michael Moore's documentary *Bowling for Columbine*, was an organic soybean farmer.

This should not be too surprising, since the rural right wing surged in the 1980s, when rising interest rates and falling commodity prices crushed many debt-laden independent farmers. A simplistic message laying the blame for this collapse on industrial farming, bank lending, the federal government, the New World Order, the United Nations, globalism, Jews, and immigrants found an audience among the newly disenfranchised. Organic farming not only provided a libertarian economic alternative to the "system," but it also dovetailed with doctrines like the "salubrious living" promoted by the Church of the Creator, which advocated "eating fresh wholesome food in its natural state" as well as the perpetuation of the white race. The Southern Poverty Law Center, which tracks these extreme groups, reported that deep ecologists on the left found common ground with the militant rural right in their antiglobalist agrarian agenda. Both might be surprised to know that they are bedfellows with that last bastion of socialism Cuba, whose renowned organic farms and widespread organic city gardens are the result not so much of political belief as economic necessity, after an embargo limited foreign chemical imports to the country.

The organic movement contains an extremely wide spectrum of participants. They may be driven by health and nutritional concerns, a family or personal history of illness, fear of pesticides, environmental ideals, adherence to principles of agrarianism or biodynamics, spiritual or religious beliefs, a desire for high-quality fresh food, left- or right-wing politics, a commitment to sustainable farming, economic necessity or economic opportunism. This diversity has always been a strength of the movement, since it increases the pool of potential consumers and prevents any one interest group from controlling its fate. At the same time, it has led to pitched conflicts, especially between those who are determined to grow organic farming above all and those who primarily want to protect family farmers from economic annihilation. But one belief about food unites all—they are the alternative to the status quo.

Before this alternative movement could take off, it had to be popularized. J. I. Rodale, perhaps the most influential figure in the American organic food movement, grew up on the Lower East Side of Manhattan, the son of Polish Jewish immigrants who owned a grocery store and wanted him to become a rabbi. He trained as an accountant instead and embarked on a career as a manufacturer, then a publisher. When he stumbled upon the work of Albert Howard in a British magazine in the early 1940s he became an evangelist for the nascent organic movement. "I had been mildly health-conscious since young adulthood and the methods I resorted to for prevention of catching colds and elimination of regularly recurring headaches were legion, but none were effective," he later wrote. "Sir Albert Howard's idea made common sense. Surely the way food is grown has something to do with nutritional quality."

Rodale wasn't the first American to see the value of an organic method. His predecessors included Franklin H. King, who, skeptical of new developments in American farming, had retired from the Department of Agriculture and, like Howard and McCarrison, traveled through the Far East, in 1907. His *Farmers of Forty Centuries,* another canonical text of the organic movement, described how Chinese peasants maintained soil fertility for four thousand years with manure and night soil, composting and crop rotation. By the time Rodale stumbled upon Howard's work, even the U.S. government had been forced to take cognizance of the ruinous consequences of conventional farming. In 1938, as topsoil blew off the Great Plains, leaving tens of thousands of farmers destitute, a USDA report, *Soils and Men,* discussed the way agricultural practices depleted the soil. The report is still cited in organic circles, as an early argument for a sustainable alternative in agriculture. As for the agricultural use of the term "organic," it first appeared in the work of an influential British biodynamic farmer, Lord Northbourne, in 1940.

Rodale brought an entrepreneur's zeal to building the movement from his farm in Emmaus, in northeast Pennsylvania, where he experimented with organic farming and composting. In 1942, he launched the magazine *Organic Farming*, with Howard as associate editor. He was, as they say, ahead of the curve. When he sent out ten thousand magazine samples to farmers, he got back only two dozen subscriptions. Undaunted, he renamed the magazine *Organic Gardening and Farming*, then dropped the word "farming" altogether. *Organic Gardening* still exists today.

Rodale likened chemical fertilizers to whipping a horse, speeding up growth but hastening tiredness. He blasted "vegetable factories"—large-scale farming—and in the early 1960s condemned the practice of giving animals vaccinations, tranquilizers, and other medicines. As a result, he was lambasted as a cultist, comic chemist, disciple of the muck-and-mystery school, part of the lunatic fringe, pseudoscientist, humus worshipper, and apostle of dung.

Undaunted, Rodale invited additional controversy by promoting his interests in alternative health. He launched *Prevention* magazine in the 1950s, offering summaries of medical research and articles on alternative treatments of the day, earning the enmity of the American Medical Association, which kept a file on him for decades. This wasn't just a passing interest: Rodale's father had died of a heart attack at age fifty-six, and over the years, five siblings had succumbed to heart disease, too. His mother suffered from diabetes, and Rodale himself fell ill frequently. To steel himself, he took more than one hundred nutritional supplements daily. He ate sunflower seeds for his eyesight and pumpkin seeds for prostate health. Meanwhile, he hypothesized that sugar caused juvenile delinquency and that white flour—in fact, all wheat—was the source of colds. He eschewed plastic and aluminum utensils and tin, copper, and silver polish as well. As for medical treatment, "I do not say we should ignore doctors when we are sick. But sickness and health are two entirely different things and each one should have its own specialized treatment."

In *Pay Dirt,* published in 1945, Rodale warned about the dangers posed by DDT, which had been introduced only five years earlier. When Rachel Carson eloquently expanded the critique of DDT in her book *Silent Spring* in 1962, sparking the environmental movement, she gave substance to Rodale's campaign. Carson herself was not an organic food proponent—she distanced herself from Rodale, whom she viewed as eccentric— but together they created a platform upon which the American organic movement could grow.

For sixteen years, Rodale lost money on *Organic Gardening,* but the times were catching up with him. In 1966, a free-form anarchist group known as the Diggers drove around San Francisco in a bus called the Yellow Submarine, scavenging food and then distributing it free to the local freaks in "feeds." In an essay titled "Sounds From the Seed-Power Sitar," one Digger wrote it was time to return to the land, "to straighten out our heads in a natural environment and straighten out our bodies with health foods and do Pan's work, toe to toe with the physical world." The freaks would feed each other, and this free-food system would ensure "the healthy, organic, harmonious evolution of the tribe."

In 1969, the summer of Woodstock Nation, circulation of *Organic Gardening* jumped 40 percent. By then, Carson's *Silent Spring* had spread far and wide. In April that year, several hundred members of the Robin's Hood Park Commission took over an empty lot in Berkeley, planted vegetables and trees and grass, put out park benches, and tacked up a sign: PEOPLE'S PARK:

POWER TO THE PEOPLE. The commission set up a free-food store, with "no owner, no manager, no employees, and no cash." Poet Gary Snyder called the event a guerilla strike on behalf of the "non-negotiable demands of the earth." That same year, an oil spill marred the beaches of Santa Barbara, and pictures of oil-drenched birds landed on front pages. The polluted Cuyahoga River caught fire in Cleveland. "Rising concern about the 'environmental crisis' is sweeping the nation's campuses with an intensity that may be on its way to eclipsing student discontent over the war in Vietnam," warned the *New York Times*. News stories about DDT, soil erosion, the population explosion, and world hunger made the front pages.

This sense of doom only heightened in the coming years. "The more we strive to reach the popular science future, the more likely we are to achieve environmental disaster," wrote Garrett De Bell, editor of *The Environmental Handbook*, a guide for the first environmental teach-in in the mid-1970s. Organic food was part of the alternative solution, appealing to baby boomers and their distrust of chemicals and processed foods and corporate poisons developed since World War II. The goal was to avoid "anything complex, anything you can't pronounce, anything chemical, synthetic or plastic," writes cultural critic Warren Belasco. Natural food was a "liberated state of mind, a symbol of opposition to mass production, efficiency, rationalization." Any white food—sugar, flour, rice—was out; brown rice and whole grains were in. Meanwhile, *The Whole Earth Catalog*, the do-it-yourself bible of the counterculture, called Rodale's *Organic Gardening* the "most subversive" publication in the country.

The Natural Order of the British organic pioneers had evolved into a starry-eyed, left-leaning vision, not unlike Howard's circle of life, but with the psychedelically charged possibility of transforming the food chain. "There's No Reason We Can't Exchange Our Goods And Smoke Our Money," read one headline in an alternative newspaper. Cooperative ventures linked organic farms with small markets, creating an alternative system based upon enlightened values. Food co-ops had "an almost religious spirit that seeks to satisfy the human needs forgotten in the plastic-coated world of a corporate supermarket," journalist Daniel Zwerdling wrote. "Some of the people who work and shop at co-ops seem almost starved for a sense of communion with the earth and with their food, and the co-ops help provide it." Paul Hawken, the organic food entrepreneur turned environmental author, said in one interview: "Massive scale and centralization of power and capital is the antithesis of what we had in mind when we started the natural and organic-food business in the U.S." But as the organic food movement drew more adherents, that massive scale and centralization became integral to feeding the growing tribe before food giants could get in and corrupt it. Production, distribution, and making money chaffed with the original ideals, leaving the movement "conflicted and vulnerable," Belasco writes.

Meanwhile, the food and medical establishments fought back against this growing alternative movement. Aside from Rodale's nemesis, the American Medical Association, the Federal Trade Commission filed charges against Rodale for alleged false-advertising claims in the 1960s. They died in court after a lengthy battle. Establishment nutritionists, funded by food companies, claimed that the whole-grain, whole-food dogma was nothing more than fiction (until the 1980s, when the industry realized it might actually be profitable). The founding chairman of Harvard's nutrition department, Frederick Stare, wrote that "food additives are like friends . . . Eat your additives, they are good for you." Stare called the back-to-nature "mania" a "hoax, perpetrated by opportunists." Modern technology was superior to nature and should be embraced in the production and manufacturing of food. Earl Butz, secretary of agriculture in the Nixon administration, said in 1971: "We can go back to organic farming if we must—we know how to do it. However, before we go in that direction, someone must decide which 50 million of our people will starve."

These arguments are still advanced by critics today who now claim that manure and compost introduce pathogens into the soil and make organic food unsafe. Yet manure is used by farmers of all stripes, which is why conventional farmers—who produce 350 million tons of it a year—have failed to join the chorus. In fact, with conventional farmers packing more and more animals onto vast factory-style farms, manure itself has become an ecological hazard. In June 1995, an eight-acre manure lagoon burst through its dike in North Carolina, spilling 22 million gallons of manure into a local river—twice the size of the Exxon *Valdez* oil spill. The pollution from these confinement farms has become a source of lawsuits in rural communities, and the subject of new EPA regulations.

Organic farms actually account for only a fraction of the manure used in agriculture, yet they face the most stringent regulations over its use. Under organic rules, raw manure must be spread on fields no fewer than ninety days before harvest, to ensure that potential pathogens in the soil will die. Other farmers face no such restrictions. Organic compost must also be produced under a regime that brings the temperature high enough, and maintained long enough, to kill pathogens, with the results recorded each day. Again, these regulations do not apply to conventional farms. Municipal sewage sludge—60 percent of which is spread on conventional farm fields because of ocean-dumping restrictions—is banned on organic farms because of concerns that the sludge may leach heavy metals.

As for the issue of whether compost is safe, the USDA Agriculture Research Service's Environmental Microbial Safety Laboratory estimates that proper composting reduces E. coli and salmonellae pathogens by 99.999 percent. The first study comparing pathogens on organic and conventional produce, at the University of Minnesota, found contaminates at slightly higher levels on organic produce, but concluded it was "not statistically different" from conventional samples. The lethal E. coli O157:H7, caused primarily by cattle fecal contamination in meat-processing plants, which has led to numerous recalls of hamburger meat, as well as to deaths, was not detected on any sample and the researchers deemed all the food tested safe.

These arguments about the dangers of organic food amount to a PR sideshow compared with a growing body of mainstream research into the consequences of conventional agriculture. By 1989, for example, the NAS found that conventional farm practices increased soil erosion; that the application of chemical fertilizers fostered the growth of algae in streams, bays, and estuaries, choking off oxygen and killing aquatic life, to devastating effect in the nation's fisheries, and accounting for half of the nation's water pollution. The leaching of these nitrate fertilizers into water sources has since been associated with bladder and ovarian cancers, and possibly colon cancer. The NAS noted that toxic pesticides ended up in drinking-water supplies; that illnesses on the farm were associated with pesticide use; that rampant pesticide use was leading to chemical resistance among insects and to reducing populations of insect predators; that large-scale confined livestock farms had higher rates of disease, which in turn was being fought with medicines and antibiotics that had shown up in food.

Although avoiding these practices may result in lower yields—or output per acre—that also is changing as organic methods grow more sophisticated. And even assuming some yield sacrifice, the trade-off might be worth it, as a Swiss study, comparing organic and conventional farm systems over twenty-one years, found in 2002. Organic crop yields were on average about 20 percent lower, but they required only half to two-thirds as much energy and fertilizer, and 97 percent less pesticides, a finding that takes on added significance considering that the production of chemical fertilizers and pesticides consumes one-third of the energy used in conventional farming. Wheat yields were only 10 percent lower. The organic soils also had far greater biological activity, hosting up to three times as many earthworms, and the organic fields supported a more diverse animal population, including endangered species.

"This study is as complete a picture as we have from anywhere," said Phil Robertson, a Michigan State University agricultural ecologist, in an accompanying article in the journal *Science,* which published the findings.

Rodale, the "Guru of the Organic Food Cult," would not have been surprised had he lived to see these results, but he died of a massive heart attack in 1971, while appearing as a guest on the *Dick Cavett Show.* He was seventy-three. His empire has endured, as a rare family-held publishing company in a business dominated by conglomerates. The family publishes *Men's Health, Runner's World, Organic Gardening,* and *Prevention,* in addition to books, and runs the Rodale Institute, a nonprofit organic-research organization, still based in Emmaus.

It was not until 2003, however, that the sixty-year-old company scored a major hit, publishing Agatston's *South Beach Diet* and selling five million books in several months. While the doctor did not tie his message to organic food, he did spin a nutritional theme about the virtues of whole grains and complex carbohydrates central to the organic movement. No doubt, Rodale would have been proud.

I saw how far the organic ideal had evolved, when I visited Austin, Texas, in May 2003. The city was baking in ninety-five-degree heat and dripping with 90 percent humidity, but I decided to walk from my hotel to the Austin convention center, several blocks away, where the newly formed Organic Center for Education and Promotion was due to hold an open board meeting.

I walked into the room and grabbed a "natural" soda, while the board members arrived: a casually dressed group of people who had been in the organic food business for years and were now leading significant companies, like the dairy cooperative Organic Valley, the retailers Whole Foods and Wild Oats, the soy milk company White Wave, and Small Planet Foods, which owns the Cascadian Farm label. Now that these entrepreneurs had made a bit of money, they were plowing some of it back into a nonprofit research-and-promotional institute for organic foods, not unlike the way conventional agribusiness sponsors research initiatives. But this kind of organized thrust was new for the organic industry, if only because the type of money that could back it was quite fresh.

The group thought the public lacked understanding about the benefits of organic food and hoped to fund research to substantiate a health-claim label for their products. Britain's Soil Association had published a report, "Organic Farming, Food Quality and Human Health: A Review of the Evidence," which pored over more than four hundred scientific studies to try to establish a scientific basis for the value of organic food. The studies had found that pesticide residues were rarely present in organic crops and that organic fruits and vegetables had, on average, higher vitamin, mineral, and phytonutrient content. Now the group in Austin wanted to advance the argument. What work could be done to evaluate existing studies, and what additional studies could they fund to further substantiate the benefits of organic farming? And ultimately, what would it take to make a health claim for organic foods that could meet the standards of the Food and Drug Administration?

Those questions were being asked only in the most tentative fashion, and mostly as background chatter at a meeting that largely focused on matters like fund-raising. The stated mission, though, was clear. What the organizers wanted to prove, with a bevy of rigorous scientific studies, was what Howard had asserted seven decades before: that organic food is better for human health.

Currently, the "organic" label does not reflect a health claim, as USDA officials have pointed out repeatedly. The Organic Foods Production Act of 1990, which regulates organic practices, defined organic agriculture only as an "ecological system of production." The "organic" label means that the food was produced using organic methods sanctioned by the USDA. No food producer can say, for example, that consuming organic food may reduce the risk of cancer because organic food has been shown to have fewer toxic pesticides. If such a health claim were substantiated and allowed, it would imply that the conventional 98 percent of the food supply was less healthy. While organic food was conceived as healthier, and consumers view it this way, the law severs an explicit link. "It's a terrible irony," said Urvashi Rangan, an environmental scientist at Consumers Union active in organic regulations.

Part of the reason for this limiting definition was pragmatic. The organic industry—and its proponents in Congress—knew that any attempt to establish a health claim would have killed the law. What lawmaker from a farm state would vote for a bill that called a constituent's crop nutritionally inferior? Plus, the law was facing stiff opposition at the USDA, which had rarely been receptive to alternative agricultural methods. Kathleen Merrigan, a former senate staffer who worked on the organic food bill, recalls being sabotaged by USDA officials who wouldn't respond to requests or who lost information. The bill only got through the House of Representatives when it was rewritten to remove any research funds for organic farming. The young organic food industry won legitimacy, but only by distancing itself from its core idea of the connection between soil, food, and health.

What the founders of the Organic Center for Education and Promotion wanted was to reestablish that link, not with alternative nutritional theories or Eastern mysticism, as so many others had done in the past, but with hard science. In essence, they were trying to do what the conventional food industry had been doing for years, and with similar aims. Like every other health claim the food industry has won, this one, too, would not only undermine critics but also boost sales. And this thrust wasn't underway only in the United States, but also in Europe, where Danish, Dutch, Finnish, German, Italian, French, and British researchers were launching similar investigations into the nutritional value of organic foods.

Are organic foods healthier? A researcher might parse this question any number of ways, looking at pesticides in the diet— like Lu and his colleagues—or studying the nutritional makeup of the foods. But these approaches compartmentalize the answer in a way that chafes with the original organic concept. Health as the organic pioneers conceived it encompasses the whole system, not just you or me. To hold a similar view today, health would have to take into account the environment, the quality of drinking water, the incidence of cancer among farming families, the pesticide-poisoning incidents suffered by farmworkers, the risks to infants and children, and perhaps even the pleasure and taste of well-grown food. But health is affected by a host of factors, not least of which is wealth, for the wealthiest people tend to be the healthiest. Once basic needs are met, people make better choices, like avoiding smoking, and eating more fresh fruits and vegetables. Organic food is a component in that universe of decisions, but as McCarrison argued nearly a century ago, it should not be considered alone.

In buying organic food, consumers become actors in this larger picture of health, contributing to consequences they may not even understand. In a direct way, they are also providing the investment in research and development that the government has largely avoided making in organic farming until very recently. Agribusiness has not pushed deeply into this area, either, since, unlike research into genetically modified crops, the results cannot be patented, owned, and licensed. The only funds to improve organic methods have come from consumers who buy the fruits of this labor. Indeed, if there is an unsubsidized free-market sector in American farming today, it is to be found in organic agriculture.

The methods were developed by highly pragmatic and individualistic farmers, spurred by sixties counterculture, environmentalism, health, even spirituality. But whatever their original motives, the innovators pushed forward, tweaking old methods and coming up with new ones, and taking their cues from the results they could see in the soil, the environment, their crops, and, above all, with consumers. In the end, they only succeeded because they gave consumers what they wanted.

It was an approach I began to understand when I looked into a food I consume with passion: strawberries.

2. *The Organic Method*

Strawberries in Two Versions

*An organic farm, properly speaking, is not one that uses certain
methods and substances and avoids others; it is a farm whose structure
is formed in imitation of the structure of a natural system; it has the
integrity, the independence, and the benign dependence of an organism.*
—Wendell Berry, *The Gift of Good Land*

I came across Swanton Berry Farm at the farmers' market in
Berkeley, California, one glorious Saturday morning in March,
at the opening of the strawberry season. The farm's stand sat in
front of a beat-up white commercial van, with UNITED FARM
WORKERS OF AMERICA and CERTIFIED ORGANIC signs promi-
nently displayed. I could smell the strawberries as I approached,
then waited my turn and bought two boxes, which the vendor
put in a paper bag. As I walked away, I pulled out a plump berry
and popped it in my mouth. The fruit was tender, not mushy,
releasing a gush of sweetness that mingled with the rounder,
deeper note of strawberry flavor, and while not all the berries
were quite as sweet, every so often I'd get another wallop. As a
couple of friends and I walked past the farm stands on the street,
with their oranges, lemons, mixed greens, herbs, olive oils, and
artisan breads—so abundant compared with the scarcity back
home this time of year—we finished off an entire box. So I

swung back up the street to buy more, since we'd obviously need at least three for dessert that evening.

To say I had flown across the country to taste these strawberries would be a stretch, but not much of one. I had called the farm's owner, Jim Cochran, when I learned he was a central figure in the creation of the organic strawberry industry on California's central coast. Strawberries rank second after apples in sales of American fresh fruit and, like them, are routinely found on lists of foods with the highest pesticide residues. When the USDA tested 518 samples of fresh strawberries in 2000, it found pesticides on 91 percent. Two-thirds had two or more separate residues and a third had from three to seven. In all, it detected twenty-five different chemicals. The $1.1 billion California strawberry industry isn't an anomaly in pesticide use, ranking fifth in total pounds used in the state (wine-grapes rank number one). But the strawberry industry has been faced with the imminent demise of one of its most cherished chemical aids, the soil fumigant and neurotoxin methyl bromide. Central to the growing regime and the linchpin of the industry's success since the 1960s, the chemical was set to be phased out by an initial date of 2005 under a United Nations treaty designed to protect the earth's ozone layer. Could organic methods offer a true alternative, altering the widely accepted belief that strawberry growers need pesticides, especially their valuable but toxic fumigants, to farm successfully?

If you look only at yield—the amount produced per acre—the answer is clear. Organic methods of production produce about 15 to 20 percent fewer strawberries than conventional methods. Organic growers also have to farm in a rotation, either hopscotching to new fields or growing different crops on the land each year to avoid crippling soil diseases. But the bigger picture is far more complicated. For farmers, profits, rather than yield, matter most. If the market price fails to cover the cost of the crop, high yields don't matter. The focus on yield also ignores the larger cost of chemicals to the environment, communities, and health—measured in the size of the ozone hole over the Antarctic or the potential impact of drifting pesticides on a nearby school. These so-called external costs, which society must bear, don't show up in yield studies.

In any case, farmers don't choose an agricultural method or system like a product from the shelf. Once farmers work a certain way, breaking out requires not simply changing a few practices but altering the conceptions of their farms, land, and even way of life. For a conventional farmer, switching to organic production means jettisoning an entire production system that evolved over a half-century and cutting ties with a ready-made network of researchers, pesticide experts, advisers, and companies. For a lot of farmers, it just looks too risky.

Cochran didn't face this dramatic choice because he was a relative newcomer when he began farming. Like so many other pioneers in organic farming, his decision to farm without chemicals meant inventing a new method along the way. In many parts of the country, you can find this kind of innovator, whose work on farms created the foundation for the organic food industry. In strawberries, a cornerstone of that foundation was laid by Cochran.

Swanton Berry Farm sits on a breathtaking stretch of beachfront, two hours south of San Francisco, where the fields angle gently down toward the Pacific Coast Highway and then to the blue ocean. Sea salt mingles with the aroma of strawberries, and a near constant breeze chills the air. Because local activists fought to preserve this coastline from real estate development in the

1970s, all that remains now is what was here before: cove beaches, where kite surfers ply the waves; sharp cliffs that fall into the water; the occasional home grandfathered into the land-use restrictions, and farms like Swanton Berry, which rents this property from a seven-thousand-acre private land trust. Cochran also grows on land belonging to the state park service and on a couple of privately owned parcels. In all, he farms about two hundred acres, with twenty-five acres in strawberry production.

A sign beside the two-lane highway says STRAWBERRIES UP AHEAD, but the place looks like any other farm: a couple of barns, a former Army-barracks building, a dirt parking lot. The barracks, moved here decades ago to house Mexican farmworkers, now serves as an office, kitchen, and store—though "store" might be overstating it. Cochran places boxes of strawberries on a counter and has a container where you can leave your money if no one's around.

The morning I visited him, Cochran grabbed two pint-sized strawberry shortcakes (an example of how he is "vertically integrating" his business) out of a refrigerator, and we sat down at a picnic table beneath a photograph of Cesar Chavez, who founded the United Farmworkers Union in the early 1960s. At fifty-five, Cochran is lean, silver-haired, and sharply opinionated but also funny—a useful combination in a highly contentious field. He remains the only organic grower to have signed a labor contact with the union.

Cochran started out in 1979 by helping about two hundred Latino sharecropping families in the Salinas Valley, two hours south, set up a co-op, Confederacion Agricola de California. "They marketed together, bought equipment, but they borrowed too much and management was spotty," he said. The co-op grew strawberries conventionally, but having read Rachel Carson's

Silent Spring as a teenager, Cochran was curious about an alternative. When he talked to the co-op workers about going organic, "People didn't care," he said. "They told me to try it myself." So in 1983, he left with a friend to start a small farm.

Finding land proved a challenge on the central coast of California. Bordered by coastal-range mountains and the Pacific Ocean, the region boasts some of the richest agricultural acreage in the world. Toward the northern tier of this region, in the Pajaro Valley and town of Watsonville, where the cool ocean air makes an ideal spot for growing strawberries, the now century-old strawberry industry took root. Land rents for up to $2,500 an acre a year, though the choicest parcels have long been carved up. So Cochran and his partner looked an hour north, in Davenport, just north of Santa Cruz. In a place called Swanton Canyon, they found a two-acre cow pasture that rented for about $400 an acre. The soil wasn't as rich, the climate cooler, water access spotty, but the rent allowed them to conserve cash. They bought a $2,000 tractor, which Cochran still has, though it rusted out badly because they didn't have a barn to park it in. For the first two seasons, they grew both conventional and organic strawberries, but then Cochran's partner left to pursue a safer course—an MBA degree. Cochran stuck with the farm, going entirely organic in the third year. He worked in construction in the winter to make ends meet.

In organic circles, a few others also grew strawberries, but Cochran was only vaguely aware of them. Mostly, he encountered critics. When reps at TriCal, a big chemical supplier in the region, heard of his organic farm, "They told me I was crazy," Cochran recalled. "They offered to come out and fumigate my fields for free." Even old-timers who had farmed before chemicals were widespread told him he would have a hard time making it. Conventional wisdom held strawberries could be grown on the same land only once every ten years, or even every twenty-five, because soil diseases would decimate the crop.

Cochran gradually moved onto nearby parcels, and he found the strawberries did well in soil where brussels sprouts had previously grown. They grew poorly following carrots, and he ran into trouble after beans, but the berries also thrived if they followed broccoli. He read that mustard attracted lygus bugs, a tiny insect that migrates from weeds to strawberries and damages the fruit. As long as mustard was in bloom, the migration slowed, so Cochran planted mustard in sync with the berries, though it was hard to get the timing just right.

In this way, Cochran discovered what farmers had long known: Breaking up a congenial monocrop by mimicking the diversity of nature could hold in check the pests and diseases that thrive on a particular plant. Managing the habitat this way didn't work 100 percent of the time, sometimes barely 50 percent, but the more Cochran learned, the more the farm improved.

Cochran's observations were also keen. Brussels sprouts and broccoli are members of the Brassica family, and each to varying degrees inhibits a potent fungal disease, verticillium wilt. This disease can lay dormant in the soil for as long as a decade, but once a receptive host such as a strawberry plant appears, it comes alive and attacks the plant's water-conducting tissue. The leaves turn brown or off-green, dry up, and an entire field can be wiped out. One reason soil fumigants such as methyl bromide became prevalent in the 1960s was that they snuffed out this ravaging disease.

Cochran, though, wasn't the only one who noticed broccoli's uncanny protective quality. Roughly a decade later, during a virulent outbreak of verticillium wilt in cauliflower fields, a plant pathologist at the University of California, Davis, Krishna Subbarao, noticed that, while cauliflower died, nearby broccoli fields were immune to the disease. Subbarao thought this was curious since both plants were members of the Brassica family. Over several years of research in the mid-1990s, he found that a natural fungicide within broccoli, glucosinolate—similar to the substance that gives mustard its pungent odor—kept verticillium at bay. The substance feeds beneficial soil bacteria, increasing populations one-thousandfold, and they in turn attack the disease. In field tests, the incidence of verticillium dropped by 94 percent after two plantings of broccoli, compared with a five-fold increase in plots without broccoli. "I have a pile of soil from 1995, where we applied broccoli residues, and I still cannot detect any verticillium," Subbarao told me. The next step will be identifying the exact bacteria at work, an ambitious task since a single gram of soil contains ten thousand species of bacteria, only half of which have been cataloged.

"When I began to investigate this," Subbarao said, "I talked with a number of farmers, including Jim Cochran, and found they knew about broccoli, but basically had kept it a secret"—a common strategy among farmers torn between a desire to spread organic methods and an urge to maintain a competitive edge. Cochran even left broccoli off his sale's list in the early years because he didn't want people to know what he was planting. Ultimately, though, he shared his knowledge, and with Subbarao's work, broccoli became a well-known crop-rotation strategy even on conventional farms.

Cochran continues to revise his rotational strategy and has found a way to bring strawberries back more quickly. Aside from broccoli, he may put in artichokes or cauliflower and, in the winter, plant a cover crop that will be plowed into the soil to build up organic matter. Some years, he lets the ground lay fallow to rebuild its fertility, which is an uneconomic strategy on more expensive land.

Cochran also plants flowers and native grasses to attract insects that feed on pests. The insects don't work as well as pesticides, but that's the point. When chemicals knock out entire populations of harmful insects, as well as the insects that prey on them, the bugs that do survive are the ones with a genetic resistance. They establish a new population, rendering the pesticide useless. While it can take over a decade for regulators to approve a new chemical, insects can evolve immunity in a few years. For this reason, "integrated pest management" is the watchword for conventional farmers. Conventional farms that practice these methods spray only when bugs appear, rather than on a set schedule, thus reducing pesticide use.

Under organic regulations, farmers can turn to a small arsenal of approved botanical pesticides, but only if the land-management measures—rotations, cover crops, beneficial habitat—prove ineffective. Cochran tried a number of these plant-derived insecticides, including neem tree oil, which attacks insect larvae, and pyrethrins, a toxin derived from chrysanthemums. While these substances break down quickly in the field, they are not benign. Pyrethrins can cause convulsions. Sulfur, a fungicide used on organic and conventional farms, can burn skin. Rotenone, also approved for use on organic farms, is a plant-derived nerve toxin. Over time, Cochran shied away from these botanicals because they also targeted beneficial insects. "When I have used them aggressively, they have backfired on me," he said.

Cochran's caution about pesticides—of any type—is not unusual among organic farmers. A 1997–1998 survey of more than one thousand organic farmers conducted by the Organic Farming Research Foundation, a nonprofit based in Santa Cruz, found 52 percent never used botanical insecticides and just 9 percent used them regularly. *Bacillus thuringiensis* (Bt), a microorganism toxic to insects, was the most common pesticide—applied regularly by 18 percent of those surveyed—followed by insecticidal oils and soap, which about half those polled used at one time or another. These pesticides have very low impact on humans. (Even humans who ingested Bt for five days showed no adverse health effects.) Sulfur and copper were applied regularly by only 12 percent and 7 percent of the organic farmers respectively.

In comparison, crop rotations were used by 74 percent of respondents to combat pests and by 80 percent to address plant diseases. The next most-common methods were to plant beneficial habitat and disease-resistant cultivars and to apply compost. Overall, 75 percent of organic farmers said they managed diseases without any difficulty, while 21 percent cited only moderate problems. Sixty-eight percent had no trouble with insects. Weeds were the biggest issue, with 20 percent of organic farmers citing serious difficulty, which is why hiring laborers to weed is a common practice on organic farms.

Cochran felt these natural pressures forced his strawberry plants to be stronger than conventional plants, which are coddled by a chemical shield. Researchers have suggested that these internal strengths might result in a more nutritious berry, because the plant's immune system is composed of phenolic compounds that include vitamin C and antioxidants, which reduce cell damage in humans. A study published in 2003 showed that organically grown strawberries had higher levels of phenolics than conventional berries. In the absence of synthetic fertilizers, researchers believe, organic plants create more phenolics as a protective measure against diseases, pests, and stresses.

When Cochran explained his entire system—the plant breeds, compost, insects, crop rotations, the presence of disease, and the vigor of his fruit—I asked, "So, then everything's in balance?"

"No, it's not really a balance, it's more like chaos theory—where everything seems to work one way for a while, and then all of a sudden it doesn't, so you try something else," he said.

What he observed was a dynamic system, because the soil and ecology around him were very much alive. Other farmers have found that soils change progressively on organic farms. "Some of the soil fertility practices that worked well when we first started organics need to be altered and re-thought as our soils change," notes Mary-Howell Martens, an organic wheat farmer in upstate New York.

Cochran didn't always know why or how a method worked, or in what measure, because there had been little scientific research into organic production, but soon, a neighbor in Swanton Canyon took a strong interest in his work.

In 1980, the University of California, Santa Cruz, which already had an influential organic-farming program, hired ecologist Stephen Gliessman to start a Center for Agroecology. Agroecologists look at farming as part of the larger ecosystem, focusing on the wider environmental and social impact of the farmer's methods. As Gliessman writes in his book *Agroecology: Ecological Processes in Sustainable Agriculture*, conventional agriculture's primary goals of high yield and output aren't enough: "Modern agriculture is unsustainable—it cannot continue to produce enough food over the long term because it deteriorates the conditions that make agriculture possible."

Gliessman received his PhD in ecology from the University of California, Santa Barbara, around the time of the first Earth Day (April 22, 1970), and went to work in Central America, focusing on the methods of subsistence farmers. Their rotations of corn, beans, and squash, rooted in Mesoamerican agriculture, renewed fertility so that the farmers could cultivate the same land rather than continually clearing tropical forest to plant crops. At an agricultural college in Cárdenas, Tabasco, Mexico, he studied these small peasant plots in relation to a nearby World Bank–funded project for banana and cocoa exports, which relied on imported chemicals and technology. Gliessman realized the small farmers had a more sustainable approach not only for the local ecology but for their own livelihood.

Back in the United States, however, funding for research into alternative agriculture was virtually nonexistent before 1987, when the University of California first set aside grant funds for the Sustainable Agriculture Research and Education Program (SAREP). Gliessman decided to apply for these funds and study Cochran's fields.

"At that time," Gliessman said, "there was a lot of criticism of organic agriculture being snake oil or hocus pocus—that it didn't have any science behind it. We knew it did, but we had to show it."

With a $75,000 three-year grant from SAREP, Gliessman's research team created twelve plots on Cochran's farmland, designating half conventional and half organic. On the conventional land, they fumigated the soil with methyl bromide and chloropicrin, a commonly used and highly effective mix for controlling soil diseases, weeds, and pests. In this process, a tractor with a deep metal shank attached to the front end rolls down the field, pumping gas into the soil. Plastic rolls off the back, and workers shovel dirt over the edges to seal in the gas. They can smell the fumigant if it leaks, however, because chloropicrin, a component of tear gas, is used as a warning agent. (The more highly toxic methyl bromide is colorless and odorless.) The plastic is often left on the ground as a mulch to inhibit weed growth. When they are ready to plant, workers cut holes in the plastic and set the young strawberry cultivars in the soil. The rest of the conventional regime consisted of dipping the plants' roots in a preplanting fungicide, applying time-released chemical fertilizers, and spraying pesticides to control lygus bugs and two-spotted spider mites—common pests that reduce yield.

In the organic plots, researchers spread compost made from dairy waste, alfalfa, cotton-gin trash, and apples. They applied blood-meal and bonemeal fertilizers—materials that break down slowly in the soil, providing a steady supply of nutrients rather than a burst of food. In place of fumigants to control weeds, they rolled out black plastic mulch and relied on hand hoes. And instead of chemical insecticides, they released a predatory mite (*Phytoseiulus persimilis*)—which had been used in Europe but was not yet common in California—that reproduces rapidly and feeds on the two-spotted spider mite.

The team reported its first-year results, in 1990, in *California Agriculture,* the agricultural journal of the University of California. Measuring soil nutrients and pest populations, they found the predatory mites performed as well as insecticides. They also found traces of DDT in the soil sixteen years after it had been banned by the EPA. (This is not unusual on crop land that has been converted to organic production, since older, now-banned pesticides may persist in the soil for decades.) As for production, the study found that while the organic plots had a 38 percent lower yield in the first year, profits were only 9 percent lower, which showed how the price premium for organic strawberries offset lower productivity.

Ironically, the bulk of that July–August 1990 issue of *California Agriculture* was devoted to looming state and federal bans on some of the most widely used chemicals in agriculture.

"Growers face an urgent need to find alternatives to many chemical pesticides targeted by such legislation, but they fear those alternatives will be unavailable or either more costly or less effective than conventional pesticides," one article stated. While the article suggested a thorough research agenda to look for pesticide alternatives, it wasn't clear Gliessman's work would be on the agenda. Even as broccoli became central to Cochran's strawberry system, another article in the issue stated crop rotations and fallow periods were no longer widely practiced. Organic agriculture was still off the map, even as the universe of chemicals was narrowing.

California Agriculture did not publish Gliessman's next article on the field trials until the January–February issue of 1996—several years after the project had been completed and after the article went through a brutal four-year review. "They would send it out to people, criticize it, ask for more input, make changes, sit on it six months, and finally give it back to us. We'd work on it, send it back in again and the same thing would happen. I've never seen a paper get torn apart like that," said Gliessman.

He viewed the opposition as political, for the article demonstrated the viability of an organic operation. Cochran's organic plots yielded fewer berries, but the deficit shrank steadily over the three years. Expenses fell, too, because the additional labor needed for weeding still cost less than chemicals. After lagging, the organic plot earned more than the conventional field in the third year ($9,738 per acre vs. $6,087) helped by the higher price for organic strawberries. While the article ignored the long-term economic impact of rotations—broccoli would earn only a fraction of what strawberries brought in—it showed a farmer could make money with organic strawberries.

After his SAREP grant dried up, Gliessman was unable to find additional funding. It would be another decade before Subbarao substantiated Cochran's rotational method, and it took until 2004 for the USDA to award Gliessman a $507,000 grant to pursue research in organic strawberries. Overall, organic agricultural research is still in its infancy. While land used for organic research doubled between 2001 and 2003 to 1,162 acres, this represented only 13/100ths of 1 percent of all public agricultural research lands. The roughly $8.5 million appropriated for organic-farming research each year also compares with a $2.5 billion federal agricultural research budget.

Looking back over twenty years, entomologist Sean Swezey, the director of California SAREP, said Cochran's methods proved groundbreaking. Farmers now plant "trap crops" such as mustard and alfalfa to lure lygus bugs; the predatory mite, *P. persimilis,* has become the standard way to control the two-spotted spider mite in both conventional and organic strawberry fields and broccoli is a common rotation.

The only approach that hasn't been replicated among other organic farms is Cochran's contract with the United Farm Workers. Labor practices were never codified into the certification standards for organic farms, even though social justice was a powerful strand in the early organic movement. Most farmers wanted to address these social issues on their own.

Driving to his fields one day, Cochran pulled his Volvo station wagon over, got out, and walked into the knee-high foliage by the side of the road. He picked a tiny wild strawberry from the grasses.

"This is the native plant," he said.

Fragaria chileonsis grows from the northern reaches of Alaska to the beaches of South America. In 1602, when Spanish explorer Sebastian Vizcaino came ashore in Monterey Bay—perhaps an hour south of here—he found wild berries growing in abundance in the middle of winter. Native Americans cultivated patches with irrigation networks. Entire villages would decamp to the fields when the berries ripened, evolving into strawberry festivals begun by the earliest Spanish settlers.

Cochran found the plant quite hardy and easy to grow, but getting it to produce our idea of what a strawberry should be— "well, that's the harder trick." In pursuit of this ideal, horticulturalists have bred cultivars for at least four hundred years and nurtured them over the past half century with an intensive, chemical regime designed to ensure a standardized, profitable product, with repercussions far outside the strawberry patch.

First appearing in Greek and Roman texts, wild strawberries were enjoyed as an ornamental and medicinal plant, treating melancholy, fainting, inflammations, and diseases of the blood. Cultivation began sometime in the fifteenth century, and the fruit was sold on the streets of London by the sixteenth century, when it appeared in the works of William Shakespeare. ("The strawberry grows underneath the nettle, and wholesome berries thrive and ripen best neighbour'd by fruit of baser quality.") The native European variety, *fraise des bois,* now a culinary specialty, became quite popular.

With the discovery of the New World, however, explorers and settlers located the distant parents of the modern strawberry and shipped them to Europe. The patriarch in the line, *Fragaria virginiana,* was discovered by the English upon their arrival in the Virginia Colony in the 1600s—both in the wild and in patches cultivated by Indians—although its first appearance in Europe may owe to Canadian explorers in the 1500s. Not much more than a botanical curiosity, the plant languished there for nearly a century, until its mate, *F. chileonsis*—the variety Cochran pulled out of the grass—arrived from the Pacific coast of South America in the hands of a French spy.

Amédée Francois Frézier first came across the variety while posing as a merchant during a reconnaissance mission to Chile, then a Spanish colony. "The fruit is generally as big as a walnut, and sometimes as a hen's egg, of a whitish red, and somewhat less delicious of taste than our wood strawberries," he wrote. "The berries are brought back in such abundance to the city of Concepción (that) for half a real, which is the lowest money, one gets one or two dozens, wrapped in a cabbage leaf."

He sailed home in 1714 with five plants, not realizing all were female. While they grew vigorously in the king's garden in Paris, they failed to fruit, deflating Frézier's claims. The story would have ended there, were it not for *F. virginiana,* imported earlier from North America. When gardeners in the coastal region of Brittany planted the two species near one another, the Virginian plants pollinated the Chilean ones. Growers soon recorded berries up to seven and a half inches in circumference, vindicating Frézier after all. By the mid-eighteenth century, the cross of the two, *F. ananassa,* became a commercial success in England, Holland, and France. A century later, the cross had returned to America, where farmers bred more than eight hundred varieties. Breeding let the human hand direct evolution to emphasize certain traits—such as size, sweetness, yield, drought and disease resistance, and hardiness—that nature in its imperfection and diversity failed to ensure.

The Wilson strawberry was the first ringing American success, because it vigorously adapted to various soils, expanding the strawberry industry fiftyfold from 1850 to 1880. The Marshall, which originated south of Boston and was known for its flavor, size, and deep red color, later gave rise to the freezer industry in the Pacific Northwest.

Chance discoveries often proved as profitable as carefully executed crosses, since the berries bred like mad between the porous borders of wild and cultivated fields. The Sweet Briar, found near an irrigation ditch in Shasta County, California, in the late 1900s, proved superior to any other variety. Joseph Reiter and Richard Driscoll, founders of Driscoll Strawberry Associates, introduced it to the Pajaro Valley in 1904 and renamed it the Banner, giving birth to California's strawberry industry. In 1921, the first railcar of Banner strawberries took off for Chicago, beginning the long process of concentrating production in the fields of California. The same year, the state's first freezer plant was built to absorb excess supply.

As soon as strawberries were grown on a large scale, however, crippling diseases and pests struck. A field of cultivated strawberries presented, in effect, a super-sized habitat in which pests and diseases could thrive. Without the checks and balances of nature, more plants meant more pests.

This was not unusual in California's rapidly evolving landscape. From 1810 to 1942, close to 570 species of trees and 260 vines were brought into the state. "Along with them came new pests, which in their native habitat might be fought off by predators, but once in a different environment, only human intervention could stop them from spreading," historian Steven Stoll writes. Among the invaders were the San Jose scale, grape scale, flea beetle, berry moth, leafhopper, blister mite, wooly apple aphid, codling moth, cottony cushion scale, red scale, red spider mite, and Hessian fly—all new to California since the gold rush. Farmers in the late-nineteenth century fought them with petroleum, sulfur, tobacco juice, and whale oil, with no firm idea what worked and what didn't. Today, entomologists estimate that on average a new insect is introduced to California every sixty days, with economic damage of $3 billion a year. A quarter of the state's crops are lost to pests and diseases. Globally, pests, weeds, and disease destroy about 37 percent of all crops, despite the annual use of 5.6 billion pounds of pesticides.

Stoll tells a prophetic story from these early years of California fruit farming, showing how the chemical response to pests developed. In 1868, a nursery in San Mateo County received a shipment of Australian lemon trees infected with the cottony cushion scale, a pest that clings to branches and leaves. In its native habitat, the scale would have been contained by predators, but in California it spread and soon became one of the deadliest citrus pests ever to enter the state. Growers threw alkalis, oil soaps, and new arsenic-based chemicals at the pest, but its waxy skin shielded it from poisons. The growers resorted to digging out citrus groves and burning them, but after new trees had been planted the pest returned. Growers thought there might be a natural predator in Australia, since the country was not afflicted with the pest, and enlisted a USDA specialist to visit Melbourne, in 1888. He returned with a lady beetle (*Rodalia cardinalis*), which was released into California citrus groves and caused the scale to vanish overnight. With this success, some argued pest control should focus on "nature's way," rather than chemicals.

Others weren't swayed, though, since the lady beetle wasn't effective against many other pests. Better to spray and wipe out all the insects quickly than experiment with targeted biological solutions. While the state Board of Horticulture discovered thirty-seven beneficial insects by 1906, the University of California did not issue a single farm bulletin on the subject until the 1950s. "The university, largely by winning the allegiance of orchardists to chemical cures, rendered itself the central institution in the matrix of industrial farming," Stoll writes.

Farmers facing this onslaught of pests were so desperate, they fell prey to hucksters selling fraudulent or improperly mixed chemicals. The nation's first pesticide law, passed by California in 1901, was written not to protect public health—as we might think from the vantage point of the twenty-first century—but to ensure the purity of the substance. All pesticides had to be registered with the state so that farmers could make sure they were getting what they paid for. Paris Green, made of copper and arsenic, and another substance called lead arsenate were the toxic pesticides of choice. Lead arsenate went on to become the most widely used substance before World War II. Its toxicity was not even questioned until the 1930s, when farm interests opposed attempts to curtail its use. We now know lead accumulates in the body and damages the central nervous system, especially in infants and children.

For much of the last century, pesticides were seen as a miracle, an incontestable sign of progress that allowed farming to expand and crops to thrive. They did provide this sort of miracle as long as their risks and toxicity were unknown or patently ignored. DDT, developed in 1939, quickly replaced arsenic and lead during the Second World War as a broad-spectrum agricultural insecticide and was also sprayed widely in a successful campaign to eradicate malaria. Pictures from the era show children playing behind DDT spray trucks; the spraying of public beaches; and nurses with special guns, fumigating beneath the clothes of children.

But DDT had a downside. It turned out to be bioaccumulating, rising in concentration as it went up the food chain, from the insects in lakes that were sprayed to the fish that consumed them to the birds that ate the fish and died, giving Carson the title *Silent Spring*. For humans, DDT and the metabolites it breaks down into increase the risk of low-birthweight babies, premature births, impaired lactations, and height abnormalities in children, according to a U.S. toxicology assessment. DDT also has been deemed a probable carcinogen by the EPA. Finally, it is highly persistent and fat-soluble, which is why more than three decades after it was banned by the EPA, it is still detected in food. Between 1993 and 2003, residues of DDE (a metabolite of DDT) were found in 37 percent of carrots, 39 percent of spinach, 7 percent of potatoes, 44 percent of beef fat, and 15 percent of cow's milk, although at levels below what the FDA views as a health risk. Residues will remain in livestock and fish for decades to come, at ever-diminishing levels.

Following blanket spraying in agricultural applications, insects quickly built up resistance to DDT and "benign" pests became a far greater threat once predators were wiped out. These secondary pests became primary ones, requiring new pesticides to combat them, such as the organophosphates that replaced DDT. These neurotoxins were attractive because they were not bio-accumulating and could be used in smaller quantities. Yet only later were their mechanisms—and effects on children—better understood, leading to their reevaluation and, in some cases, withdrawal from the market. In this historical progression, each chemical class was replaced by a new one, which only later was found to pose its own health risks. At the same time, growing insect resistance prompted continued chemical replacements.

Cornell University entomologist David Pimentel estimates that despite a more than tenfold increase in pesticide use since 1945, crop losses due to pests have nearly doubled. The NAS counted over 440 pesticide-resistant insects in 1986 and found the number rising. An international survey identified 289 herbicide-resistant weeds by 2004, with the biggest number in the United States. The adoption of genetically engineered crops has allowed freer use of herbicides, but this has also led to a rise in herbicide-resistant weeds.

The strawberry industry conformed to this evolution of chemical use, though it took until the 1960s to get the formula right. The industry's first response to the problems that monoculture wrought had been far more benign—to breed a strawberry that would resist diseases.

This began in earnest in the 1920s, when the popular Banner variety was hit by "strawberry blight," later identified as *xanthosis,* causing its leaves to turn yellow, and stunting growth. It took a decade to figure out the blight's viral nature, spread by aphids from mother to daughter plants in nurseries and then shipped around the state. Driscoll and Reiter also faced a devastating case of verticillium wilt in the 1920s, when eighty acres of strawberry plants collapsed in a Palo Alto field where tomatoes had previously grown. From then on, growers made sure their fields had been free of tomatoes for at least a decade and moved fields every year—often ripping out the trees in old apple or prune groves, which they considered lower risk. But these lands were in short supply. Farmers escaped to the foothills of the central coast, but after wet winters, plants died from *Phytophthora* fungus, or late blight—the cause of the Irish potato famine. Then the industry was hit by spider mites, which prompted the state legislature to appropriate funds to the University of California with a directive to get these diseases and pests under control.

Plant pathologists at UC Berkeley tested more than one hundred plant varieties, some from as far away as England, in 1925, and two hundred and fifty varieties from the USDA a year later. They created tens of thousands of hardy hybrids, including the remarkable Shasta and Lassen cultivars, which soon came to dominate the California strawberry industry. On the backs of these breeds, the industry grew to $30 million by the 1950s, capturing a third of the national market. But soil diseases continued to hold back the full potential of these plants.

Then, in the mid-1950s, agricultural researchers made a remarkable discovery that would allow growers to stay on the same soil year after year. When methyl bromide, which dates to the nineteenth century, and chloropicrin, an element in tear gas first tested in the soil after World War I, were pumped into a strawberry field, they synergistically controlled a host of diseases, including verticillium wilt, *Phytophthora* root and crown rot, anthracnose, black root rot, and charcoal rot. The gas kept a host of weeds in check, wiped out insects, and killed rodents, too. Growers could ease their worries about losses and low yields, as long as they blasted their fields with enough gas to keep all threats in check. By 1965, nearly all the strawberry fields in California were fumigated with methyl bromide–chloropicrin.

With this advance, breeders could focus on traits such as the berry's aroma and size, ease of harvesting, yield, hardiness in shipping, and long shelf-life. Two plant pathologists at the University of California, Stephen Wilhelm and Albert Paulus, wrote in 1980 that even a tenfold advance in breeding disease-resistant plants would not equal the benefits derived from soil fumigation. This was the premise of the green revolution in the 1960s and 1970s: Develop new plant varieties and protect and nurture them with as many chemicals as needed, leading to an explosion of yield and output.

In the strawberry patch, statistics tell the story well. Before fumigation, the yield was around ten thousand to twelve thousand pounds of strawberries per acre. After fumigation took off in the early 1960s, yield shot up. It hit thirty-nine thousand pounds per acre by 1978 and continued to rise to sixty-two thousand pounds per acre in 2003. With just 2 percent of the market before World War II, California now supplies 86 percent of the nation's strawberries, and Florida is a distant second. Production in other regions of the country could not keep up in the face of this competition and largely shut down.

A higher yield can have enormous financial benefits for a farmer, since it means more revenue per acre of land. A University of California Cooperative Extension report on strawberry production costs spells out the return at various prices. Consider a tray of strawberries (eight one-pound boxes) that fetches $7 wholesale. At that price, an acre yielding four thousand trays will return a profit of $154 after costs—or break even. If the farmer has a great year and gets seven thousand trays per acre, the profit jumps to $11,249 per acre. Higher yields require more laborers to pick the berries, but the greater revenue more than covers the additional harvesting costs. According to these estimates, on a strawberry ranch of twenty acres, seven thousand trays per acre at a price of $7 per tray nets a $250,000 profit. As one grower put it, "When you hit it, you can hit it big." If everyone hits it big by pursuing the same strategy, however, supply can swamp demand, pushing down prices and wiping out profits.

Still, the modern cultivar gave strawberry growers what every business craves—a desirable product—and the chemical regime of fumigation, fertilizers, and pesticides created an artificial ecology in which the plant could thrive. In 2002, growers applied 8,274,926 pounds of pesticides in California strawberry fields, 89 percent of which were soil fumigants. In Monterey County alone, 2.36 million pounds of methyl bromide and chloropicrin were pumped into strawberry fields. But take away a key element, such as methyl bromide, and the plant, the farm, the entire system, could wilt like a field without water.

People have died from breathing methyl bromide when it was used improperly to fumigate homes. Farmworkers have been hospitalized and people evacuated from their homes when the pesticide leaked from containers or drifted the wrong way. But methyl bromide has a benefit compared with other pesticides: It does not cling to food as a residue, when used as a soil fumigant. Nor does it leave a toxic footprint in the soil, because the gas evaporates. But this quality turned out to be its undoing, for as methyl bromide rises into the stratosphere, its bromine atoms break down the ozone layer, allowing more ultraviolet radiation to reach the earth, where they in turn can cause skin cancer and cataracts, weaken the immune system, and even hinder plant growth.

Deemed an ozone-depleting substance in 1991, methyl bromide now fell under the United Nations Montreal Protocol. Negotiated after the discovery of the ozone hole over Antarctica, the treaty banned chemicals such as chlorofluorocarbons once used in aerosol cans and refrigeration, because the chlorine atoms within them attacked ozone. Since the bromine atoms in methyl bromide are fifty times more potent than chlorine, the treaty set a target to phase out the fumigant in the developed world by 2005. In a controversial decision, developing nations got another ten years. "Critical" uses—such as quarantining fruit shipments to prevent the spread of pests—were exempted from the phaseout.

Meanwhile, its status as a neurotoxin made methyl bromide a focal point for environmental, farmworker, and public-interest advocates in California. The nature of this "category-one acute toxin"—the highest in the EPA scale—is not in dispute. On the opening page of *Methyl Bromide: Risk Characterization Document,* volume 1, *Inhalation Exposure,* the California Department of Pesticide Regulation (DPR) notes that early symptoms of inhalation of the toxin include malaise, headache, visual disturbances, nausea, and vomiting. Delirium and convulsions eventually set in, followed by suffocation, heart attack, and death. A nonlethal dose can still have neurological effects and cause skin lesions, but as with most toxins, the severity depends on the amount and duration of the exposure and the age and health of the person exposed. Since two hundred to four hundred pounds of methyl bromide are injected in every acre of strawberry fields—compared with most pesticide applications of one to five pounds—the potential for both acute and nonlethal poisoning is great.

Cochran recalled getting a whiff of gas while working the fields in Salinas, since it would leak out before workers could shovel dirt over the plastic to contain it. (Now workers are required to wear respirators.) "You'd get all jittery, and it smelled awful," he recalled. By the time Cochran smelled the tear-gas agent chloropicrin, the concentration of odorless methyl bromide was likely one hundred times higher than its chemical partner.

The only way to mediate this risk, short of banning the substance, is to protect workers in the field and come up with ways to prevent the gas from drifting into nearby communities. Over the course of a decade, with environmental lawsuits and pressure mounting, California's DPR gradually tightened its restrictions on methyl bromide. By 2004, the DPR had mandated permeability limitations on tarps covering fumigated fields, notification for nearby property owners of fumigation, renotification when requested, minimum buffer zones between fields and nearby buildings, the minimum gap between fumigation and the start of a school session (thirty-six hours, when the school is within three hundred feet), time limits for application workers in the fields, record-keeping of hours worked, the type of gas masks workers should wear in various fumigation situations, the duration between fumigation and the cutting of field tarpaulins, the method of cutting tarpaulins, the wording on methyl bromide warning signs, the distance between these signs, and so on. These regulations, which are far more stringent than any at the federal level, added another layer of costs to the growing regime, causing an uproar among strawberry farmers. The DPR was thus under fire on two fronts: from farmers who viewed the measures as extreme and from environmentalists who criticized the agency for being too lax.

Drifting pesticides account for about half of all reported poisonings in California fields, but they can also threaten nearby homes and schools. Children and pregnant women are especially vulnerable to low-level exposures, which can cause symptoms similar to a cold or the flu. While acute-poisoning incidents can make headlines, more subtle harm can result from "subchronic" exposures that last a season for people who live by the fields, or from "chronic" exposures over a lifetime. The health effects of these exposures are much harder to estimate and must be extrapolated from tests on animals, which involves guesswork. A more accurate method of testing humans to determine toxicity is widely opposed, since that would mean poisoning people. (The EPA has come under fire for suggesting such testing.)

In 1992, the DPR began reviewing toxicity studies in which animals were exposed to the gas at various levels. Once the lowest toxicity level was determined, it was cut a hundredfold to get the maximum level for humans—taking into account variations between animal subjects and humans and then the physical differences among humans as well. Based on these studies, the DPR set a limit on "acute" inhalation exposure at 210 parts per billion (ppb), meaning this was the maximum concentration anyone should encounter in a twenty-four-hour period.

More controversial and difficult to measure were "sub-chronic" exposures. No regulated limits were set for these seasonal levels, but the DPR relied on a "target level" of 1 ppb for children and 2 ppb for adults, extrapolated from a 1994 study of the gas's effect on dogs. Any exposure above these levels in a six-week period would constitute a health risk, though the big unknown was how prevalent the gas actually was in the ambient air. The only way to find out was to sample farming towns during the fumigation season.

In 2000, the California Air Resources Board in conjunction with the DPR tested for pesticide drift and found methyl bromide concentrations above target levels at four sites in Salinas and Watsonville, three of them schools. One, the Pajaro Middle School in Watsonville, is a low-income, largely Latino school in which 60 percent of the students are children of farmworkers. With tractors rolling across fields near the school's baseball field, the school had an average ambient air concentration of 7.73 ppb methyl bromide in 2000, far above the 1 ppb target for children.

When the test results were publicized in early 2001, they caused a stir in the local media. The DPR called the air levels "unacceptable." The Pajaro Valley Unified School District, in Santa Cruz County, passed a resolution calling on the state to "commit all necessary resources" to analyze and resolve the health concern, but acknowledged that "the implementation of regulations on the application of methyl bromide could significantly affect the agricultural and farming community in the Pajaro Valley." In the media, parents were reluctant to speak up. They didn't demonstrate or call for a ban on the substance, perhaps because they knew that the result could well mean a loss of jobs. Dave Riggs, the president of the main growers' lobby, the California Strawberry Commission, called the figures "preliminary" and said, "We need to think about a balanced approach that protects the public and allows farmers to stay in business."

That spring, the DPR floated a number of proposals to reduce methyl bromide exposure, including enlarging the buffer zones around schools and capping the amount of gas that could be applied. "To achieve the 1 ppb target reference concentration," one DPR memo said, "methyl bromide use should not exceed . . . approximately 18,000 pounds per township per month." Since methyl bromide use in nearby townships (thirty-six square-mile blocks) was above that level, growers lobbied heavily, calling the proposals "draconian" with "devastating economic consequences." By June, just before the start of the 2001 fumigation season, the DPR backed down. It announced there would be no new restrictions after all, since the 1 ppb "target" was not the equivalent of a regulated ceiling that must not be exceeded.

Working with a farmworker advocacy group, California Rural Legal Assistance, a retired farmworker whose child attended Pajaro Middle School sued the DPR. Under a settlement reached in 2002, the agency agreed to put in restrictions around schools and set a firm subchronic level for exposure—rather than a vague "target"—when it reissued its methyl bromide regulations.

A year later, the DPR proposed the regulations, but in the interim, the agency considered a new industry-sponsored study on methyl bromide exposure. This study, which had been recommended by an independent peer-review panel, was specifically designed to determine subchronic exposure levels in dogs over a period lasting six weeks. It proved crucial in the battle over methyl bromide, showing just how political the science of toxicology has become.

Although environmentalists criticized the study for being industry funded, this was not unusual. Companies seeking permits to sell toxic chemicals fund virtually all the studies regulators review before making their decisions. Setting aside this apparent conflict of interest, the issue then becomes how to interpret the findings. The industry-backed scientists predictably argued methyl bromide showed no toxicity even at the highest concentration tested, 20 parts per million (ppm). State health scientists and environmental advocates argued the gas was toxic at the lowest level, 5 ppm, based on twitching and tremors in one exposed dog. The DPR viewed this finding as inconclusive, because dogs exposed at higher levels did not exhibit these symptoms. Plus, the twitching might have resulted from an unrelated illness.

At the end of the review, the DPR determined that 5 ppm was the lowest level with *no toxic effect*—the so-called No Observed Effect Level (NOEL). Although on the low end of the toxicologists' opinions, it was still ten times higher than the 1994 study upon which the previous subchronic exposure targets had been based. "This consensus was, however, not unanimous," a DPR report stated. "In establishing the 5 ppm as the NOEL, the staff recognized that there were uncertainties to this determination."

Extrapolating from the NOEL—by accounting for the differences in dog and human respiration rates and adding an uncertainty factor of one hundred times—the DPR raised the subchronic exposure level to 9 ppb from 1 ppb for children, and to 16 ppb from 2 ppb for adults. Watsonville's Pajaro Middle School could now be declared "safe," as could the fifty-one other townships in California with ambient levels of methyl bromide 1 ppb or higher in 2002. Forty-five of these townships applied more than 18,000 pounds of methyl bromide a month—the ceiling discussed by the DPR in 2001. One township in Ventura County applied 232,592 pounds in one month, for an estimated air concentration of 4.64 ppb, though "it is likely that air concentrations of certain sections within the township are higher than this estimated concentration," a DPR memo stated.

The new subchronic exposure level essentially allowed growers to keep fumigating as before. The DPR decided that a safe township limit was actually 266,194 pounds of methyl bromide per month, since only that level would lead to an air concentration of 9 ppb. No township used that much methyl bromide. As the agency concluded: "DPR has not found any imminent health hazard to communities from seasonal exposures to methyl bromide in recent years, based on air monitoring of high-use areas."

While the DPR argued it had erred on the side of caution, critics were not assuaged—even those in the California Office of Environmental Health Hazard Assessment, which also evaluates pesticide risks. This is also unlikely to be the last word on methyl bromide. After the DPR had reconsidered exposure levels, the National Cancer Institute, the National Institute of Environmental Health Sciences, and the EPA published an epidemiological study of fifty-five thousand farmers and their spouses in Iowa and North Carolina, which found a 14 percent higher risk of prostate cancer from several pesticides, the risk being most pronounced with methyl bromide. Men exposed to the pesticide had two to four times greater chance of developing prostate cancer than those who were not exposed; the greater their exposure levels, the greater their risk. Although the EPA is now reassessing regulations on methyl bromide in a much-delayed review, it has previously listed the fumigant as a "group D" carcinogen, which means its cancer-causing properties are uncertain because of a lack of studies.

Determining the "safety" of pesticides has always been a moving target, especially for neurotoxins, whose mode of operation is only partially understood. Historically, the amount of pesticides a farmer sprayed was based on efficacy in the field, not on health concerns. Only later have regulators gone back to review studies and reconsider the chemical's safety. No studies have even considered the toxicity of methyl bromide in combination with chloropicrin, though the chemicals have been paired for nearly forty years. Are they more toxic in combination, or less? It is this type of uncertainty that gives pause when deciding whether the chemicals are "safe." For students at Pajaro Middle School, "unacceptable" exposures one year were called "safe" the next. Yet this conclusion rested entirely on one new study, and even then, the conclusions were debated.

By the late 1990s, stiffer regulations and the looming phaseout under the Montreal Protocol caused methyl bromide use to fall, but not dramatically among strawberry growers who had not found suitable replacements. Researchers had studied herbicides, insecticides, soil solarization (in which plastic sheets placed over the ground heat up the soil and kill diseases), biological controls, crop rotations, even broccoli and new disease-resistant cultivars. The primary alternatives, though, were other fumigants, which, while not a harm to the ozone layer, are still highly toxic.

One substance, 1,3-dichloropropene (Telone), listed by the EPA as a probable carcinogen, was banned by California in 1990 after regulators detected high levels in the Central Valley air. Its maker, Dow AgroSciences, then came up with a less hazardous way to deliver the chemical, through drip irrigation lines, and the state ended the ban in 1995—only the second time it had ever done so. A mixture of Telone and chloropicrin has replaced about 20 percent of methyl bromide use, but regulatory limits prevent wider application. Other growers have switched to 100 percent chloropicrin, but Thomas Trout, a researcher with the USDA Agricultural Research Service, told me, "if there's any off-gassing, the neighbors get on the phone, because it's tear gas." Europeans avoid chloropicrin because the stigma of tear gas from World War I remains so strong. With the chemical's potential to damage the lungs, the DPR has launched a review similar to the one it carried out with methyl bromide. Metam sodium has grown in popularity, though it is also a probable carcinogen and responsible for drift poisonings in California, including an incident in 1999 that forced 150 people from their homes and sent 30 people to the hospital. Trout has studied about twenty other fumigants. Propargyl bromide was effective, but proved impractical because of its risk of exploding during transport—not a great attribute in a post-9/11 world. Methyl iodide, another carcinogen, has been struggling with regulatory approval.

"We've been working on this for nine years, looking at quite a lot of chemicals, but we keep coming back to the same standard fumigants," Trout said.

With this paucity of alternatives, growers pursued a more effective strategy: They lobbied the Bush administration to save methyl bromide. In the spring of 2004, American strawberry and tomato growers (who also rely on the chemical) attended a meeting of the Montreal Protocol with U.S. negotiators to push for "critical use" exemptions to the looming phaseout under the UN treaty. Growers worried that developing countries would steal U.S. markets, since they could use the fumigant until 2015. Several growers told me, though, that Mexico has been unable to match American quality in the fresh market. China was viewed as a looming threat in the frozen market (as it is in much of the produce industry) though, as of 2002, it ranked twentieth in global strawberry exports. The United States ranked number two in exports, after Spain, with sales 135 times greater than China's.

This made me wonder why American growers viewed the phaseout as such a threat. If California growers seriously applied alternatives now, they would have a competitive advantage once methyl bromide use ended in the developing world. Scrapping the pesticide could even be a selling point with consumers. This type of response was not unprecedented, since the Netherlands had banned the fumigant in the early 1990s and has since managed with alternatives. "Many farmers worldwide successfully grow crops without methyl bromide," said Margot Wallstrom, the environment commissioner for the European Union.

The April meeting in Montreal was heated, with conventional growers arguing with organic farmers and environmentalists in the hallways. At the negotiating session, Washington fought hard and eventually won "critical use" exemptions for methyl bromide at a level roughly twice that of all other nations combined.

In this climate of tougher pesticide regulations, ever-encroaching suburbs, environmental concerns, and changing consumer tastes, organic strawberries began to look more attractive to a few conventional growers such as Tom Jones. Jones farmed twenty acres on a two-hundred-sixty-acre organically certified parcel near Salinas, rotating with farmers who grew artichokes, broccoli, and cauliflower. He had been hopscotching around these fields for nearly a decade, never growing on the same ground, nor encountering troubling soil diseases on the land. The day I visited, raised beds of rich black topsoil stretched into the distance, with strawberry plants evenly spaced at the center of each row; a small crew of Latino workers with long-handled hula hoes removed the few weeds growing near the young cultivars.

Jones was a Driscoll grower, meaning his company, Windward Farms, based in Watsonville, licensed proprietary varieties from Driscoll. He grew them, then sold the berries back to the company for marketing. Driscoll depends on growers like Jones to provide the berries, while the growers rely on the company to provide a superior plant and ready market. Jones was the first Driscoll grower to try organic cultivation in the mid-1990s, prompted, he told me, by the declining effectiveness of pesticides. Although his conventional acreage still represents the majority of his crop, he prefers organic production. Jones's motivation isn't environmental, it's economic. "My primary concern is sustaining our workforce with good wages, health insurance, and incentives and if we can't grow a crop, or get a good price, we can't sustain the workforce to the level we want," he said. Four-fifths of U.S. farmworkers earn less than ten thousand dollars a year, live in substandard housing (or squatters camps), and work long hours, often without health insurance. The majority of the estimated 150,000 farmworkers in California are undocumented immigrants. In an industry that outsources picking work to crews of low-wage migrant workers, Jones kept 250 farmworkers on staff.

The organic premium allowed Jones to pay a higher wage in his organic fields, and gave him a comfort zone when dealing with pests. "The first year we were here, we had a lygus infestation and I thought we were dead," he said. "Every plant had two or three bugs. But it ended up being a ten percent cull for two weeks and then the bugs were gone." He wouldn't have been as patient in his conventional fields. "If you find two or three lygus bugs on a conventional plant, you can't wait it out, because you can't take that loss." The smaller profit margin on the conventional crop meant he had to ensure as high a yield as possible with pesticides.

But his experience in the organic fields influenced his growing practices on his conventional land, which may be the biggest indirect effect of organic food production. Though he still sprayed and fumigated his conventional fields, he thought he had reduced his pesticide use by nearly 50 percent since the early 1980s. "We used to spray every week," he said, "but those days are gone." Jones now relied much more on beneficial insects and other biological pest-control methods.

We drove to one of his conventional fields, which had not been fumigated with methyl bromide. When I asked why, he pointed to a house on a small ridge overlooking the field. "I would have to notify them if I fumigated," he said. "Would you want to knock on their door and tell them?" This was emblematic of a larger conflict in California, as suburban home-buyers searching for affordable housing encroach on farm communities. Unlike disenfranchised farmworkers, these homeowners vote and have backed environmentalists seeking more stringent pesticide restrictions. Still, Jones supported an extension on methyl bromide, so that growers could gain time to develop alternatives and avoid losing their farms to competition. When I asked him whether he could forgo fumigation altogether, he said, "Sure. But not if every one else is fumigating. Then, I wouldn't be competitive."

Although he would have preferred to grow all his berries organically, land was scarce. A year after I met with him, Jones lost his lease to the organic parcel in Salinas. He remained out of organic production for a season, then found sixty acres of certified organic grazing land in the eastern part of the Salinas Valley, and negotiated a long-term lease. The improvements he made to the land would accrue to him, at least during the lease.

By 2003, 1,290 acres of California strawberry fields, 4.6 percent of the total, were organically certified. While growers like Jones made the switch, others held back, wary of the method and worried about losing money. Organic growing means applying compost and organic fertilizers that the plants absorb more slowly than chemical nutrients; fighting pests with beneficial insects and limited botanical insecticides rather than chemical pesticides; figuring out how to farm in the presence of diseases rather than in their absence; working out the economics of a lower yield and higher labor costs for jobs such as weeding; setting up crop rotations on expensive land or swapping fields to avoid growing the same crop every year on the same soil; and identifying cultivars suited for organic fields. For a conventional grower, organic farming can look a lot like the crapshoot farming was before soil fumigation became widespread. "It's incredibly difficult to accept the organic method because it's an entirely different mind-set," said Vanessa Bogenholm, a former conventional grower who now farms organically in Watsonville. "There's no chemical switch."

For those who can work out the method, the results can be profitable—or, more to the point, sustainable. Cochran called me at 5:00 A.M. one day to discuss a business arrangement that would distribute shares in his farm company to his employees and give him a way to retire eventually. His ideal wasn't a family farm, but an employee-owned company, where workers would build up equity they could sell back to the company when they left.

"The idea," he said, "is to give them some incentive to stick around—something a yearly bonus doesn't do."

The key to the arrangement was the farm's board of directors, which would ensure the integrity of Swanton Berry Farm's organic and environmental mission and be the last word on any major change in the company. That way, the values on which his company had been built—and marketed—could be preserved. But the foundation for this was his spectacular fruit, which he delivered direct to the stores of his largest customer in the Bay Area, Whole Foods, the day they were picked. The high quality of the fruit justified the price, and the price supported the mission. In the past year, Swanton Berry Farm had doubled in size. "I'm having more fun that I've had in years," he said, before rushing off to work at 6:00 A.M.

This farmer had found a way to avoid pesticides, increase yield and profitability, and give consumers a product they wanted. This didn't happen immediately for trailblazing organic farmers, but the ones who made it in the long run invariably figured out how to deliver high-quality products consistently. They did so without teams of USDA researchers, or replacement chemicals, or company reps telling them what to do and when to do it—without this elaborate agricultural network that supports conventional growers but also locks them in to a singular approach.

The goal of this enterprise wasn't to get rich—a fool's dream in farming—but to make enough money to sustain the mission. It was never easy. To see how this worked, I turned to an organic farm in the mid-Atlantic. Jim and Moie Crawford had made a living for thirty years selling their organic produce literally on the streets of Washington, D.C., and they had influenced a generation of young farmers to follow their path. I wanted to know how they created a market for their goods as part of the growing local food movement. They let me see.

3. A Local Initiative

From Farm to Market

And we've got to get ourselves back to the garden.
—JONI MITCHELL, *Woodstock*

Three-thirty in the morning. Pitch-black out. Not even the birds are awake. I can hear Jim Crawford rustling around in the bedroom above me, on the second floor of the farmhouse. I rise up off the couch in the living room, go upstairs to brush my teeth, and return downstairs just in time to see Jim and his wife, Moie, walk out the kitchen door and into the chilly night. I follow them a few minutes later, up a slight rise on the dirt road to the barn, where two delivery trucks are parked in front of a cement loading dock.

Crawford is already pushing around a large pallet-jack, packing boxes of produce into the back of the sixteen-foot Nissans. The doors of two walk-in coolers stand wide open, thick ribbons of clear plastic keeping the cold air inside. A pallet of peaches from a nearby orchard sits near the doorway. The night before, Crawford had gone back and forth about whether to cool them. "People like 'em ripe," he said, "but not too ripe." He decided to put them in the cooler because last week's batch had gone too far. Behind the peaches are boxes of sweet corn, tomatoes, basil, kale, squash, and lettuce—two days' harvest from

Crawford's organic farm and from the farms of his surrounding neighbors who market together through a cooperative he co-founded.

He spots me and nods.

"You can sleep another half hour, if you like," he says. I nod back. Too early to talk.

Ten minutes later he's sweating and still hasn't had any coffee. At age sixty, he has told me he doesn't know how much longer he can keep up this pace. The apprentices, who are in their twenties and signed up to work on the farm for a year, straggle in, and soon the two trucks are loaded. They climb into the first truck and pull away, the logo of New Morning Farm— a big tomato with the tagline HOMEGROWN, HOMEMADE—on the back door. We settle into the second truck with cinnamon buns and a thermos of coffee and my contribution, a day-old carrot muffin. Crawford turns the key, shifts into gear, and we're off, rolling down the dirt road into the dark hills of south central Pennsylvania to the market in Washington, D.C., two and a half hours away.

The Crawfords are at the center of a growing movement toward regional food consumption, of eating close to home. Their farm is organic, a deep personal and philosophical distinction for the couple. They are also independent, in the mold of the family-owned farm that is central to the ethos (if not always the reality) of the organic movement. These attributes—local, organic, and independent—form a potent identity in what is the largest segment of the organic marketplace, fresh fruits and vegetables, worth more than $4.3 billion a year.

Like other small-scale farmers, the Crawfords have found creative ways to sell their goods outside of supermarkets, because they don't produce enough volume at a cheap enough price to make purchases worthwhile for a large chain. There are exceptions to this rule—as we shall see—but they are rare. On Saturdays, Jim runs his own market in front of a private school in northwest Washington, where he sells produce from their own farm and from the co-op. On Sundays, Moie has a stand at the FreshFarm Market in Dupont Circle, sandwiched between Buster's Seafood and Twin Springs Fruit Farm. There are about thirty other vendors at this market, a boon for customers when compared to the 1,500 to 2,500 miles supermarket food usually travels before it reaches a shopping cart. In fact, at the FreshFarm market, Moie can sell only products the Crawfords grow themselves.

Using these channels, the Crawfords have built an organic brand infused with locality, freshness, friendship, and taste—qualities that can lead a customer to return again and again, even if it's more expensive. A survey of 3,500 people in Ohio found that 59 percent would be willing to pay 10 percent more for locally grown food. Thirty-nine percent were willing to pay a similar premium for organic food. Another survey of 1,500 people in eight Midwestern states, Seattle, and Boston reported that more than 75 percent would choose food labeled "grown locally by family farmers" as their first choice for produce or meat. "Grown locally-organic" was the second-highest choice, though the researchers said it might have come in first had the words *by family farmers* been added. About 25 percent said they would pay a premium of 6 to 15 percent for food from small local farms.

Unfortunately, most of these farms have now disappeared. One percent of the population now farms, compared with 23 percent just before World War II; from a peak of seven million farms in 1935, just two million remain. As the number of farms has declined, the size has increased. The largest 2 percent (or 46,100 farms) account for half of all sales. The organic sector has not been immune to this trend. Researchers at the University of California, Davis, found that 2 percent of California's organic farms, or about twenty-seven growers, accounted for half of all organic sales in the state in the mid- to late-1990s.

In Huntington County, New Morning Farm is surrounded by shuttered barns and vacant fields that Jim refers to as "dead farms." The bankrupt dairy farm up the road was sold off a few years back to a weekender from New Jersey. Of thirty-five local fruit orchards, only three are left. Pennsylvania still has more farms than any other state in the northeast, and agriculture ranks as the state's top industry, but the number of farms fell 45 percent between 1964 and 1997. In nearby Cumberland Valley, along I-81, industrial warehouses that serve as distribution hubs for goods destined for stores in the mid-Atlantic sit next to the cornfields of Amish and Mennonite farmers. Frequent signs offer acreage for sale along two-lane highways filled with tractor trailer trucks and the occasional horse and buggy. These soils are considered among the best in the nation and have been productive since the seventeenth century. Nearby Lancaster County was the most productive farm county east of the Mississippi in 2002, yet with the rise in real estate values, "a lot of farmers feel pressure to sell," local USDA extension agent Steve Bogash told me.

The Crawford's ninety-acre farm in Hustontown, Pennsylvania, with twenty-five acres under cultivation, is an exception to the rule of fading family farms. The couple has inspired about twenty apprentices to start their own organic farms over the years; Jim and Moie regularly speak at farm conferences. Awards adorn Jim's ramshackle office and their living room, recognizing the Crawfords' efforts to build a "sustainable" farm at a time when that is a rarity. They have raised two children on the land (one in college in Pittsburgh, the other a Cornell University graduate living in New York City's East Village). And they are actually *working* the land for a living, rather than more recent back-to-the-landers sinking midcareer earnings into organic hobby farms.

Jim Crawford doesn't hold any special claim in the world of farming. He isn't an especially "elegant" organic farmer; others have far more complex rotations and cover-crop systems. He has studied them, applied them when he could, but he does what works best on his land, in his harried life. He is ever the pessimist, grousing about the weather, and doesn't bank on luck, because the farm was set up, more or less, to get by without it. While this has been a struggle, there is no mistaking that he and Moie have achieved a measure of what Crawford views as the gold standard: a modest middle-class life supported by selling locally grown organic food from their independent farm.

Of course, when you bring that up, he'll say, "Well, it took years. I mean we lived on nothing for years." He never takes it for granted; he knows how precarious this life is, how he's bucking the odds, how he still might not get out of the business with enough money to retire. The anxiety associated with that uncertainty always hovers nearby.

This morning, as we drive down the dark road away from the farm, he's clearly troubled. He's usually talkative, opinionated, never at a loss for words. Now he's quiet. After a few minutes, he apologizes for the mood and tells me his usual driver has taken the day off. Crawford is worried that the replacement driver—one of the young apprentices—doesn't know the best route to Washington. When I ask whether the sub has driven it before, Jim says he has. His anxiousness strikes me as odd, but I don't say anything. Moie had recognized his edginess the evening before, telling Jim to calm down. Everything was fine. All the boxes were packed. Ready to go! But as on most market days, with thousands of dollars riding on one trip, Crawford can't shake it. He tells me he had nightmares the night before. "We've got five and a half hours to sell all this stuff and if anything happens, an entire week is shot," he says. More than a week, considering the work of seeding, planting, weeding, irrigating, harvesting, washing, cooling, and packing—as much a marvel of planning and logistics as nature.

Now it all comes down to a truck ride.

Two years ago on the way to market, the truck he was driving hit a deer a few miles down the road from the farm. Crawford had to call on his cell phone for another truck, then reload the produce, hoping to arrive before his customers went home. "We're moving a whole store every weekend—no one really understands that," he says. "Nothing can go wrong!" Not twenty minutes later, a deer lurches out of the dark on Jim's side of the truck. I can see the animal's eyes, its nimble legs, as it darts into the road. Jim doesn't have time to swerve or brake. Somehow, we miss it. The truck speeds on, dawn barely visible, as we wind down Cove Mountain toward the interstate and the city.

Crawford began farming in earnest when he was twenty-eight, after deciding, on the opening day of his second year of law at Washington's Catholic University, to leave the school and never return.

That summer, in 1972, he had rented a seven-acre farm near Berkeley Spring, West Virginia, with a few friends. While they viewed it as a place to hang out, Crawford was determined to try growing vegetables and cleared a plot a hundred feet square. "They were dropping acid, I was hoeing the ground," he said.

During his childhood south of Boston, in Norwood, his father kept a small vegetable garden in the backyard. Milk was delivered daily from nearby dairies. A farmer down the road, in

Walpole—"Mr. Buttimer, I didn't know his first name"—ran a roadside stand and sold produce door-to-door. Crawford watched the farmer in the fields, as a kid, and tried to get a job with him, in high school, but Buttimer turned him down. Years later, long after he had become a farmer, Crawford returned to Walpole and found Buttimer still selling vegetables by the side of the road.

Talking about why he quit law school and began farming, Crawford circles back to those memories. But the decision also came at a time when the anti–Vietnam War, environmental, and back-to-the-land movements intersected. Crawford had attended Rice University in Houston on an ROTC scholarship and upon graduation, in 1965, entered the Navy as an ensign. He had studied French, German, and Russian, so was assigned to the Naval Intelligence Command as a foreign-language specialist. However, he was denied a high-level security clearance for work on Russia—due, he thinks, to his civil rights work in college and a brief period when he considered becoming a conscientious objector—and was shipped out to Vietnam just before the Viet Cong launched the Tet Offensive in 1968.

His yearlong tour, mostly in Danang and Saigon, studying enemy troop movements, solidified his antiwar views. "I felt the misunderstanding between two cultures was so great, it was like a fog that no westerner could see through," he said. "All we saw were grenades going off and people dying and nobody knew why." By the end of his tour, he was a lieutenant and still had a year to go. But by then, he felt the need to take a public stand and upon returning to the States wrote a statement opposing the war. The Navy discharged him.

Once out, he launched full-time into the antiwar movement, then applied to law school. After a year of night classes, he rented the place in West Virginia. "I just wanted to do something I liked, rather than the right thing, the thing everyone said I should do," he said. "I just wanted to be Mr. Buttimer."

This was the era of the *Whole Earth Catalog*, with its articles on self-sufficient living; Rodale's *Organic Gardening*, a bible for young farmers like Crawford; and the well-known example of Helen and Scott Nearing, who had run a subsistence farm in New England since the 1930s. A generation of young people trudged to the Nearing homestead in Vermont, and then in Maine, to share the couple's vision of a simple life.

In their influential book, *Living the Good Life,* first published in 1954 and reissued in 1970, the Nearings said society "had rejected in practice and in principle our pacifism, our vegetarianism and our collectivism. Under those circumstances, where could outcasts from a dying social order live frugally and decently, and at the same time have sufficient leisure and energy to assist in the speedy liquidation of the disintegrating society and to help replace it with a more workable social system?"

The answer was a farm.

The aim was to be as "independent as possible of the commodity and labor markets," to be free of the stresses of urban life, and to avoid exploitation of the planet, people, and animals. The Nearings wrote a ten-year plan to achieve these goals, avoiding money as much as possible and selling maple syrup for what cash they did need. The farm was organic; they kept no animals, not even cats and dogs (because they "live dependent subservient lives"); they built stone houses by hand, logged, and planned meticulously. Their diet was vegan, with fruit in the morning, vegetable soup and whole grains at lunch, and a big salad for dinner. They snacked on nuts, honey, and peanut butter and avoided refined flour, sugar, and white rice. Like Rodale, they opposed food additives and food processing. Instead of refrigeration, which would shackle them to distant electrical interests, they made do with root cellars.

The Nearings said they were not trying to escape life, but were seeking a more worthwhile existence, a life that valued "simplicity, freedom from anxiety or tension, and the opportunity to be useful and to live harmoniously"—an approach that can be traced back to Thoreau. Distractions were gone, materialism for its own sake discarded. Their time was split between chores, which took half the day, and reading and writing, music, and social activities. All was part of an integrated whole, each portion as valuable as the other, and all fulfilling.

The Nearings had reduced their footprint on the earth in a way that they found spiritually rewarding (though they were atheists), creating a blueprint for four to five million young people moving back to the land, whether on communes or independently. "We yearned for psychic rewards and spiritual wealth, not money, so we planned to generate mere trickles of cash flow from our cottage industries, manual labors and crops," writes Eleanor Agnew in her memoir *Back From the Land.* "The payoff was to be freedom." This wasn't the first rural return in the twentieth century—a wave had taken place in the 1930s—but the 1970s movement was larger and more significant. Its adherents were swimming against the tide of American consumerism, rampant energy consumption, environmental degradation, and existential doubt. "The land," nature, a farm, could offer the kind of off-the-grid authenticity missing in the Vietnam era. Agnew makes the point, however, that the movement ultimately lost steam because its ideals of purity played out, in her case, by hauling well water up a hill in the middle of winter, heating it on a stove, and washing clothes by hand while dealing with two young children. She eventually returned to the modern world.

Scott Nearing, however, stayed true to his ideals and died three weeks after his hundredth birthday. Helen lived to ninety-one. Their approach filtered through to the simplicity movement articulated by Duane Elgin, among others, in the 1980s. The movement's goals were restraint, conscious living, minimizing distraction, and avoiding blind consumption, although the tether to rural life was loosened. "The objective is not dogmatically to live with less, but is a more demanding intention of living with balance in order to find a life of greater purpose, fulfillment and satisfaction," Elgin wrote in his book *Voluntary Simplicity*. This meant not renunciation, but paring down to focus on things that mattered, "outwardly more simple and inwardly more rich." This movement has since morphed into a far more consumer-friendly version, by making modern life more manageable rather than jettisoning it altogether. Time Inc.'s stunningly successful magazine *Real Simple* is devoted to stylish living and time-saving tips and products for the harried woman; the status symbol is not a composting toilet out back, as it was in the 1970s, but a Toyota Prius in the driveway. This conceptual evolution parallels organic food's growth from a small alternative movement to the mainstream.

While aware of the Nearings, Crawford was never a homesteader. His four-room farmhouse in West Virginia was "pretty rough"—with a woodstove, basic plumbing, and asphalt-shingle walls—but reflected his finances rather than his ideals. Rodale was the larger model, and Crawford made the trek to the pioneer's farm in Emmaus, Pennsylvania. "If you were an organic farmer, it was something you had to do," Crawford said.

He, and later Moie, were on the fringe of the back-to-land movement. Most of the homesteaders around them in West Virginia did not last more than two years. Crawford could think of no one who maintained that pared-down existence. The Crawfords did last, though, because they had a more practical model, which now means telephones, cell phones, a dishwasher, air-conditioning, a gas grill, cars, trucks, and a new addition on their old farmhouse that doubled its size (though they still rely on a wood furnace for heat). "We had ideals—we were environmental, we believed in healthy food, we wanted to live in the country, and we wanted to be independent—but we didn't really want to drop out," he said. "We wanted to make a living from farming. This was a business from the beginning."

That first summer in West Virginia, Crawford became friendly with the two couples in a nearby commune, the Good Heart Farm, who had grown up on farms and were passionate about organic agriculture. In the evenings, their talk about ecology and family farms echoed the agrarian idealism taking root at the time. Crawford wasn't yet an organic farmer, but when he brought his vegetables to a dinner at Good Heart Farm and set them down next to the organic ones grown at the commune, he thought, "Well, why eat the stuff with chemicals if this stuff is grown without it?" From then on, he was organic.

Even with the commune's help, his first two years were bleak. He peddled tomatoes in the House of Representatives office building on Capitol Hill and knocked on restaurants' doors. By the spring, he had set up an organic farm-stand—the "co-op market"—in a parking lot in Adams Morgan and began running it with the commune. (The spot is still going strong thirty years later, though Crawford passed it on to an organic farmer who lives down the road from him.) He liked the whole business of farming—planting the seed, watching the crops grow, driving his beat-up pickup truck to the market, and selling the vegetables in the city. One nearby farmer who sold tomatoes to a cannery for three dollars a box channeled as much as he could to Crawford, who got ten dollars at his market in Washington, a profit they split. Crawford thought local was more important than organic, since the only way to keep these farms going was to buy what they grew. If they could manage the transition to organic in the future, all the better. While the movement was motivated by agrarian, organic, and local ideals, consumers liked buying fresh food direct from the farmer. "That was the kernel of the whole direct-marketing piece," he says. "I knew I could always make a profit."

Crawford also tried Buttimer's model, though instead of selling vegetables door-to-door, he drove from corner to corner in Georgetown, standing on the back of his pickup truck and ringing a bell to announce his presence. "People would come streaming out of their homes," he said. After half an hour, he'd drive around the block and do the same thing. "I could sell as much as I brought in—which is still the case today," he said.

Crawford met Moie through mutual friends, and during his third season, she joined him in his West Virginia shack. That year, the commune, dashed by personality conflicts, disbanded. "That was hard for me to watch, because I was just in awe of them," Crawford said. But having seen the benefits of cooperation, he thought about how he might design a system that would work longer term.

A few years later, with help from their families, the couple bought the farm in Hustontown for $40,000. The rich dark bottomland was deposited by the twisting Aughwick Creek that runs by the western edge of the property and eventually feeds into the Susquehanna River and the Chesapeake Bay 150 miles to the east. Behind the creek looms a steep wooded hill. Walking on the property one brisk night, Crawford told me he had convinced a neighbor to build his house back from the hill's ridge, so neither would see each other's lights. "That was very important to me," he said. As we walked down the road, the farm was nearly pitch-black, aside from Crawford's flashlight.

"Folks, we've got some nice peaches today," Jim bellows at the New Morning Farm market outside the Sheridan school. Customers stroll around the open boxes of vegetables and come over to ask questions. He knows most of the customers and enjoys the repartee. He asks one customer about his vacation, hugs a little girl who runs by ("her grandmother was one of my first customers"), explains the difference between white and yellow peaches, and entices people to "try the fava beans!" He'll be on his feet for six hours, then pack up the crates and take his crew to lunch before driving back to Pennsylvania. He looks a little worn today, but he doesn't flag. "It's been a good day," he says, "better than I thought for this time of year." Back on the farm, Crawford empties several lockboxes on the dining room table, forming a huge pile of cash. Over the next hour, he counts it out with several apprentices. It adds up into the thousands.

One of the allures of farmers' markets is meeting people like Jim or Moie, along with the artisan bakers and fishmongers, buffalo ranchers, orchard owners, and cheese makers who fill the stalls. Though they don't have a lot of time to talk in the frenzy of the market, you can still ask how the crabbing's been down on Chesapeake Bay, or whether the eggplants are coming in, or how much longer spring mix will be available before it gets too hot and bolts. This type of local "foodshed"—as sociologist Jack Kloppenberg dubbed it—ties producers to consumers, countering the anonymity of the modern food chain, reducing the distance that food travels from farm to table, and keeping money in the local farm economy.

In the conventional food system, farmers get about 20 percent of the good's final retail price—a percentage that has steadily shrunk as shippers and packers, distributors, advertisers, food processors, retail chains, restaurants, and other middlemen take an ever-bigger slice along the way. The profit on each item—tomato, bushel of wheat, or steer—is razor thin, and unlike processed and packaged food, farm commodities in the mainstream food system have no "value added" that would make the product distinct and command a premium. Farmers have to sell an awful lot of tomatoes or soybeans or peaches to make a decent living. These economies of scale are the basis of monocultural farming, since it is highly complex and expensive to run a large, diverse farm. Easier to grow one crop cheaply on a massive scale and ensure a high yield with fertilizers and pesticides. Then these large farms compete with each other to drive down prices and win market share.

Crawford saw the logic of massive expansion, even if he eschewed it. If he made $1,500 an acre in profit on one crop, he could keep adding acres and make more money, but then he'd be just another large-scale farmer who wouldn't have time to go to the market on the weekend. He'd seen some of his neighbors do just that, including one—Lady Moon Farms—that set up a winter farm in Florida and became the largest organic grower on the East Coast. Crawford opted out of this high-volume game, but in doing so, reached an entirely different market segment, since part of what he was selling was the small farm. In fact, longtime patrons liked his approach so much, they lent him $1,000 to $20,000 each, in return for interest-bearing "turnip notes." This cut his lending costs, gave his customers a higher-than-bank-market rate, and tied them into his venture, solidifying his customer base. At the height, Crawford borrowed $250,000 from more than forty customers, in the 1990s.

In Dupont Circle's FreshFarm Market, diversity was also an attribute, not the handicap it was for larger farms. Here, farmers have carved out niches within the local foods niche. Heinz Thomet, the bearded, wild-haired, superlative, Swiss-born organic farmer who runs Next Step Produce, sells fresh gingerroot, figs, wheatgrass, fava beans, and purslane in addition to the more usual fare of eggplants, cucumbers, and tomatoes. He planted kiwis on his southern Maryland biodynamic farm to differentiate himself further and expects his first crop in a few years. He's first in the market with strawberries and is done with them by the time the rest of the farmers come in with their crops in June. This crop selection, like the farmers' market itself, offers a product few supermarkets can match. Chefs are the cheerleaders for these goods, but clearly people want to shop these venues, too, which is why the market is jam-packed when it opens at nine on Sunday mornings.

Bernadine Prince, who was then a development officer at American Farmland Trust—a nonprofit foundation devoted to preserving farmland—started the market in 1997 with a local chef, Ann Yonkers. They wanted to channel more local produce into the city and create a market to help small farms. (Farmers keep all revenues, after a 6 percent fee to the organizers.) Yonkers saw the market as "a showcase for our regional bounty—a place where we could have a conversation about local food and local farms. It's impossible to have that conversation in America because no one sees the farmer." Rather than focus on policy, the usual mode in Washington, they wanted to make the point with fresh food. "Nothing is more persuasive than a perfect peach or a ripe tomato," she said. "The food carries the message."

The city had several farmers' markets, but they often included produce from the main wholesale market. Others, like Crawford's, were small, private affairs. In a meeting to form the Dupont market, the Crawfords and Chip and Susan Planck, from Wheatland Vegetable Farms in nearby Loudoun County,

Virginia, told Yonkers and Prince the market should be for "producers only," meaning the goods should be sold by the people who made or grew them. The organizers also wanted to limit the participants to the Chesapeake Bay watershed, within 150 miles of Washington, although exceptions have been made. "The message is that this food is different, that the people producing it are different, that the way of farming is different and it's an alternative way of feeding ourselves—and it's economically viable," Yonkers said.

In seven years, revenue at the FreshFarm market, which is open for just three to four hours a week, topped $1 million a year. The venture was eventually spun off from the American Farmland Trust, with Price and Yonkers forming their own nonprofit organization operating six markets in the area. By 2004, Washington had twenty-seven farmers' markets, up from twelve in 2001. Yonkers and Prince plan at least four more.

The nation's capital isn't unique in this regard: The USDA counted 3,706 farmers' markets in 2004, double the level a decade earlier and up from 340 in 1970. San Francisco's bustling Ferry Plaza Farmers' Market has become such a robust tourist attraction, with five thousand to eight thousand visitors each Saturday, that farmers now grumble about lost business because the tourists merely gawk. The farmers' market in Madison, Wisconsin, boasts over 150 local farms. New York City alone has 47 farmers' markets, with 70 producers at its anchor Union Square Greenmarket in the peak of summer.

While these direct farm outlets supply less than 2 percent of the nation's produce, they are a highly visible outlet for organic fruits and vegetables. About 80 percent of all organic farms sell some portion of their crops direct. A USDA survey of 210 farmers' markets in 2002 found that a third of the vendors were organic, compared with less than 1 percent of all farmers. "Are you organic?" and "Are you certified?" were the most frequently asked questions at one farmers' market in Seattle, a manager in the survey reported. Farmers' markets in Florida and California could not find enough organic growers to meet demand. This was causing farmers to shift to organic methods, especially in Washington state and New Mexico. As for price, managers reported that organic farmers tended *not* to charge a premium over conventional goods, showing that produce prices are largely a function of the market channel—local, direct sales—rather than the method of farming. As it is, the prices farmers receive in farmers' markets are 200 to 250 percent higher than prices paid by wholesalers and distributors.

But while the direct channel is attractive, it doesn't work for all farmers. "Some farmers aren't into marketing, they just want to grow," Crawford told me. Others live too far away from markets, and still others do better growing specialty crops than diverse assortments. Local and direct sales are meaningless for organic soybean farmers in Iowa, whose entry into the market was spurred by Japanese demand in the early 1980s, or organic wheat farmers in the Midwest, who found a market in Europe at that same time. Farmers' markets certainly aren't a panacea for the crisis faced by farms caught in what's been called the "shrinking middle."

These middle-sized independent farms with annual sales between $100,000 and $250,000 are too small to provide the huge volume, low-cost pricing, and year-round availability sought by mainstream buyers, but too big, specialized, or remote to make selling direct practical. While they still make up about half of all farms, and are the bedrock of the "family farm," their numbers have been dwindling since the 1970s, as has the diversity of the food supply. Richard Schnieders, the CEO of Sysco Corporation, the largest food-service wholesaler in the nation, with

$23 billion in sales, worries about this trend because demand for specialty items has grown as the supply has fallen. This means his company is pressured to find growers for what customers want. Moreover, this trend threatens to "hollow out many regions of rural America by transferring most of the agricultural economic activities that have sustained rural communities," according to a white paper by an ad hoc policy group, Agriculture of the Middle.

I heard from organic farmers in California that this squeeze was also underway in some parts of the organic marketplace. Midsize farms too big to rely entirely on direct sales now faced tough competition by larger players in the wholesale market. Erica Walz, who analyzes surveys at the Organic Farming Research Foundation, told me the organic apple market had been pressured in the late 1990s when China entered the conventional market, driving down prices and prompting Canadian orchards to switch to organic methods. The Canadian organic supply sent prices falling, forcing American growers to either get larger or scale down and sell direct.

But this type of forced choice wasn't universal in the organic market. Crawford, like others, found a way to make both wholesale and direct channels work. He sold direct but he also supplied food co-ops and restaurants, because it diversified his market. He also acted as a middleman for his neighbors who'd rather stay on the farm, selling their produce at his farmers' market. This helped the farmers, but it also satisfied his customers by increasing the variety of goods. When he found a luscious Italian extra-virgin organic olive oil, Olio Beato, he decided to sell it, too—the only olive oil he offered at his market. Then there were the oranges he got in the winter from an organic co-op in Florida, when he was selling a lot of potatoes, turnips, and beets. For New Morning Farm, all these channels generated $700,000 a year in sales, which actually put it in the category of a large farm, bigger than 96 percent of all farms in the nation. In acreage, though, it still ranked as a small farm (less than fifty acres), underscoring how this diverse business concentrated revenue.

Despite their high visibility, farmers' markets actually tend to be an alternative rather than a main outlet for organic produce. A 2002 survey by the Organic Farming Research Foundation found that only 13 percent of organic vegetables were sold direct to customers. Natural-food stores, supermarkets, restaurants, and food-service suppliers were a more vital market. Fifty-three percent of organic vegetables were channeled directly to retail stores and 34 percent to wholesale channels—the vast majority locally. While some fear wholesalers and supermarkets will siphon away the sales from farmers' markets, farmers don't see this as a zero-sum game: It's a way to diversify sales and survive.

Crawford woke up to the potential of the wholesale channel in the late 1980s, as demand for organic produce exploded from local food co-ops. But he couldn't handle all the orders by himself. "It was a lot of work, and he knew there was a bigger market than what he was supplying," said Chris Fullerton, an apprentice at New Morning Farm in the early 1990s. "Growers were stepping on each others' toes, driving vans making the same deliveries. Jim figured, 'Wouldn't it make more sense just to have one driver?'"

A few of his friends had set up a farming cooperative in New York state called Finger Lakes Organics, which coordinated growing schedules, handled marketing, made deliveries, and ensured customers a supply of high-quality produce. In 1988, Crawford and two other farmers met to form a similar venture in Pennsylvania. "We scraped together about fifteen names of organic farmers we knew, called the Rodale Institute for others, sent out a mailing, and got six or eight farmers to a meeting," he said. They applied for a state grant, but the business plan they wrote up didn't qualify. "We were sitting in my living room, with the news that we didn't get the grant, and we said, 'Shit, we can't stop now!' I had an apprentice who was willing to work on the project, and had room in my coolers, so we put in an extra phone line, printed up a brochure, figured out whose truck would be used for deliveries, and we were in business," Crawford said. The absence of grant money turned out to be a blessing, he felt, since it forced the co-op to become self-sufficient without the crutch of nonprofit support that would one day be withdrawn. Crawford had seen too many sustainable-agriculture ventures collapse once well-meaning foundations turned their attentions to the next new thing.

Their co-op, Tuscarora Organic Growers (TOG), named for a range of mountains in south central Pennsylvania, had sales of $20,000 the first year. By 1992, sales had hit $150,000, and they now exceed $1 million a year. "It really makes a nice curve when you plot it out," said Fullerton, who became TOG's manager in 1993, when he was twenty-four.

"My first job was digging boxes of financial records out of the snow," he said. The fledgling TOG immediately took all his time, which was fine, because the only parts of farming he really liked were the spring planting of seedlings and the harvesting of winter storage crops. "The rest of it, like harvesting tomatoes in the middle of the summer, I could do without," he said.

Fullerton, who grew up in Hawaii and majored in ecology and environmental policy studies at the University of Redlands, in Southern California, found that the job satisfied an idealistic streak. "I realized that this business was a chance to really do something to help local farmers, rather than just studying the problems or talking about policies. I could help make local sus-

tainability real," he said. But in the beginning, the stress of running a business, of making a sale and ensuring a market for the
farmers who depended on him, was so great he often vomited
when he got to work in the morning. For advice, he subscribed
to business magazines like *Inc.*

TOG was set up to serve its farmers, who own the business
and vet all major decisions. Their operations range in size from
two acres to sixty. Growth has been carefully controlled to meet
the marketing needs of the farmers and the ability of the co-op
to run the business—not to meet demand. Still, Fullerton saw
opportunities to expand, and he pushed them, especially when
Austrian-born chef Nora Pouillon opened the door to upscale
Washington restaurants.

When Pouillon arrived in the United States in the 1960s,
accompanying her then husband, a journalist, she was appalled
by the food. "I felt nothing had any taste in this country," she
says. "There were no seasons anymore. You went to any supermarket and they sold all the same thing. There was no diversity.
No flavor. And too much processed food. Too much frozen
food." The childhood summers she had spent on a farm in the
Tyrol Alps had sealed her love of fresh food. "This farm family
was completely self-sufficient. They grew everything and made
everything they needed to live. Even the soap. The roof
shingles. They harvested wheat and thrashed it, ground it up,
and made bread. They milked the cows and churned butter and
made cheese. I mean, I saw all of that from age three." In the
United States, she searched for a reminder of those flavors as she
began to cook professionally. Even before she opened Restaurant
Nora—the nation's first organic restaurant—in 1979, she scoured
the Yellow Pages for local beef sources; drove out to Potomac
Vegetables, a forty-year-old organic farm in suburban Virginia,
for produce; and set up a network of local artisan suppliers,

much as Alice Waters had done at the famed Chez Panisse in Berkeley.

Pouillon was the first to approach Fullerton about this market. "Your stuff is wonderful, let me introduce you to some chefs," she told him. Fullerton arranged each year to bring chefs by the busload to TOG's farms (though one Amish farmer was taken off the itinerary because he felt the activity "immodest"). The tours typically ended with a lunch at New Morning Farm, prepared by the farmers. When I attended one year in June, the farmers had roasted over an open pit two lambs coated with a spice rub, making for a crunchy exterior and succulent meat. Crawford asked if any of the cooks would carve the lamb, and a couple quickly filleted the carcasses on a large wooden plank. On a side table, the farmers put out spring potatoes, quiche, asparagus, salads, beans, roast carrots, rhubarb pie, upside-down apple cake, fresh strawberries, and vanilla ice cream from the local organic creamery. After the meal, each farmer stood up to talk about his or her crops and thank the chefs who bought the produce.

This was the type of connection Fullerton strives to make, and it gets results. Each year the co-op has grown 10 to 20 percent, mirroring the organic food industry's growth as a whole. Originally six growers, TOG now counts more than twenty-five; 1,500 cases of produce were delivered its first year, and it now loads 60,000; instead of using a beat-up pickup truck, Crawford rents his four $50,000 Nissan trucks part-time to TOG. While New Morning Farm was the biggest TOG grower at the start, it now ranks fifth. Restaurants make up 45 percent of TOG's sales, with natural-food co-ops and grocery stores accounting for another 45 percent. Crawford and other growers who buy from TOG for their own direct-sale markets make up the remaining 10 percent. With sales booming, TOG has tripled its warehouse space, using state and community development loans, and now delivers three days a week to Washington and Baltimore in the height of the season. Those loans and about $20,000 in grants are the only outside support TOG has received.

"The benefit for farmers is not necessarily that we'll be able to work wonders and get a higher-than-market price, but that we're going to get that market price," Fullerton told me. "The advantage is *getting access* to the market."

As a cooperative, TOG aims to pass 75 percent of the sale to the farmer. If a case of basil wholesales for $10.00, TOG pays the farmer $7.50. The remaining $2.50 covers TOG's expenses, debt, and year-end staff bonuses, if sales targets are met. That's the cost of paying a business to sell, organize, and deliver the food. That $10.00 basil will then be marked up to $15.00 by the retailer, meaning the farmer gets 50 percent of the final price — not 100 percent, as in a direct sale to the consumer.

"Some farmers who are used to selling direct get outraged at that," Fullerton said. "They think if they sell this pint of strawberries for three dollars at the farmers' market, then that's its inherent worth. But they're not thinking about the marketing costs, the driving costs — all the work that goes into making the sale." In other words, they're not thinking about the *value* the middleman provides. So while middlemen and "marketing costs" are often derided in agrarian circles, the real question is what service they bring to the farmer, which is crucial for anything other than direct sales.

Another marketplace pillar for TOG was organic certification. Inspectors visit organic farms each year to review farm methods, crop rotations, seed sources, compost, and other aspects of the organic regime to make sure they meet U.S. regulations. The inspector then submits a report to an organization accredited by the USDA—such as Oregon Tilth, the Northeast Organic Farming Association (New York), Pennsylvania Certified Organic, Quality Assurance International, or any of the fifty-six domestic or forty-three foreign certification bodies. The report details the farmer's practices and raises any red flags. The reviewer then allows the farmer to remain certified or begins a process to suspend or revoke certification, if the methods violate regulations. This structure provides a third-party review of both the farmer's methods and the inspector's assessment, protecting the integrity of the underlying product. (Inspectors and their organizations are also banned from any business relationship with the farms.) And this integrity, in turn, creates a viable market for TOG to sell "organic" produce.

Many farmers grouse about the costs of this regime, largely in the form of record keeping. Some farmers complain the paperwork keeps them busy two hours a day, while others say they can't afford the cost of getting certified, which runs to several hundred dollars. (Congress has appropriated funds to offset some of those costs.) The regulations also do nothing to ensure the varied and conflicting ideals that gave rise to the organic movement: of protecting small farms, concentrating on local production, and supporting alternative food networks, social justice, farmworker rights, or even nutritious food. Companies or farmers can evaluate whether to enter the organic market as a business decision, and grow "organic" food to the minimum standards. That is the cost of defining the movement by a set of rules governing production methods.

Still, it is hard to see what the alternative might be for a nationally, and now internationally, recognized label. To ban food from large farms? All processed food? Food grown beyond 150 miles of the consumer? These designations would leave some organic producer (and buyer) behind. But smaller farmers do appear to be opting out of certification in increasing numbers, since it does little to enhance their direct sales if they can otherwise convince customers that they are organic. Only half of all organic farmers at farmers' markets are certified, a USDA survey found. The rest describe their produce as "chemical-free," "no harmful insecticides," "sustainably grown," "good bugs at work here," "no spray," and so on, because they cannot use the word *organic* without being certified, if they sell more than $5,000 annually. These farms are also likely avoiding wholesale channels, where their goods would be identified as conventional.

Talking about the issue at the dinner table one night, Crawford told me he recognized certification might not be worth the cost for someone selling at a farmers' market, since the consumer could talk to the farmer about his practices (if they knew what to ask). But certification ensured a farmer wanting to sell grain to Europe or Japan, or to sign up with TOG, or to sell to local food stores or Restaurant Nora, that she could. The customer, by relying on the label, would more or less know what he was buying.

While Fullerton felt organic certification was key to TOG's business, the co-op had not cracked the mainstream market in any big way. Nor did Fullerton aim to. He knew tiny TOG could be whipsawed by a big buyer. In one instance, TOG sold hundreds of pounds of basil to Whole Foods, which used it to make pesto for their prepared-foods counters. Then, one day, the buyer called to say they wouldn't be needing the basil any longer: The chef had changed the recipe.

"What do you mean, changed the recipe? He isn't using basil in his pesto any longer?" Fullerton asked.

Actually, the buyer admitted, the chef had decided to buy pesto rather than make it himself.

"Well, should I tell my farmers to plow under their fields?" Fullerton asked.

While he might have cursed, Fullerton didn't blame Whole Foods, because he saw it as a mismatched partner for TOG. He knew TOG couldn't provide palates of produce all year long, like much larger California producers. Unless a regional manager made a special effort, Whole Foods wasn't going to become a steady buyer of TOG's diverse goods, like the restaurants, co-ops, independent grocery stores, and delicatessen that quickly bought the basil Whole Foods no longer needed. They were a better match for TOG's scale.

"TOG's always been about two things," Fullerton told a group of visiting chefs. "First, it's been about creating a system for marketing produce so that farmers can do what they do best—farm. Secondly, it's about community, about the ecosystem that we are all a part of. So if a restaurant goes under, a farmer won't be left holding unsold goods, or if a farmer's crop fails, others can fill in to make sure you get your produce." A market brought these two worlds together. While the endeavor was informed and even created by ideals, it was propelled by commerce—a point the chefs, busy in their kitchens, or the farmers in their fields, might have missed.

February now. Snow covers the Pennsylvania State University campus, two hours north of the Crawfords' farm, where a "Farming for the Future" conference is underway. From California to Iowa to Minnesota and Vermont, winter's the time for these agricultural conferences. More than 1,500 people have come, a fair number in their forties and fifties, with weathered clothes and scruffy work boots. A smattering of Amish are present, with their familiar beards and dark attire, the women with hair coverings, a skinny boy furtively looking at a television set playing a video. Then there are the rural folks with John Deere hats, overalls, and work shirts, and a younger generation with knitted wool hats, Indian-weave shirts, sneakers, beards, and a tattoo or piercing—college-age kids looking to get back to the land.

The conference is sponsored by the Pennsylvania Association for Sustainable Agriculture (PASA), a nonprofit organization the Crawfords helped found, to support organic and sustainable farmers. The sessions include panels on how to establish a relationship with a chef, grow various heirloom vegetable varieties, sell grass-fed beef, and manage shallow-till plowing. It's all nuts and bolts: How to run your farm, sell your produce, and care for your soil in a way that might make a living and also protect the earth and the rural community. This premise unites the group. Dairy farmers, ranchers, horticulturalists, and vegetable farmers like Crawford are here. Many have been coming for years. "I always get pumped up when I get here," Crawford tells me. "Can't you feel the energy?" One of the keynoters, Cheryl Tevis, an editor with *Successful Farming* magazine and from Des Moines, Iowa, contrasts the hopeful air at the conference to other farm gatherings she attends. "Most are suffused with despair," she tells the crowd.

The evening I arrived, Crawford urged me to talk to his friend Jack Hedin—"very smart, went to Yale, worked out in California on a couple of farms"—who apprenticed at New Morning Farm a decade earlier and now ran an organic farm with a partner in southeastern Minnesota. About six feet tall and in his late thirties, Hedin's chosen profession was apparent in his massive shoulders and arms. Looking at this crowd, you wouldn't know the nation faced an obesity epidemic. Just then, Fullerton walked up, the only computer-bound worker in the bunch besides me, as evidenced by our midsections. We went downstairs to grab a bite in the bar, and after a couple of beers, the talk veered to California.

"I mean, Jim, doesn't it just get you?" Hedin said. "They can grow anything I can grow, better, at any time of the year, except for one crop—fall raspberries. I mean, I hate California, don't you, Jim?"

Crawford smiled and didn't say a word.

"They've got perfect weather," Hedin continued. "They grow year around, but I couldn't get used to that, either. Jim, you know how things start to slow down in October? How you begin to look forward to the winter? Well, when I was out there, I couldn't believe it. They took two weeks off and then were sprouting lettuce again in the greenhouse. It was a hundred and one degrees in October. I couldn't deal with it. I got sick. I had to take a few days off and go down to San Francisco."

Hedin had eminent respect for California farmers. His friends at Full Belly Farm—four partners who had long run a highly successful and influential organic farm in the Capay Valley, about ninety minutes north of the Bay Area—hired him regularly for a few winters, and his oldest son had been born in a small shack on the farm. But he was about to be competing with organic farms from California in the wholesale produce market. Winning the ear of a sympathetic Midwest produce manager at Whole Foods, Hedin had just reached a deal to sell the store organic heirloom tomatoes and sweet corn. If it worked out, the deal would put his organic farm, Featherstone Fruits and Vegetables, on a much sounder economic footing. On Crawford's advice he had asked Whole Foods for a contract. "He was going to borrow like $100,000 to do this and I told him, 'You better get a contract,'" Crawford later told me. "I wouldn't trust 'em. But Jack thinks this is his ticket."

When Hedin gave a presentation about his business—which relied on a farmers' market, co-op stores in the Twin Cities, and a Community Supported Agriculture (CSA) scheme in which customers pay $400 upfront each season to receive a box of vegetables every week—I realized why the Whole Foods deal was so important. On the third page of a handout Hedin passed around, a spreadsheet listed the farm's gross sales, net profit, payroll, and loans over the past seven years. The more I studied it, the tighter my stomach grew. Sales had started at $35,000 in 1997, with a gross profit of $7,200. The figures rose the following years on the revenue side, but income was something else. By 2001—year four at Featherstone Farm—Jack and his partner, Rhys Williams, had grossed $128,000 but made only $20,000 in profits. By 2002, sales climbed to $152,000, but earnings were still $22,000. Maybe these profits came *after* the partner's salaries, I thought, so I looked at the payroll line. But payroll was only $42,000 total for seven seasonal migrant workers, a couple of farm interns, and a part-time office worker. The partners' take-home pay came out of these profits and from debt.

Over the seven years, the farm had amassed more than $100,000 in loans from family members and its customers and was now angling for another $90,000 bank operating loan to ramp up for the Whole Foods deal. The money had gone toward greenhouses, trucks, tractors, used cargo vans, and a stream of chisel plows, weeders, seeders, and transplanters—much of it second- or third-hand and requiring time to repair or rejigger. (I found that a surprising number of organic farmers rely on tractors and farm equipment dating to the 1960s or even earlier.)

Hedin was speaking about "work-life balance" now. His wife, Jenni McHugh, worked off the farm, as a midwife, and they had two sons he wanted to spend time with, but he felt

pressure to make the farm viable. He had tried to work less—
fifty hours a week instead of seventy—because of the kids, but
now the pendulum was swinging back toward more hours. "I
have to make money or I can't justify this to my family any
longer," he said. "My goals have shifted and now I need money
instead of time."

Several months later, I visited Hedin and McHugh in
Rushford, Minnesota, in the southeast corner of the state. For
several years they had been living in a six-family cohousing
community on a 550-acre farm in the Wiscoy Valley. Streams
cut deep into the land—the Mississippi River was forty miles
to the east—forming depressions and valleys between the rolling
hills and expanses of flat land, covered with corn, soybean fields,
and pasture. The families shared a communal meal once a week
in a central building, swam in the pond they had dug beside
Money Creek, which ran down the valley, and played baseball
on the grass field they had graded flat. Hedin and Williams,
whose family was also part of the community, rented forty acres
from the group for their farm.

After he gave me a tour of the farm one morning, we rode
up the hill to another field he had rented to grow the tomatoes
for Whole Foods. Hedin was proud of his heirlooms. He was
also a bit amazed that he and one other farmer in the Upper
Midwest were providing the bulk of them for the chain's Midwest stores, and receiving a higher price than he could get at a
farmers' market. So far, the plants were looking good, the leaves
a rich green, with tiny flowers that would bear fruit. Oats and
buckwheat grew between the rows to keep down the weeds.
Each row was set twelve feet apart, wide enough to get a flatbed
truck between them at harvest and to increase airflow, reducing
the threat of mildew. Hedin explained that the heat enveloped

the top of the hill, creating better growing conditions for a crop like tomatoes than the valley below, which had richer soil but cooler, more humid air that could promote disease. The downside was that he had to truck in water to feed the drip irrigation lines.

"Last year, we had twelve hundred plants, this year we've got nine thousand," he said. If all went as planned, 45 percent of that year's revenue would come from the Whole Foods contract. His biggest fear was a hailstorm, but so far he had been spared.

Hedin and his partner had decided with trepidation to sell to Whole Foods, and not only because the company would become their biggest customer. They also felt strong loyalty to customer-owned co-op stores in the Twin Cities, where the movement is especially strong. (Whole Foods has opened only two stores in the area that compete with the co-ops.) Many of these co-ops buy from a central produce distributor, Co-op Partners Warehouse, a $4 million business that had been instrumental in supporting local farms. Although Co-op Partners also bought a lot of its produce from California, it often paid a higher price for locally grown food. The price Hedin got for his zucchini, for example, was nearly double the price from the West Coast. Co-op Partners supplied stores such as the Wedge, which took a lower markup on locally grown food to keep the retail price below what it would have been otherwise. This not only helped keep small farms running but also gave the co-op's members what they wanted—local food. For these consumers, a tomato was not just a tomato.

"Thank God for them," Hedin said.

Even with these loyalties, Featherstone Farm was having a hard time achieving sustainability, facing challenges that aren't always recognized by proponents of a purely local food system.

Featherstone was not near a premium market such as New York or the Bay Area. Hedin would come home from the farmers' market in Rochester with his truck three-quarters full if it was raining, or if a festival in town lured people away. Customers also had their own backyard gardens. "They would come up and say, 'Wow, you've got beans already. Doesn't look like mine will come in for another week or two,'" he said. That meant he could sell them beans this week but not the following.

The farm's subscription operation, or CSA, also had its difficulties. These schemes, which began on two farms on the East Coast in 1986, now number more than 1,700 across the nation and are strongly associated with the organic movement. But a 1999 survey reported that the farms' median CSA income (with half above and half below) was $15,000. While the CSA guaranteed an income for a portion of Featherstone's crops and let customers share in the farm's risk, the operation had to be augmented with the other revenue streams.

Despite the ideal of a highly diversified farm, Hedin also found it difficult to grow everything they needed to satisfy their CSA customers. He felt it best to concentrate on crops suited to the soil and microclimate of the farm, rather than grow 150 as some other CSA farmers do. To supply the CSA, Featherstone had teamed up with another farm, so each could specialize and combine to give their customers a wider range.

Then there were transportation issues. Sending a rickety van to deliver produce to Rochester or the Twin Cities meant tying up a worker for the whole day and getting a gas bill to boot. When he sold to Whole Foods, an empty truck on its way back from a Twin Cities delivery drove down the dirt road to his farm, loaded up the pallets, and charged him sixty dollars to haul it to the company's regional Midwest distribution center outside Chicago. It freed up his time, cut transportation expenses, and added an energy-efficient benefit from utilizing a truck that would have otherwise run home empty and that allowed him to forgo his gas-guzzling van. (In the larger scheme of things, however, this still wasn't energy efficient, since Whole Foods would then send a loaded truck from the distribution center to the Twin Cities, returning a portion of Featherstone's produce to Minnesota.)

Hedin's deal was not standard for the natural-foods chain, which doesn't send trucks to small farms around the country to gather produce and fill its refrigerated shelves. Much of what Whole Foods stocks is from big producers such as Cal-Organic, owned by the biggest vegetable company in the nation, Grimmway Farms, in Bakersfield, California. Whole Foods isn't alone or unusual in this decision. Co-ops also stock Cal-Organic, because, as one produce buyer told me, the company delivers high-quality goods. Plus, buyers can use one company to get a lot of what they need.

Still, Whole Foods has recently stepped up local food offerings, promising when it opened a new store in New York City's Union Square in 2005 to buy up to 20 percent of its produce in the tri-state area.

Featherstone Farm's deal with Whole Foods worked out well, amounting to nearly $100,000 in business in 2003. The heirloom tomato plants I saw growing on top of the hill came in especially robust that summer and the natural-foods chain took as many cases as they could provide because severe rains on the East Coast had decimated the tomato crop that year. Whole Foods diverted West Coast produce to the East to make up for the shortfall, leaving Hedin and other local growers with a bigger slice of the Midwest market.

If all went well at Featherstone Farm, if it avoided hail and rain damage and kept its customers happy, the farm would gross

$400,000 a year. Debt payments would take at least $35,000 off the top, leaving Hedin and Williams with $40,000 each in take-home pay after expenses. This was the *best-case* scenario, one they had not yet reached, because a storm or cold weather, or emergency borrowing, or the need for a new truck, undermined their plans. Their hope was to become big enough and profitable enough to pay down their debt. If that happened, the cash from produce sales would cover the farm's expenses, wages, salaries, and capital improvements. In short, they would achieve sustainability.

That was the dream, anyway.

When I was at the farm, Jack and Jenni invited me to dinner. We sat down with their two boys at the picnic table beside their trailer home, on a rolling hillside with the fields below. Jenni had made some green beans picked earlier in the day, a baked tofu dish, rice, and a berry cobbler with fruit from the farm. But when I began to ask about the farm, I could sense the tension the venture engendered. They were expecting a third child, and while the trailer was comfortable, I sensed this was not what they had in mind when they started out. It was now eight years on and hard to say whether this farm, for all its progress, was "sustainable" in their conception of the word, in a way that made sense for their family.

As with any start-up, you could argue these were the lean years. But a start-up is predicated on the assumption that the business will take off, that a profit will ensue and an asset will grow in value. The farm was on the right track, but it was taking an awful lot of work and patience to wring even a basic living from the land. I later told Hedin that given what he was making after a sixty- or seventy-hour workweek, he was in effect giving his customers a food subsidy. He had certainly traded

the prospect of a much higher salary, in any number of professions, based on his education. But he didn't buy the argument.
His job was to make the farm work, whatever the circumstance.
It wasn't a question of whether he was being forced to subsidize
his consumer, but of figuring out how to make a decent living
while selling at a price his customers would accept. So far, this
was an elusive balance, even in the organic marketplace, though
Hedin and his partner had by no means given up.

Crawford, too, had his challenges, though over thirty years he
had designed a farming and retailing business that worked. Still,
it bothered him that he made more money as a retailer than as a
farmer. When he sold TOG's offerings, for example, he marked
up the price 50 percent to be assured of a decent profit. He didn't
have to worry about losing one-third of his crop to plant diseases
or a hailstorm, or about the cost of field labor or the myriad other
concerns that add up to the expense of growing a crop and making it back, with a profit, at the time of sale. All he had to worry
about was picking up produce at TOG's warehouse and reselling
it, without damaging it along the way or returning home with
too many unsold boxes—an easier game than farming.

We talked about this one day sitting in his office—a small
building with a window looking out over the lower field, where
tomatoes grew. His wood desk was littered with papers, in-
voices, and Post-it notes. Behind him, the intercom crackled
with questions from Moie or Fullerton or one of his workers.
Shelves of rough-hewn lumber were piled with papers and seed
catalogs. His mud-covered rubber boots sat by the door. He was
sounding pessimistic.

"I don't want to look at my life's work as an economic model
of conformity. I choose this life for idealistic reasons. And I

don't regret thirty years of pretty shitty income. But if agriculture depends on people like me, it's not going to work," he said.

He pulled out a spreadsheet from a presentation he had given a couple of years earlier. Despite his high revenue per acre, his fields hadn't made much money because of loan interest and high labor costs. Crawford refused to hire the skilled migrant farm laborers who commonly work the orchards, nurseries, and vegetable farms in central Pennsylvania—and the rest of the nation. Productivity from high school kids, other local workers, and interns he hired each year was lower—and thus his costs higher—than it might have been with migrants.

"I'm very tempted to use migrants," he said, "but it so goes against my grain. I'm totally Don Quixote about it—it's stupid in some ways."

Even if he paid a fair wage, Crawford didn't want to benefit from the economic desperation of people looking for work in the United States. I wondered if this was nearsighted, since he would be giving a job to a skilled laborer who wanted and needed the work. In any case, his three-decade stance on this issue lasted only one more season. Hedin and friends in New England who employed Mexican and Hmong workers convinced Crawford the issue wasn't whether to hire migrants but how to treat them in terms of hours, wages, and housing. This was low-wage work, but Hedin, Cochran, and organic farmers I talked with had the same seasonal staff return to their farms year after year. These growers had helped some workers with their immigration status, and made loans so others could buy homes. This was not universal, nor overseen by any third party (except in Cochran's case with his UFW contract). But labor is crucial to produce farming—organic or conventional—which is why migrant workers are hired throughout the industry. If you were going to hire migrants, there were ways to do it right.

Crawford finally hired two migrant workers in 2003, but his Spanish was sparse, the workers lacked transportation to the farm (he ended up buying them a car), and then the one who drove decided to seek other work, leaving the second worker stranded. It seemed a comical attempt to enter a labor market with which he was unfamiliar. But once that bridge was crossed, that compromise made, Crawford noted an improvement in productivity and profitability. Eventually, he offered housing to two migrant workers on the farm. (The interns also live there.) He had also made massive investments in equipment and buildings—into the six figures over a few years—and decided to raise prices. He realized he had kept prices too low for too long when the FreshFarm market opened. "We were in this ridiculous situation where we were charging less when we had no competition," he said. "When we saw what others were charging, we raised our prices!" His customers didn't flinch, because the prices were still competitive with other venues with high-quality produce, such as Whole Foods.

These measures, which came none too soon with retirement looming, meant his stalwart customers would not have to worry about whether their farmer would be selling to them the following year. He had achieved sustainability.

"It's a predictable, strong economic model, but it took us a long time to reach this point," he said. "If this had happened fifteen years ago, we'd be in good shape."

He and Moie were now pulling $100,000 out of the business annually—an above-average farm income, considering that only 10 percent of all U.S. farms earn more than $50,000—and had some money left over to save toward retirement. But they wouldn't be able to retire on the savings they could amass ahead; the model that proved economically viable had kicked in too late. The Crawfords' only hope now was to bring in a new farmer who might learn the business and then gradually buy them out. Perhaps a former intern; Crawford wasn't sure. That act still had to be played out.

While Crawford grumbled about how unprofitable farming was, it was clear he had made choices along the way that fit into his ideals of what the farm should be. He avoided migrant labor for years, relying on interns, untrained in farming and apt to leave after one or two years. He planted many crops, in line with the principles of biodiversity, rather than growing a more manageable number. He remained in a beautiful, craggy valley, with hilly slopes, less than ideal for crop farming.

"He could have made decisions that would have been more economically lucrative, but it would not have fit into his idea of the right thing to do," Fullerton said. "But, at the same time, he always has recognized the importance of compromise—that you can't be totally idealistic."

Crawford had walked a fine line, designing a business that worked for the scale of the farm, played into his strengths as a farmer and marketer, and reflected his own balance of ideals and practicality. The model could be adapted if it followed these principles: that marketing is as important as farming, on a smaller scale, and takes as much, if not more, time and devotion than the fields themselves. The number of certified organic farms has increased around the country—from three thousand in 1993 to seven thousand in 2001 to nine thousand in 2004. The total is probably closer to between fifteen and twenty thousand, including farms that use organic methods but are uncertified. These are small numbers compared to the two million U.S. farms, but the significant thing is that they are growing—unlike other independent farmers, who are disappearing from the landscape. The work of the coming generation will be to build on the examples of Crawford and Fullerton, establishing more viable market outlets so that organic farmers have places to sell.

This experiment in creating a local "foodshed" is just one slice of the organic market, just one of the interpretations of the organic ideal. Others have taken a very different path, doing whatever they could to increase sales, drive down prices, and compete with conventional farmers in mainstream markets. This means growing organic food on a large scale, shipping it nationally, and making sure prices are competitive so people will buy it at the supermarket. While this approach increased the size of the organic market in the 1990s, it sent shock waves through the movement, since it appeared at odds with small-farm ideals. I soon saw this tension play out in a California company pursuing this expansive track: Earthbound Farm.

4. A Spring Mix

Growing Organic Salad

My definition of fresh *is that the perfect little lettuces are carefully hand-picked from the hillside garden and served within a few hours.*
—ALICE WATERS, 1982

It would be hard to miss the corporate offices of Earthbound Farm, the largest organic produce company in the nation. The operation is just off Highway 101, a half-hour inland from the central coast of California and five minutes from San Juan Bautista—a picturesque small town best known for the nineteenth-century Spanish mission tower James Stewart warily climbed in Alfred Hitchcock's *Vertigo*. Beside green fields that stretch for miles toward the Gabilan Mountains to the east sits a squat 205,000-square-foot processing plant—the biggest of five the company has erected at a cost of more than $110 million. Out back, a row of refrigerated semitrailers lines up, waiting to pick up the twenty-two million servings of organic salad the company sells each week. In front, a huge refrigerated truck idles while a forklift unloads plastic bins of cut lettuce fresh from the fields. The bins whiz by me, headed for a submarine-sized vacuum cooling tube. Within twenty minutes the lettuce is chilled to thirty-six degrees, beginning a cold chain that will continue as the salad is washed and bagged and sent to supermarkets around the country, where it is sold within seventeen days.

I'd come to the plant to talk with Drew and Myra Goodman, a couple in their midforties who founded Earthbound on a two-and-a-half-acre garden plot two decades earlier. From these humble roots, they created a company with $360 million in sales, ranked fourth-largest in the $2.5 billion bagged-salad industry. With a 5 percent share of the packaged salad market, they have triple the market penetration of most organic foods. Earthbound bagged lettuce could now be found in three out of four supermarkets. The Goodmans grow produce on nearly twenty-six thousand acres, mostly in California and Arizona, but also in Mexico, Canada, Chile, and New Zealand (for Kiwis).

But for all their success, their company was controversial in organic circles. Myra, a svelt and casually fashionable woman with long dark hair and a New York accent, mentioned that Earthbound employees attending California's Ecological Farming Conference, the premier annual event, had covered up or removed their ID badges to avoid open hostility from other attendees. "They felt like Jews in Nazi Germany, like they shouldn't be there," Myra said. When she complained, the conference organizer pleaded with her to remain a top sponsor.

What irked the organic critics wasn't simply Earthbound's size—clearly antithetical to the ideal of the small diversified farm—but the way the Goodmans had achieved it. "They were aggressive and predatory," one farmer told me. The accepted story seemed to be that they had stolen the organic salad market from smaller farmers, overproducing and dropping the price until these competitors were driven out. If true, this version of Earthbound's corporate history could be read as a parable for the mainstreaming of organic food, altering the character, ideals, and practices of the founding generation. Would this move toward industrial-sized organic farming undermine the identity of organic food itself?

The Goodmans felt no need to apologize for their success or sidestep the criticism when I brought it up. Drew, a broad-shouldered man who was friendly, though less effusive than Myra, said he simply felt Earthbound was in a different market than small farms since its customers were Safeway and Wal-Mart, not white-tablecloth restaurants or farmers' markets. In these mass markets they had to compete on price with other mainstream players. Plus, the couple made clear, they had never really sought to become Big Organic. It just, well, happened. They had even thought about selling the business and returning to "a simpler life." Their PR pitch emphasizes these roots: Young couple just out of college starts out on a small organic farm in Carmel Valley, selling baby lettuce to chefs and at a farm stand; a light bulb goes off; they put the lettuce in ziplock bags and become the first to sell bagged spring mix to stores. It's a huge hit. Their company grows like crazy—partnering with big farmers, winning supermarket-chain accounts—until it becomes the number-one organic produce company (and third-largest organic food brand after Horizon Organic milk and Silk soy milk).

Behind their obvious marketing smarts, the Goodmans had entrepreneurial zeal, making the right moves to expand at the right time—perhaps because they came into the organic world without a heavy ideological bias. The couple believed in the premise of organic agriculture but were not going to limit their horizons by remaining small, local, and tied to natural-food stores. They replaced the organic idealists' counterculture baggage with practicality, growth, and business. Jeff Larkey of Route 1 Farms, in nearby Santa Cruz, told me that in the 1980s, Drew would drive to his farm in an old Volvo station wagon to pick up lettuce. "You could even sense back then that they had this business mentality, you could kind of see it, so in a way it's not surprising what happened," he said. But if the Goodmans were different, they were not unique in the organic movement: Many of the founders pursued growth and the mainstreaming of organic food in order to have a larger impact on agriculture and on consumers. (This is, after all, how I slipped into the movement: through the attractive entry point of Whole Foods.)

But to make sense of how two college kids raised on the Upper East Side of Manhattan—the son of an art dealer and the daughter of a jewelry manufacturer—ended up with the biggest organic produce business in the nation, if not the world, it's necessary to leave them for the moment and take in the landscape. Because the issue of *where* they started, it turns out, was as crucial to their success as all that followed. Had they begun farming on the East Coast, they would probably still be selling at a roadside stand, or at a farmers' market, if they were still farming at all. But they hadn't begun on the East Coast. They had pursued a decidedly Californian model. This was only something I understood after visiting the Salinas Valley, the Salad Bowl of the World, where it all began.

The moniker, it turns out, is accurate. Leaving the college and beach resort town of Santa Cruz, a strongly liberal enclave with a long history in the organic movement, I drove south on Highway 1 to the Salinas Valley. The road narrowed and then entered a plain with huge fields on either side, the ones to my right just inland from the sea. These weren't small family farms nestled in quaint valleys, like back East, but vast fields clearly driven by the acquisitive urge of business.

The Jeffersonian ideal of small-scale yeoman farmers, which lives on so strongly in the American imagination, was never central to California farming, because California farms were founded not by American settlers but by Spanish colonial land grants. The word "farms" isn't even used much in the valley, but "ranches," a holdover from the nineteenth-century Spanish *ranchos*. These vast land parcels, granted by the Spanish and Mexican colonial authorities to the aristocracy, were taken over (often fraudulently) by whites in the 1850s, after California joined the United States. The result was not shoestring family operations but huge "bonanza" wheat farms that employed cheap migrant workers—Indians, along with Chinese immigrants and whites—and shipped wheat to Europe over the transcontinental railroad, completed in 1869. Some farmers even called for the importation of southern slave labor, envisioning a plantation-ideal in the West. Smaller farmers criticized the feudal-like conditions in the countryside and the monoculture of wheat, joining in the call in 1884 to ban Chinese immigrants. But, ironically, by the 1890s, with a global glut in grains, these smaller farms had become fast-growth, capital-intensive businesses that needed immigrant labor, too. With irrigation, fruit supplanted big wheat, foreshadowing what would happen time and again in California agriculture. One crop would take over the formerly predominant one, and efficiencies and marketing savvy would be applied to make the new product highly profitable. That is, until too many farmers got into the game, leading to overproduction and falling prices and the desperate attempt by growers to avoid bankruptcy by finding the next hot item. There was no reason organic farmers would be able to avoid this fate.

The huge scale of California farming was apparent in the endless crews of farmworkers I saw bending over strawberries or artichokes, or working beside huge lettuce-harvesting machines, in the morning sun of the Salinas Valley. I never saw a white person among them, other than managers. This was the type of expensive farmland Cochran could not afford when he began farming strawberries just north of here. I was told much of the land was managed by lawyers for absentee landlords, descendants of the original deed-holding families who now lived scattered across the country and owned the land through trusts. High rent and high volume went hand in hand, since growers had to produce enough to pay rents and still make profits, while high productivity continued to boost land prices. Monterey County, in the heart of the Salinas Valley, produced $3.3 billion worth of agricultural goods in 2003, third among all California counties and thus third in the nation. This valley is the source of 90 percent of the nation's salad greens.

To get a better understanding of the valley, I visited the National Steinbeck Center, which honors Salinas's most famous native son. Oprah Winfrey had recently sent John Steinbeck's *East of Eden* to the top of the bestseller list, and the novel's epic tale of brother against brother through three generations of the Trask family could be read as a metaphor for the struggles in the salad business that dominate the valley today. The center had just opened an exhibit called Valley of the World, which I caught after eating lunch—a giant chef salad, with conventional lettuce from a local producer—at the center's café.

In a breezy fashion, the exhibit told how the valley was settled, through cattle ranches and the tanning industry of the nineteenth century, the dairies of the early twentieth century, the rise and fall of the sugar beet industry, and the ascendance of fresh vegetables and lettuce. The exhibit emphasized the way a new technology, company, specialty crop, or immigrant labor group supplanted the previous one. After the Chinese in the nineteenth century came the Japanese, then the Filipinos, then the Okies fleeing the dust bowl, and finally the Mexicans, whose presence rose once Japanese Americans were interned in concentration camps during World War II. There were portraits of several families who, in one way or another, had "made it" in the new land. What the exhibit didn't elaborate on was the way new immigrants had been brought in to undercut any hard-fought advancements in wages or working conditions the previous group had won. This practice continued until the present, with the publicized victories of the United Farm Workers eroded by a new wave of undocumented workers from Mexico and by the outsourcing of field labor to independent contractors. Indeed, the central conflict in California agriculture has not been between big and small farms, but between business owners and wage labor.

The exhibit showed that so-called grower-shippers were at the heart of the valley's business structure. These companies made money by participating in all segments of the business—not only in farming, but in cooling, packing, marketing, and distribution. Many of these companies were built on family relationships that went back generations. When I spoke on the phone with Tanimura & Antle's president, Rick Antle, he referred to the company as a "family farm"—a comment that left me nearly speechless considering it is the nation's largest lettuce grower, with forty-seven thousand acres of farmland. But, in the context of California, he was right.

The Tanimura family had lost everything during World War II when they were sent, along with other Japanese Americans, to a barbed-wire-ringed "relocation camp" in Poston, Arizona, for three and a half years, while two of seven brothers served in the U.S. military. When they returned to the Salinas Valley, the brothers worked as field laborers and saved enough money to buy a twenty-acre farm. Soon the Tanimura brothers were supplying "Bud" Antle's produce distribution operation with lettuce. By 1971, Antle's firm had grown into the largest marketing company for head lettuce in the United States, and the Tanimuras had grown in lockstep. A decade later, the families formed Tanimura & Antle. Their grandchildren, such as Rick Antle, and nieces and nephews show up at work today.

"We still do everything fifty-fifty," George Tanimura, one of the original brothers and now the reigning patriarch, in his late eighties, told me at the barnlike corporate headquarters. He was dressed like a farmer, in a plaid shirt and work pants. This was the story of how a California family farm evolved.

Even this brief tour of Salinas made clear that the fields, packing plants, and crews I saw each day were part of a story as old as the valley itself. But so, too, was another vision, of an agrarian California. In the 1930s, Steinbeck thought that the Okies could populate a new strata of family farms, since they were in effect displaced Jeffersonian yeomen. He advocated a new era of small farms, set up through state and federal land grants. (But his vision also had a racist tinge, since he thought foreign migrants should not be given land ownership grants because they were "a peon class" in comparison to hearty yeomen.)

Contemporary small-farm advocacy rose again with the sustainable and organic farming movement, since these farms in the 1970s and 1980s flourished outside the realm of conventional agriculture. Earthbound Farm found itself in the crosshairs of this movement for pursuing its market on a large scale in the 1990s and driving prices down. But the rise of Big Organic—whether practiced by the Goodmans or another company—might have been expected. Success in farming breeds imitation and the infrastructure—and perhaps, more importantly, the entire culture—of the Salinas Valley is geared toward growth. When an observant grower identifies a new, profitable niche, it is not a question of whether to tackle it, but how, before the next guy gets in the game and drives the price to the floor. That process was as evident with organic spring mix in the 1990s as it was with bonanza wheat in the 1870s.

Spring mix began on a very small scale, like a lovely little side plate of greens in a multicourse gourmet meal. The greens were grown in gardens in Berkeley, two hours north of the Salinas Valley but a world away. There, a number of chefs, among them Alice Waters of Chez Panisse—perhaps the most prominent voice in establishing a link to small, local, and organic farms—developed a new California cuisine that later swept the nation. An important component of the menu was a salad of baby lettuce, which for Chez Panisse became a signature dish. It quickly took the Bay Area by storm and amounted to a shift in the way salad was perceived and consumed—a shift that would eventually affect the American palate. For Waters, baby lettuce wasn't just a dish, but an expression of an approach to good food simply prepared.

In *Chez Panisse Menu Cookbook,* Waters explains that she was richly influenced by living abroad in France at age nineteen, when she had something of an epiphany. "It was the first time for so many foods," she writes in the cookbook's introduction. "The idea of ever opening a restaurant hadn't entered my conscious mind but I experienced a major realization: I hadn't eaten *anything,* comparatively speaking, and I wanted to taste *everything.* I began to see a pattern—a technique for looking at food, examining it, and understanding it." She lived near a farmers' market and absorbed the love of fresh ingredients, ate languorous dinners with friends, and then sought, when she returned home, to recreate the experience. "It was important that I was driven, as if I had a sense of mission," she writes. "I didn't envision success. All I cared about was a place to sit down with my friends and enjoy good food while discussing the politics of the day. And I believed that in order to experience food as good as I had in France I had to cook and serve it myself." The radical idealism of the time and the locale—Berkeley in the late 1960s—was crucial to this confidence and the culinary concept. "We all believed in community and personal commitment and quality," she writes. "Chez Panisse was born out of these ideals. Profit was always secondary."

Waters opened the Berkeley restaurant in a two-story wood house, in 1971, when she was twenty-seven. While she emphasized fresh, local, and seasonal produce, in the early days, she had to rely on wholesale markets because she couldn't find farmers to supply her. For the baby-lettuce greens, cooks would attack forty or fifty cases of large-leaf lettuce, stripping the outer layers to get at the small, tender leaves inside. Waters didn't add the mixture of lettuces known as mesclun—the precursor to spring mix—until a visit to a farmers' market near Nice, in southern France, several years later.

"It was very particular to the region," she told me. "Farmers would bring it to the market, display it on a big tablecloth, and sell it by the pound." Derived from the Provençal word for "mixture," mesclun may contain young greens like rocket (similar to arugula), small lettuces, chicories, dandelion greens, mâche, chervil—as many as twenty-three ingredients. In her book, Waters describes the experience of discovering the greens: "How well I remember buying armloads of mesclun, as my friend Martine exclaimed, 'But Alice, you are not buying to feed the restaurant!' The commingling of colors and textures, and the contrasting flavors of these diminutive lettuces tempted me to eat the salad right from the sink." For Waters, a well-made salad with dressing was "analogous to the balance of nature in many ways."

Hoping to add mesclun to the restaurant's menu, she returned home from France with the seeds in hand and planted them in a garden behind her house. Up came dandelion, frisée, mâche, and watercress. Needing more, she convinced friends and patrons to grow the greens in their gardens, trading meals for produce and keeping track of the transactions in a leather ledger near the front door. "Foragers Alice knew would bring these wonderful little things, like miner's lettuce, nettle, indigenous things that were in a lovely mixture," said Todd Koons, who joined Chez Panisse in 1987 soon after he graduated high school. Koons cooked, "foraged" for fresh ingredients, and started a garden with the head chef, Jean-Pierre Moullé, on a half-acre plot owned by a local doctor. They grew lettuce following the biodynamic and intensive French methods of Alan Chadwick, who ran the farm gardens at the University of California at Santa Cruz and influenced a generation of organic farmers in northern California. (The farm garden would later grow into the Center for Agroecology, where ecologist Stephen Gliessman worked during his research with Cochran on his organic strawberries.)

Another crucial player in the budding salad market was Le Marché Seeds, a home-based company in Dixon, east of the Bay Area. Georgeanne Brennan, who had lived in southern France in the 1970s, and Charlotte Glenn—both former high school teachers—founded the company in 1982. They traveled to Europe to research seeds, then imported and sold them to farmers and gardeners, including Koons, first in the Bay Area and then nationally. The pair introduced to the United States a number of now-common lettuce varieties such as Lollo Rossa, Rouge d'Hiver, Merveille de Quatre Saisons, and Reine de Glace—as well as Lacinata kale and Chioga beets, which are often found at farmers' markets.

By the time Le Marché was active, organic farmers and gardeners were growing heirloom varieties (those at least fifty years old) rather than the common supermarket offerings of iceberg, romaine, and red- and green-leaf. After all, they were pursuing an "alternative" to the mainstream—in their farming methods, way of life, crop varieties, and marketing networks. Digging around to find out who first grew mesclun in the Bay Area— many think it was Waters, though many farmers cite Le Marché as their first seed source—I became aware of how many immigrants carried seeds with them to America. In New Jersey, for example, the nonprofit Garden State Heirloom Seed Society offers a plethora of local heirlooms brought over by Italian, Greek, Chinese, and Eastern European immigrants and passed down from parent to child for generations, in backyard gardens. So, while it's difficult to say who "first" grew mesclun in the United States—I expect to hear from the grandchild of a French immigrant carefully tending the family's seeds in Connecticut— Waters, the Bay Area chefs, and Le Marché's specialty catalog helped catapult salad mix to national recognition in the 1980s. In fact, Waters counts simple mesclun mix with dressing as one of her greatest accomplishments as a chef.

Ultimately, the Berkeley gardens proved inadequate to the needs of Chez Panisse, so Sibella Kraus, a cook at Chez Panisse Café (the informal restaurant upstairs from the main dining room), set up a small network of farms to supply six restaurants in the Bay Area. Aside from Chez Panisse, the vegetarian restaurant Greens, started by the San Francisco Zen Center, and four others participated. The restaurants were far more specialized and discriminating than natural-food stores, co-ops, and farmers' markets; and the produce they wanted—baby carrots, haricots verts, baby lettuces—couldn't easily be unloaded anywhere else. The farmers worked closely with the chefs to determine varieties and quantities, and with Le Marché to see what seed was available. Among the most popular items that summer of

1983 were the miniatures: baby leeks, baby beans, baby summer squash, baby spinach, baby new potatoes, baby carrots, and of course, baby lettuce.

Relationships grew out of Kraus's farm-restaurant project, including one between Chez Panisse and Warren Weber, a farmer in Bolinas, Marin County, about an hour north of San Francisco. Weber had started farming organically in 1974 and had been selling produce to health food stores in the Bay Area. He had a PhD in English from Berkeley, hair down to his shoulders, and a team of draft horses to pull his plow (though he eventually switched to a tractor). He was, and still is, an influential figure among organic farmers in the area, having headed California Certified Organic Farmers, the state's first certification organization, in the mid-1980s.

Weber was also one of the first, if not the first, farmer to sell mesclun to consumers. I sought him out one Saturday morning at San Francisco's bustling Ferry Plaza Farmers' Market, which was five times as big as the Dupont Circle market back home. Venders sold organically grown fruits—peaches, plums, nectarines, figs, and grapes—rarely available at East Coast farmers' markets, as well as the usual tomatoes, potatoes, greens, peppers, lettuces, olive oil, grass-fed beef, breads, and pastries—a veritable feast. I met Weber at his Star Route Farm's stand and we walked to an open-air espresso bar. Tall and thin, his now silvery hair short, Weber looked like a professor, out for a morning stroll.

We sat on a sunny bench overlooking the San Francisco Bay and he pulled from his pocket a label with tiny hand-drawn lettuces and the word *mesclun* written in capital letters. "This was the original label," he said.

He got into the business when Kraus came out to his farm one day, looking for baby lettuces for Chez Panisse. At first he was confused. "What do you mean, 'baby lettuces'?" he asked.

She pointed to the tiny plants that had sprouted five or six weeks earlier. Weber was happy to quickly sell a crop that would normally take ten to sixteen weeks to reach maturity. Under a contract with Waters, he agreed to provide lettuce four to six inches high, three times a week, "shipped from the farm within one hour" of harvest.

The contract specified the produce would be grown organically, although Weber told me Waters had not been catholic about that initially. "I can remember having little discussions with Alice about organic, trying to say, 'This is important, what we're doing here. This is different.' And she'd say, 'Well, I get great stuff from these other guys and they're not organic,'" he recalled.

Waters told me she had an aversion to the word *organic*, and resisted using it on the restaurant's menu, because to her it represented "health food." "That was the worst and I didn't want to be associated with it," she said. Waters was interested in taste, size, and the way the salad looked. Only later did she tie those qualities to the way the food was grown. Weber also made the case for the importance of stewardship of the land and responsible agronomic practices, and Waters came around. Today, she is a vocal proponent of organic farming, with a public-school garden project in Berkeley and several other endeavors promoting sustainable, local farming, and local-food consumption.

When Weber realized how successful the baby-lettuce heads were, he wanted to sell them to retail stores, but he could only do so if he could package the delicate product. He talked it over with Waters, who told Koons to help Weber figure it out. Koons found a plastic fabricator who made a small container that held several baby heads, and soon Weber was in business. He packaged several types of whole baby-lettuce heads with herbs, which sold for six to seven dollars retail. Since diners were familiar with mesclun from local restaurants, they snapped up Star Route Farm's packages in stores.

"They just sold like crazy, absolutely crazy," Weber said, shaking his head at the recollection.

Other farmers joined in by the mid-1980s, including Paul Muller, a partner in Full Belly Farm. "It was one of those crops that was too good to believe," Muller said. "Regular lettuce took three times longer in the field, the boxes were more expensive, and the price was the same." In Watsonville, Dale Coke began to grow baby lettuces on a hillside farm. A former fuel-injection engineer, he had started farming organically in 1981, when he was twenty-eight and seeking a change in his life, after suffering a bout of cancer.

"We started right over there," he told me one hot, sunny afternoon on his ten-acre farm, pointing to a sloping field across the driveway from his home. Coke had first put in organic strawberries—around the same time Cochran was getting started—but added baby squash once he hooked up with Kraus's farm-restaurant project. Soon he added baby lettuce and expanded his fields.

Coke is credited with the second major breakthrough after Weber's container: coming up with the actual product known as "spring mix," now also sold as "mesclun mix," "baby salad," "European salad," and even "yuppie chow." Before Coke, baby lettuce had been sold in whole heads, meaning cooks had to rip the leaves off and wash them. Coke's innovation sprang from all the leftover lettuce he had on hand, because the chefs he sold to all wanted a slightly different mix of heads. "They'd call up on the phone and say they wanted the head with the jagged leaf, or the round one—no one knew what it was," he said. In Los Angeles, chefs preferred heads two to three inches tall. In the Bay Area, four to five inches.

Coke harvested the specific heads to satisfy his customers, but found he had invariably grown too much of one or another variety. He began to cut the baby leaves off the leftover heads, wash the lettuce in a huge bin, and run it through the spin cycle of an old washing machine he kept outside the house. He packaged the mix in three-pound bags, because that's what fit in the boxes he had on hand—setting an industry-standard bulk size that exists today.

Kraus hooked him up with Greenleaf Produce, a restaurant supplier in San Francisco, and soon chefs were clamoring for the prepared mix rather than the whole heads. Coke labeled the salad to reflect the seasonal ingredients it contained—such as autumn mix and winter mix and summer mix—but "after a while, chefs would say, 'No, I want the spring mix; I want it just like it was before,' so the name stuck."

"Immediately, we were doing the same thing," Weber said. "Everyone followed suit."

The Goodmans were among them. They had started farming almost by happenstance, after Myra graduated from UC Berkeley in 1984. Her parents had bought an investment property in Carmel Valley and asked the young couple if they wanted to live there and fix it up. The two planned to stay for a year while Myra applied to graduate school. They moved into a six-hundred-square-foot guesthouse, rented out the main home, and then took a look at the field of raspberries out back, which were quite popular in the neighborhood. The previous owner had grown the berries conventionally, but when it came time to spray, Myra was afraid to touch the pesticides. "We really felt like it was poison and figured there's got to be a way we can do this naturally," she told me. They sought advice from the library, local nurseries, organic farmers Drew knew from his alma mater, UC Santa Cruz, and back issues of Rodale's *Organic Gardening.*

They figured out the organic regime for berries, added fresh herbs, and set up a roadside stand, naming it Earthbound Farm. It was then that they heard from local chefs that they could sell baby heads of lettuce for the same price as full-size ones. Since the heads were so small, and could be planted much closer together, they could grow many more of them on their small plot of land. This way their two-and-a-half-acre plot yielded the same revenue as twenty-five acres of full-grown lettuce. Busy farmers that they were, the Goodmans got in the habit on weekends of storing ziplock bags full of small portions of washed baby lettuces they could eat throughout the week. Seeing how convenient this was, they started selling the bags to natural-food stores in 1986. And, like Weber's container and Coke's spring mix, bagged salad took off. Unable to grow enough to meet demand, the Goodmans contacted Coke, an old friend and then the leading grower.

While Coke supplied the Goodmans with spring mix, he was also overnight-shipping the salad mix to distributors and chefs in Los Angeles, New York, and Atlanta. He never advertised, and still could not meet demand. He grew from his original ten acres to five hundred at the peak. Weber, in turn, expanded to Southern California, near Palm Springs, so he could continue growing through the winter. (Growers migrate in the winter to the Imperial Valley or to the desert near Yuma, Arizona, with pickers, packers, and their families in tow, because it's too cool to grow lettuce on the central coast.)

But it was Koons, the onetime Chez Panisse cook, who saw the future. He had left the restaurant, worked in France, and was now back running even bigger lettuce gardens in Berkeley. He caught a whiff of the Salinas Valley when he consulted with a British agricultural company developing herbs and baby spinach. Though the venture fizzled when sales didn't meet projections, Koons realized the possibilities for organic spring mix.

"Nobody had attacked it on a commercial level, so I thought I'd take it on," he told me. "I realized there was a $100 million business there."

Koons was actually following a little-known and aborted attempt by his old friend Brennan at Le Marché Seeds. Brennan had visited production facilities in Europe, where bagged mesclun mix was already being sold in supermarkets, and realized she could bring the process to the U.S. market. In 1986, she partnered with a large Salinas lettuce company, Western Express, to form Opal Rose Inc. She printed up clear plastic-film bags and ran them through a salad-packaging line owned by Western Express, creating what would likely have been the first large-scale bagged organic spring mix product. (Earthbound was still processing in the Goodmans' kitchen.) Brennan took samples to supermarkets, who put in purchase orders, but at the last moment Western Express pulled the plug on the project; she said the company was worried that it would lose too much money. So ended Brennan's pathbreaking attempt to commercialize spring mix.

Koons founded TKO, in 1988, with the goal of using similar industrial processes, though he aimed at the food-service market rather than retail stores. He mounted salad washers on forty-eight-foot trailers that could follow the lettuce harvest south in the winter, developed proprietary seeds and planting techniques, and invested at least $100,000—and, by several accounts, a lot more. (He would not be specific.) Raised outside of Eugene, Oregon, where his back-to-the-land family grew their own food, Koons is loathe to be remembered as the one who industrialized organic salad mix. But he was the first, and for a time succeeded, selling the bulk mix to natural-food wholesalers and food-service suppliers. By 1993, he was doing $15 million in business and trumped Coke to become the top player in the young industry. What he didn't do was come up with the methods that would drop the price dramatically—a saving grace for his smaller competitors.

By the early 1990s, then, all the pieces for a market boom were in place. Waters and her cohorts had popularized mesclun; Brennan and Glenn supplied the seed; Weber had put the baby heads in a consumer-friendly container; Coke had developed a ready-to-eat organic spring-mix product; the Goodmans had added the convenience of a sealed bag; and Koons had ramped up production to a bigger scale. Koons even sought to enlist major lettuce companies in his expansive vision for the budding market. "They kindly dismissed me," he said. "They thought I was a loose screw."

Agribusiness didn't yet see the potential of organic food. It would take a competitive threat to open its eyes, showing just how tied together the opposing worlds of conventional and organic farming can become.

A bag of washed lettuce leaves had long been the Rosetta stone of the salad business. Packaging cut-up lettuce in a bag is an old problem of food science, because once the leaf is cut, it "respires." It breathes in oxygen, exhales carbon dioxide, and degrades, causing the cut edge to turn brown. A sealed bag speeds up the process, because the carbon dioxide builds up inside the bag. The lettuce, essentially, chokes from a lack of oxygen.

If the Goodmans had cut up and packaged heads of iceberg and romaine, they would have found out what every other Salinas processor knew: The leaves spoiled quickly. Cut lettuce in a sealed plastic bag has a shelf life of a few days, which is why for decades an industry based on hardy iceberg and romaine had kept selling whole heads to supermarkets. There was no alternative. But, with spring mix, the Goodmans were dealing with an entirely different product—whole baby leaves cut at the stem. Since the leaves weren't chopped to bits, respiration slowed. This gave the bag a shelf life of about seven days, long enough to deliver and sell in local stores.

Although the Goodmans thought they were first with packaged lettuce, the product has a long and illustrious history, even if no one had got it right on a national scale. Among the pioneers: Charles "Chick" Black, who saw a package of shredded coleslaw in Los Angeles around 1936, then started selling a similar item to his grandmother Annie Condie, who owned the Liberty Park Grocery Store in Salt Lake City. The store grew into Condies Foods, one of the oldest family-owned processors in the nation. Then there was Joseph Brock, a haberdasher in Buffalo, New York, who, facing falling sales, went looking for a new gig in 1947. He began to cut up lettuce in his garage and bag it with a container of homemade salad dressing. In his Plymouth, he hand delivered the "chef salad" to stores, and soon retailers asked for more—without the dressing. In Southern California in 1969, Dennis Gertmenian bought a bathtub for seventy-five dollars and began to wash, cut and package, lettuce in his father's warehouse. He sold the product to restaurants, but it only had a three-day shelf life. He persisted for decades, and eventually built the third-largest fresh-cut-salad company, ReadyPac. In 2004, ReadyPac bought Tanimura & Antle's bagged-lettuce business, showing just how cozy this industry is.

A company known as TransFresh, originally founded by Whirlpool Corporation, had been working on a high-tech solution since the late 1960s, creating Modified Atmospheric Packaging. By reducing the oxygen content in bags and raising the nitrogen level, food scientists slowed respiration. Essentially, the cut lettuce breathed more slowly, delaying its decay. TransFresh packed the cut lettuce in its special MAP bag for the fast-food industry, which was a more natural market than supermarkets because restaurants used the product quickly. The venture was highly profitable, since all the damaged heads in the field could be shredded for the fresh-cut product.

In 1981, TransFresh launched bagged lettuce in stores but had to pull the product because of its short shelf-life. Even in the nitrogen-rich atmosphere, carbon dioxide buildup was a problem. The bag needed to breathe.

TransFresh was by then owned by the Taylor family in Salinas, who, like Tanimura & Antle, is a three-generation lettuce dynasty. In 1988, after graduating Harvard Business School, Steve Taylor, the grandson of company founder Bruce Church, returned to Salinas to head up the MAP project. A year later, working with film manufacturers, TransFresh developed a breathable bag that maintained the right nitrogen-rich atmosphere inside by leaching out the carbon dioxide and allowing oxygen to reenter. The lettuce could breathe. TransFresh patented the result, the Keep-Crisp Bag, variations of which are still used today.

The development would prove to be what Harvard Business School professor Clayton Christensen has called a "disruptive" technology—one that reshapes an industry and leads an innovator to the top of the heap. When TransFresh started its MAP experiments, the Taylors were selling $80 million to $100 million worth of lettuce heads a year—major revenue, to be sure, but no home run in the annals of business. Forty to forty-five grower-shippers were competing over the same pie (or, should I say, bowl). Each had a modest market share, though Dole's was higher than the rest. The Taylors were in the middle with a 6 percent share.

Once their new company, Fresh Express, launched the one-pound Keep-Crisp Bag of cut iceberg lettuce in the retail channel in 1989, everything shifted. The product took about six months to gain traction on the West Coast, but then sales rocketed. Fresh Express built regional plants around the country to shred and bag whole heads shipped from California and Arizona. It began the now-standard practice of coring iceberg heads in the field, reducing shipping weights—and thus transportation costs—by half. It launched a salad blend in 1991 and became the world's largest buyer of Italian radicchio. A year later, in a development that would do Joseph Brock of Buffalo proud, it came out with the first Caesar salad kit with a container of dressing; overall sales grew by 300 to 400 percent annually for several years. To keep others out, Fresh Express paid retailers' marketing fees—unprecedented in the produce business—to get its bags on their shelves and keep them there.

In 1999, Taylor took the company out of farming altogether. Just as Crawford had learned on a much smaller scale, manufacturing and retailing were the more profitable games. Others would now grow for Fresh Express. In 2001, with salad sales at a half-billion dollars, Taylor sold Fresh Express to Performance Food Group of Richmond, Virginia, for $302 million, creating the third-largest food supplier in the nation. By 2003, when I talked with Taylor at the company's Salinas headquarters, Fresh Express salad sales were closing in on $1 billion a year. The evolution wasn't over, for in 2005, Performance Food Group sold Fresh Express to Chiquita Brands for $855 million cash, a gain of half a billion dollars in five years—all from salad.

In the process, the company's initial 6 percent market share jumped to 40 percent. Fresh Express wasn't alone at the top; Dole had matched it move for move. "It's really a two-player race at this point," Taylor told me. "Dole tries to come at it from price; we try to come at it from freshness, quickness to shelf, and differentiation."

It's hard to underestimate the impact bagged lettuce had on the valley, which had been built by the grower-shipper alliances. Now whole heads of iceberg, which had supported the entire industry for decades, weren't moving at the checkout counter like they once had, and the old-line business models began to creak. Tanimura & Antle, and a host of competitors, had to confront the fact that their number-one market was a dinosaur.

They faced a number of options, none of them particularly attractive. They could become contract growers, dependent on Dole and Fresh Express to buy their lettuce; they could launch a competing brand, picking up whatever supermarket customers the two leaders had left behind in their rush for dominance; they could pursue new niches in specialty vegetable markets; or they could try all these strategies at once. Many ended up with another course: They went under. By the turn of the century, just five big players were left of the forty to forty-five processors active in the 1980s. "We did a pretty good job of keeping them out," Taylor told me.

Ten days after I talked with him, Taylor announced his retirement at forty-seven. He told the local Salinas paper, the *Californian*, he was thinking of an eventual Republican run for Congress.

Until the mid-1990s, organic spring mix remained in its own comfortable, natural niche—growing enormously, but not big enough to attract the interest of major growers. Organic entrepreneurs such as Koons, the Goodmans, and Coke had room to grow because they weren't seen as a threat—or an opportunity—by dominant produce companies. But when the lettuce industry got blindsided by bagged salad, growers looked around for an alternative and the savvy ones noticed organic spring mix.

Stan Pura, a tall, solidly built man with thick arms and an eager handshake, was among them. He wasn't at ease like Koons was in a world of chefs, gourmands, and organic zealots. Pura's family had farmed the southern Salinas Valley for decades, first in dairy, then sugar beets and peppers, and finally fresh vegetables, shifting with each tide of the market. Pura, whose company was named Mission Ranches, had been growing iceberg, romaine, and other vegetables when he got wind of spring mix. He had seen organic lettuce fields in Watsonville—among them, Coke's—and was impressed. Spring mix, he told me, "seemed like a little specialty deal that really was under the radar."

By chance, Pura had the same accountant as the Goodmans and heard they might be interested in selling their business. (They had actually asked the accountant for a valuation of Earthbound but weren't actively looking to sell.) Pura met Drew Goodman and the two started talking business and getting to know each other while playing tennis.

Pura admits that even considering organic was a sea change in his thinking. "Everyone used to think these organic farmers were a bunch of hippies from Santa Cruz," he told me in the Goodmans' offices. Organic farmers at meetings such as the Eco-Farm Conference viewed him with equal skepticism. "If you were from conventional agriculture and wanted to get involved in organics, well, you were like taboo right off the bat," he said. While understandable, this clubby point of view could undermine one of the organic movement's core goals—changing agriculture.

But Pura persisted because he had mounting doubts about conventional farming. Pesticides were becoming less effective and ever more restricted. Many "weren't safe," he said. People in the region were increasingly worried about groundwater contamination, air quality, and population density.

"I was looking for some sustainable practices to incorporate into our conventional agriculture," he said. "But the thing blew away all our expectations, it blossomed into a business." At the same time, Pura wasn't naive about his prospects. When an industry trade journal, *American Vegetable Grower,* wrote a cover story on his company, Pura said that organics was an obvious source of profits. "It's so easy to be a relatively good [conventional] grower that you don't get rewarded for it," he said. "The only way you get rewarded in this industry is if you can do something well that's difficult to do—it's the ultimate challenge."

By 1995, Earthbound was the second-biggest company in organic spring mix after Koons's TKO. But with only a hundred acres, the Goodmans were bumping up against a lack of available farmland. Conventional growers had long tied up the choicest parcels in the Salinas Valley, leaving only second-rate fields for organic newcomers. Plus, the couple had two children by this time and Drew didn't want to farm any longer, or take the logical next step of expanding winter production to the south, into Arizona, which meant being away from home.

But the business needed to expand, because demand continued to grow for its bagged salad mix. In 1993, the Goodmans won a major account from Costco, the large membership warehouse club, and several supermarket chains soon followed. In a twist, Costco wanted a conventional product—or at least one not labeled ORGANIC—because the retailer thought organic food cost more and meant poor quality (echoing the concerns of Waters when she kept the word *organic* off her menu). Despite misgivings about compromising the brand, the Goodmans went ahead with the deal, slapping the Earthbound label on a conventional product for the first time. But the deal made sense, because they were growing some spring mix on transitional

land. During the three years it takes to transition conventionally farmed land to organic, none of the produce can be sold as
organic. The Costco deal created a channel for that nonorganic
transitional lettuce.

Even so, the Goodmans were short of land. Enter Pura. He
could grow enough conventional spring mix on his acreage to
meet Earthbound's needs and, at the same time, learn organic
farming methods as he converted his conventional land to organic production. With Pura ensuring their supply, the Goodmans could focus on processing, marketing, and distribution,
getting Pura's lettuce into stores. In this way, the Goodmans
and Pura arrived at the classic Salinas Valley model, forming a
grower-shipper partnership in 1995 they named Natural Selection Foods. (Though the company is known as Earthbound,
that is technically now just a brand name.) Stan Pura and Drew
Goodman proved to be competitive partners. "They had this
little joke," Myra recalled. "Drew would say, 'I can sell as much
salad as you can grow!' And Stan would say, 'I can grow more
salad then you could ever sell!'" As they tried to outdo each
other, the company took off.

In forming this partnership, the Goodmans and Pura also
solidified Earthbound's position at the top of the organic salad-
mix market. When in negotiations with Drew, Pura had gotten a feeler from the number-three company in the organic
salad market, Riverside Farms, whose owners had eight hundred acres and wanted to sell out. So Pura bought Riverside
Farms and added it to his partnership with Earthbound. The
same year, Koons's organic lettuce fields were flooded when
twenty inches of El Niño rain fell on the region within three
months, swelling the Salinas River. His company, TKO, the
number-one player, had to shut down production.

Pura, on higher ground, saw a good opportunity, and offered TKO's food-service customers a cheaper conventional
spring mix to make up for TKO's curtailed business. Since the
food-service industry was concerned with the mix itself, rather
than whether it was organic, the customers snapped up the
cheaper alternative. Once Pura entered the market, Koons was
finished. "It was a brilliant move," Koons told me. "By [Pura]
coming in with conventional product and lowering the actual
margin of the business, we could never get back into business.
It was a below-the-waterline hit." Koons filed for Chapter 7
bankruptcy and dissolved the company; Pura and the Goodmans picked up its assets at auction.

Having knocked out the number-one player and bought the
number-three player, Earthbound saw its sales jump from $14
million to $50 million and its land base rise from one hundred
to twelve hundred acres. Suddenly it was the only major spring
mix label in the organic market.

Koons later ran into Alice Waters at a conference on sustainable agriculture. The chef wagged her finger at him and said,
"You grew too big!" But he was really too vulnerable, brought
down by the costs associated with his high-end organic product, his inexperience, and his failure to partner with a Salinas
grower who might have filled the gap when the disastrous rains
struck.

"I was too monogamous," he concluded.

With the competition gone and his relationship with the Goodmans sealed, Pura had only to figure out how to grow spring
mix. Like many conventional farmers going organic, he first
tried an "input substitution" approach, trying to find the organic
equivalents of conventional pesticides and fertilizers. "It didn't
take too long to figure out that swapping materials wasn't going

to work, because it's really expensive," said "Amigo" Bob Cantisano, perhaps the most well-known organic farming consultant on the West Coast, who worked with Pura for about five years. "They were all strung out on Chilean nitrate [an organic fertilizer] . . . so we started pretty conservatively, with rotations, cover crops, beneficial habitat, nutritional components—extremely basic stuff," Cantisano told me.

Pretty soon, Pura began to understand how the system worked, though it wasn't easy. "You're sweating bullets out there, because your product's full of aphids, and you're wondering, 'Are these beneficial insects going to clean it up by the time it's ready to harvest?'" Within two years—and with some notable flops—Pura began to see progress. A key turning point came when he planted lettuce in the San Joaquin Valley, on a field that had been organic for four years. The soil was fertile, the weeds under control, and a good crop came in. "I was like, 'Wow, you can really do this.' That's when it hit me," Pura said. He adopted some organic methods on his conventional fields and mused that one day the entire Salinas Valley might be organic. The costs were still higher, but he found the yields on par with those of his conventional fields.

As he dramatically ramped up acreage, Pura brought large-scale production methods into the mix in an effort to whittle costs. His wife, Jamii, an entomologist, zeroed in on beneficial insects. He hired a plant breeder to develop proprietary lettuce varieties suited to the climates and regions they farmed. His key innovation—quickly copied by other growers—addressed the huge cost of hand-cutting baby lettuce, with labor in short supply. Pura's mechanical harvester cut the baby heads at the ground with a rotating band-saw blade, preventing damage to the leaves, then spit the leaves onto a vibrating conveyer belt, which culled the smallest ones and sent the remainder through an "air jump," so rocks and dirt would fall away, then misted them with water and dropped them into twenty-pound bins that refrigerated trucks transported to the plant. (Cantisano said this machine was not wholly original, but a larger version of an Italian harvester displayed at Eco-Farm one year.) All of these innovations were aimed at one goal: becoming the low-cost producer of organic spring mix. The wholesale price of spring mix fell dramatically, from about seven dollars a pound in the 1980s to about two. Growers for Earthbound now got between $0.85 and $1.10 per pound (depending on the specific salad crop).

On the processing side, the Goodmans expanded the original twenty-five-thousand-square-foot washing, spinning, and bagging lines in their facility in San Juan Bautista eightfold. (The original plant is now just a holding facility for the greens entering the production line.) Workers in thick coats haul the lettuce around the chilled and noisy processing plant in two ten-hour shifts, with a four-hour cleaning shift in between. Much of the process is automated, with multiple production lines triple-washing and individually bagging twenty thousand pounds of lettuce an hour. In 2002, Earthbound opened another huge plant, in Yuma, Arizona, to handle winter production, then set up "forward distribution" plants in Cranbury, New Jersey; Indianapolis; and Atlanta.

The company also manages the schedules of the farmers who feed into Natural Selection Foods, trying to harvest the right amount to meet demand. Much of the lettuce supply comes from Pura's Mission Ranches, but a network of farmers also works with him. About 150 other farmers supply organic fruits and vegetables to the company, so a supermarket chain can order everything from heirloom tomatoes to oranges and spring mix under the Earthbound Farm brand.

In 1999, the Goodmans expanded further and got rid of a competitor by partnering with Tanimura & Antle. This was prompted by the same concerns that led the Goodmans and Pura to link up four years earlier: the need for land. Earthbound offered a fast-growing market to the giant lettuce company, which had missed out on the bagged market dominated by Dole and Fresh Express. Within three years, Tanimura & Antle had transitioned nearly twenty-seven hundred acres of its forty-seven-thousand-acre land base to organic production. Each of the partners now owns one-third of Natural Selection Foods.

While Earthbound Farm had "industrialized" over the course of the 1990s—getting bigger, driving down costs, and eliminating the competition each step of the way—it had done so to compete against Dole, Fresh Express, and ReadyPac, the big conventional companies in mainstream markets. Earthbound's goal was to be as efficient in harvesting, processing, bagging, marketing, and distribution as conventional produce companies, narrowing the price differential between organic and conventional lettuce and prompting more consumers to try their product. At the supermarket, the forty to sixty cents premium on organic bags of lettuce that remained reflected higher growing costs. The Goodmans had matched their competitors in every other stage of the supply chain. USDA data bear this out. While organic produce often costs 100 percent more than convention-ally grown produce, this differential has narrowed to 6 to 8 per-cent in wholesale spring mix. At the same time, due to its large organic acreage base, Earthbound claims to have withdrawn seven million pounds of synthetic fertilizers and 225,759 pounds of chemical pesticides from use annually.

"We're offering an organic choice, we're doing something great for the environment, we're providing farmworkers a healthier work environment, so I can't feel like I'm doing a bad thing," Myra said.

The results of this "efficiency," though, were painfully obvious to competitors. When the price fell to two dollars a pound, smaller producers got out. Coke, the inventor of spring mix, scaled back and now farms 250 acres of vegetables for wholesale markets. Weber, who first brought mesclun to the market in his plastic container, left the wholesale market altogether and focuses on restaurants and farmers' markets. Neither seemed bitter, though they were critical. Coke thought organic had gotten too big, too divorced from local markets, though he only had praise for the organic farming methods of his friends, the Goodmans. "They're doing it right," he said. He was in a position to know, though perhaps not the best judge, since he was renting two hundred acres of certified organic farmland to Earthbound. Weber seemed to take the greatest issue with quality, since spring mix sold in supermarkets today is far inferior to what it had been before, though the flip side of this trend is that it once again opened a window for smaller growers producing a superior product.

Although Weber had scaled back, spending time now on a program to covert all of Marin County to organic farming, he was also renting organic land he once farmed in lettuce to the giant produce company Grimmway Farms. He said he had no gripe with them. Coke and Weber might have been taken out of the business, but they still had a hand in the game.

Converting conventional growers is precisely what needs to happen if organic farm land is going to expand and pesticide use decline. But this transition hasn't come without conflicts and costs.

Julie Guthman, a scholar at the University of California at Santa Cruz who surveyed organic farms in the late 1990s, highlighted several controversial developments in her book *Agrarian Dreams: The Paradox of Organic Farming in California.* One was the use of Chilean nitrate, a heavily nitrogenous mineral that helps winter crops such as lettuce, broccoli, and greens grow when cool weather limits the availability of nitrogen from compost. Critics felt it should be banned—as it was under European organic rules—not only because of the environmental costs of it being mined and shipped from South America, but also because of its potential to leach into groundwater, like chemical fertilizer. Using Chilean nitrate also goes against the organic ideal of building soils through composts, cover crops, and legumes, which fix nitrogen in the soil. Growers lobbied to use it, so a compromise was crafted in the organic regulations limiting its use to 20 percent of the nitrogen applied to a crop. But this remains controversial.

Guthman also found cases in which growers monocropped organic fields until the soils were depleted and then moved on, because the cost of the land could not support rotations, cover crops, and fallow periods. Growers in Merced County "found land to lease that was previously fallow, had it certified immediately, squeezed out two or three seasons of sweet potato production, then let it go when problems of overuse and disease inevitably arose," she writes. This was precisely the type of practice organic agriculture had been designed to prevent.

In other cases, growers "were known" to have fumigated fields with methyl bromide *before* the start of the three-year transition period to organic cultivation. While legal, this was a highly cynical move that undermined the integrity of organic cultivation. Yet, if organic agriculture was solely approached as a business, it actually made sense. The transition period is a particularly onerous time, for the benefits of organic methods have not yet accrued, yields are low, and growers must sell their crops in the lower-priced conventional market. Applying a toxic pesticide at the last legally permissible minute could mean a better crop and fewer losses during the transition.

At the margin, opportunists will always abuse rules and exploit loopholes, which is why Pura's vision of an organic Salinas Valley was complicated. If the organic market was to grow and "change agriculture," market-oriented farmers would have to come into the fold, but that didn't mean they would follow the spirit of the method. Still, this has more to do with the farmer than the size of the farm. As Guthman points out, there is nothing inherent in a large-scale farm that undermines the ideal of organic farming, at least so far as nurturing the soil. Any farm, regardless of size, can get it right *or* exploit loopholes. In the 1930s, Howard's method of composting spread to small farms in Britain as well as to plantations on the Indian subcontinent, in Africa, and in Central America. Organic innovations were not the monopoly of small farms then, nor are they today. A big farm with enough capital, commitment, and conscientious planning could create a highly ecological farming model, even if it put smaller farms out of business. In fact, this is what would be expected in a market economy as new players dove into a lucrative niche and drove prices down—whether for organic salad mix or flat-panel television screens. Cantisano, the organic consultant, seemed to view Earthbound through this dual lens.

"They're good stewards of the land and the environment," he said. "But they've also put a lot of organic farmers I know out of business with their marketing practices. They overproduce and sell crops cheap and have been doing that for the last ten years and they're highly reluctant to recognize it as a problem."

This was the price of popularity, of new producers and cost-conscious consumers entering the market with values that diverged from the pioneers. The newcomers were either ignorant of or uncommitted to the vision of organic food as part of a larger paradigm built upon smaller-scale farms, local food, and alternative distribution networks. For these supermarket shoppers, the main impetus to buy organic food was health and nutrition (in a convenient setting) not all the idealistic rhetoric. So while Earthbound did undercut smaller competitors, it also brought a cheaper and more accessible product to consumers, driving the expansion of the organic marketplace.

The key to survive—if you weren't Earthbound, with 74 percent of the organic packaged salad market—was to sell direct. At farmers' markets in the Bay Area, I found spring mix for four to five dollars a pound, far cheaper than Earthbound bags at most supermarkets. One small farmer, Vicki Von Lackum, did brisk business selling a beautiful, hand-cut product she grew, harvested, and sold herself to restaurants such as Chez Panisse for eighteen dollars a pound. She made about twenty-five thousand to thirty thousand dollars a year working part-time on a small suburban plot of land. I came across one East Coast grower of micro-greens—lettuce with a tiny quarter-inch leaf—who sold his product to New York chefs for forty dollars a pound. The market had segmented between large and small, mirroring the shrinking middle in the broader agricultural economy.

Koons, who lost TKO to bankruptcy, was also trying to create a market niche with a new company, Epic Roots. He was marketing the hell out of the small, buttery European leaf known as mâche—appearing on TV, winning endorsements from star chefs, and convincing Burger King to add it to salads. He wasn't producing it organically, because, he said, it was too hard to grow that way. Although he thought bagged mâche was another "$100 million opportunity!" he was cautious about what might happen if he succeeded. "Rick Antle told me,

'When you get to $20 million I'll be all over you,'" Koons said. Actually, it wasn't Antle but his nemesis Earthbound that eventually rolled out a competing product, organic mâche, within two years.

Such was life in the Salinas Valley.

I was pondering all this on a cross-country trip, when I switched planes in Minneapolis and looked around the airport for something to eat. One option was McDonald's, which had launched a line of fresh salads with dressings from Newman's Own, the philanthropic venture cofounded by Paul Newman. The salads had been such a hit that suppliers such as Fresh Express were caught short of lettuce and wholesale prices had spiked. I bought a salad, unsnapped the plastic container, and tore open the small bag of ranch dressing. The salad consisted of iceberg and romaine with specialty items such as frisée, radiccio, and baby spinach, and a tough piece of grilled chicken on top. The dressing was overpowering, but the salad was something I could eat on the run.

How curious that this mass-market product was related to the revolution in taste that took root in Berkeley two decades ago. You couldn't draw a straight line from Chez Panisse to McDonald's, but the roots were apparent in the specialty greens packaged with the iceberg lettuce that made up the bulk of the salad I was eating that day. Waters's accomplishment had evolved in two very different directions, changing the face of American cuisine and the aspirations of home cooks like me—who began to seek out fresh ingredients at farmers' markets—and reaching deep into the mass market, all the way to fast food. These trends mirrored a bifurcation of the organic food industry, between small-scale, specialty growers such as Weber, or the Crawfords in my town, and large-scale producers like the Goodmans who wanted organic salad in every supermarket. The small-scale pioneers viewed organic food as more than just a farming method; the idea was also tied up with the scale of the farm, the quality, locality, and freshness of the product, and the personal networks, small stores, and restaurants through which the food was sold. All were necessary to create a true alternative to industrial agriculture rather than a facsimile of it. But the problem with this vision was that organic salad outgrew the model. Given its resounding success, the product easily made the jump to the mass market and then it was up to the pioneers to jump, too. This proved too tough for some, since their values were largely incompatible with the way food was grown, distributed, and sold in supermarkets. They weren't willing to push the price of salad mix down to eighty-five cents a pound. Others, like Koons, tried but failed. Without any of the early ideological baggage to hold them back, however, the Goodmans made the leap and figured out how to ramp up organic farming on a large scale. For many, that was a resounding success, because so many more acres were free of pesticides, and so many more consumers had access to the food. But for others it was an abhorrent compromise that destroyed smaller farms and undercut what organic food was supposed to be, transforming and packaging an alternative way of life into little more than a product choice in the supermarket aisle.

As for McDonald's, salad represented "healthier" fast food at a time when the chain faced obesity-related lawsuits for its highly caloric burgers and fries. "The pundits will say it was because we were sued. Well, that's what they say. It was never about that," McDonald's then chief executive Jim Cantalupo said in an interview. "Salad was a big indicator of that—there was a huge market out there for it. And why not tap it?" Salads led to new growth and profitability at the fast-food company, even while the bulk of its customers continued to eat burgers. Health, or the appearance of it, like the concept of "fresh," has often been a selling point in the mass market—as true for McDonald's salads as for organic food. I didn't appreciate the full scope of this principle, though, until I looked into the age-old ways food has been intertwined with the concept of health. Organic food was just the latest, potent twist in this quest, which became even more clear when I looked closely at my breakfast.

5. Mythic Manufacturing
Health, Spirituality, and Breakfast

And God said, Behold, I have given you every herb bearing seed,
which is upon the face of all the earth, and every tree, in the which
is the fruit of a tree yielding seed; to you it shall be for meat.
—Genesis 1:29, King James Bible

For breakfast I often eat a bowl of Autumn Wheat cereal made by the natural-foods company Kashi. The cereal is part of Kashi's Organic Promise line and has an earnest tagline, "true taste, true nourishment, true to nature"—the kind of motto that's easy to embrace because it can mean whatever the consumer wants. I like to think I'm immune to this marketing hyperbole, which attempts to turn the food into an aspiration or something "true," and that I simply eat the sweetened shredded-wheat biscuits because I like them and want to support organic farming.

Yet, even while I may not buy the company's marketing language, I'm pursuing an agenda of virtuous consumption, too, since the cereal supports something Good and is Good for me. The food's extraculinary appeal triggers my own consumptive choice.

On the cereal, I pour soy milk, usually Silk, the second most widely purchased organic packaged-goods brand. I like its taste (helped by organic cane sugar) and find it easier to digest than dairy milk. Being half-Japanese, I've eaten soy products from a young age. By high school, I was buying soy milk in New York City's Chinatown, where on East Broadway I could find the highly sweetened, bottled beverage in the refrigerator case of a crowded, dank, superlative tofu shop that has since shut down. I did not need a great leap of faith to try soy milk, like many Americans did who began to buy it in the late 1990s, prompted by health claims. Pouring soy milk on cereal felt natural, with Silk an especially good version of what I'd been drinking for years.

Autumn Wheat and Silk, though, had another link rooted in a kind of culinary evangelism that swept them into the market. Whole grain cereal and soy milk represented more than food to their creators; they were viewed as a superior form of vegetarian nutrition and a path toward health and even enlightenment. Whole grains—as opposed to white flour—were overtly tied to Christianity, vegetarianism, and even abolitionism in the mid-nineteenth century. Soy's supporters had a spiritual bias as well, but by the time it arrived on the counterculture scene in the 1960s, the impetus came from the East—from Buddhism, principles of "right livelihood," and idealistic notions about how to feed the planet with a cheap source of vegetarian protein. As Steve Demos, whose company invented Silk, told me: "We were going to change the world, one bite at a time."

Although separated by a century, the ideas that gave rise to these products were as intertwined as the soy milk and cereal in my breakfast bowl. The health impetus at the core of organic foods expressed ideas that stretched back to the nineteenth century, which is why the movement has proved so enduring today: Health food has long been part of the cultural zeitgeist. Whether aiming to clear out the digestive tract or the heart's arteries, or restore vitality and reach a higher state of well-being, these foods pointed the way ahead. What better way to start the day?

Curious about the religious impulses behind food, I called a friend, Natan Margalit, a Boston-based rabbi and anthropologist. Didn't kosher dietary laws spring from a particular interpretation of food, with some moral or ethical basis? In some cases they did, he said. Kosher slaughtering drains the blood from the neck of the animal since, the Bible tells us, blood is life and should not be eaten. This method of slaughter was also meant to reduce the animal's suffering. The prohibition against eating meat with dairy can also be read as respect for the mother-infant bond. But in some cases, the laws were just God's word, rules that needed to be followed to lead a virtuous life—an equation nearly as common in the secular world as in religion. By eating or avoiding certain foods, one could enter a higher state of being, either religiously, in the eyes of God; in health, in the judgment of your physician; or in those feelings of wellness and balance typical of the contemporary lifestyle arena.

Whole grains have held this extraculinary appeal at least since the mid-nineteenth century, when they became the symbolic center of perhaps the earliest anti-industrial food movement. By the 1830s, Sylvester Graham, a Presbyterian minister, was preaching that whole wheat flour was better than mass-produced white bread. (The graham cracker is the sullied remnant of his crusade, just the kind of commercial product that would have caught his ire.) Though white flour had been favored by the rich as far back as ancient Greece, Graham thought that refined flour—along with alcohol and sex—caused disease. His concern was not entirely misplaced, because of the routine addition of heavy ingredients such as chalk, pipe clay, and plaster of paris to bread, which was sold by the pound. He fingered other additives as well, including aluminum, zinc sulphate, sub-carbonate of magnesia, and copper sulphate.

Many of these ingredients were used to whiten the flour, since milling techniques were not refined enough to produce truly white flour until the late-nineteenth century. As any natural-food devotee knows, white flour is made by removing the highly nutritional wheat germ and fibrous bran found in whole wheat flour—the staff of life, which Graham and every health food advocate that proceeded him said should be maintained. In damning the consumption of white flour and promoting whole wheat, he articulated the earliest health food diet in the emerging consumer market.

For Graham, at stake was not just health, but the well-being of society. Graham was a proponent of vegetarianism as a way to control sexual passions, for he thought meat-eating led to masturbation and masturbation made one stupid; in this way, sex and meat were not only immoral but unhealthy. The threads throughout his work were purity, restraint, and temperance. In an early echo of the simplicity movement, he found an enemy in contemporary life which overstimulated the body and senses. (It will come as no surprise that the Nearings baked whole-grain bread, since it was sustenance for a simpler, purified, and healthier life.)

Whole-grain bread also sprang from Graham's reverence for the pioneer, whose way of life was fading with the growth of cities and markets in the mid-nineteenth century. In Jacksonian America, wheat was for the first time shipped from the Ohio Valley to be processed in distant eastern bakeries, which Graham considered morally inferior to the home hearth. He urged women to mill their own flour, since only a wife or mother could truly make bread. This wasn't domestic drudgery, but God's work. Anything sold by a baker was lacking in fiber, actual and moral. (Not surprisingly, a mob of bakers attacked Graham at a talk in Boston in 1837.) His exotic views should not obscure the larger point: Whole wheat "Graham flour" represented a return to a pristine past and was a reaction against early mass markets, industry, urbanization, the rapid pace of modern life, and the decline of the pioneer homestead—ideas that would be reprised in twentieth-century agrarianism and its cousin, organic food.

Whole-wheat bread wasn't new, since peasants and the working class had always eaten it. Yet, more-costly white bread, along with meat, was what they wanted to consume. Graham turned this hierarchy on its head, urging his well-educated and urbane followers to covet what the lower class ate. Handmade whole-wheat bread was better for you—an idea that reappeared with McCarrison, Rodale, Lady Eve Balfour, and the rest of the organic pioneers, and that resonates to this day. The $5 to $6 loaf of artisan bread has transformed what was once common into a luxury item, because what is now common at the supermarket is inferior, both gastronomically and nutritionally.

While contemporary consumers have switched to whole grains to stave off cancer, heart disease, and weight gain, Graham's followers were looking for an antidote to dyspepsia, the gastro-intestinal ailments that arose from the consumption of pork fat, bacon, eggs, coffee and cream, and pie for breakfast—the first of three heavy meals. This was sustenance for the laborer or farmer, who could easily burn off the calories, but produced something akin to pizza-induced heartburn for the less-active urban set. In combating this malaise, some proclaimed the virtues of raw food, others ate nuts and milk. Graham championed whole grains grown in virgin soil—a luxury afforded by the westward expansion. (Among his eccentric ideas was that manure "debauched" the soil rather than renewed it—an idea reprised to me one day by a vegan organic vegetable farmer.)

Graham was not alone in these beliefs or practices. Fruitlands, a transcendentalist community founded by Bronson Alcott in Harvard, Massachusetts, in 1843, sought to strengthen the spirit by pursuing a simple, self-reliant life of Platonic conversation and animal-free food. The community avoided meat, eggs, butter, and cheese, and it banned coffee, tea, molasses, cotton, and rice because they were produced by slave labor. In today's ergot, Fruitlands's adherents would be called fair-trade vegans. Alcott argued that if grazing land were put under cultivation, the world's population could eat on one-fourth the acreage—an equation similar to one put forward in the early 1970s by Frances Moore Lappé in her highly influential *Diet for a Small Planet*. The members of Fruitlands drank only water and ate grains, fruits, and herbs, attempting to restore the purity of Eden. They favored "aspiring" vegetables, those that grew upward toward heaven, but forbid tubers and other root crops mired in the earth. Like many back-to-the-landers more than a century later, they barely lasted a year.

The Fruitlands ideals were already in vogue among British Romantics, who eschewed certain tainted foods and developed principles of alternative consumption. Percy Shelley was among the most vocal, ascribing the slave trade and "a variety of violent acts" to meat eating, which was the root of all evil, the original sin. When Mary Shelley wrote *Frankenstein*, in 1816, she made the monster explicitly vegetarian. The Romantics' preoccupation with diet can be read as a reaction to colonialism, to rising consumerism and industrialism in the late-eighteenth and nineteenth centuries, and to their products—such as refined foods. A bestselling antislavery pamphlet from 1791 equated sugar with the blood of slaves in the West Indies. For every pound of sugar, two ounces of human flesh were said to be consumed.

Graham traveled among those who, on both sides of the Atlantic, criticized large-scale food production—then the slave plantation—and pursued conscious consumption. He was president of the American Vegetarian Society—founded in New York City, in 1849, on a platform of abstinence, women's rights, and vegetarianism—which had a number of illustrious members, including author Harriet Beecher Stowe and the journalist Horace Greeley. Like the organic movement more than a century later, it also had its commercial wing, since another member was the entrepreneurial Dr. James Caleb Jackson, who ran the Jackson Sanatorium in Danville, New York. These food movements were never content to remain small, insular affairs, but wanted to spread the message and offer products so that others could adopt their regimes.

Jackson—who emphasized a daily regimen of exercise, vegetarian food, temperance, and water cures—came up with a breakfast food called Granula. It might qualify as the first bulky, tasteless health food, for it consisted of "Graham flour" and water. Had Jackson thrown this concoction on a hot stone, he would have had flatbread or chapati. Instead, Jackson would bake whole-wheat bricks, crumble them into bean-sized pieces, bake the beans again, then pulverize them. He dished up this whole-grain breakfast cereal for the guests at his spa, and, lest they be without the special food when they checked out, Jackson launched Our Home Granula Company. He went down in history as the inventor of cereal.

Jackson identified the product, but others would run with it. Dr. John Harvey Kellogg, who was raised in Battle Creek, Michigan, by a family of Seventh-Day Adventists, was the most prominent. He expanded the health principles of the church, which were a simple vegetarian diet, hydrotherapy, exercise, and abstinence from coffee, tea, alcohol, tobacco, and spices (since they could inflame desire). Kellogg was said to have existed on a diet of graham crackers and apples, one coconut per week, and the occasional dish of potatoes and oatmeal during medical school in New York City. In 1876, he became medical director of the Seventh-Day Adventist's Battle Creek Sanitarium, which grew into a world-renowned health spa. A year later, after he married, Kellogg wrote a book entitled *Plain Facts for Old and Young Embracing the Natural History and Hygiene of Organic Life*—a treatise not on organic food but on the evils of sexuality, especially masturbation. His brother Will K. Kellogg, eight years younger, managed the sanatorium's business affairs while the doctor lectured, wrote (he penned eighty-one books, many of them in the "self-help" category), and directed the health programs.

Guests at the spa would be massaged and pummeled, pampered and coddled, and treated to over two hundred types of water therapies, including "salt baths, steam baths, hot water baths, cold water baths, showers, douches, fomentations, and a high-powered enema machine that could put fifteen gallons of water through the bowels in a matter of minutes," the authors of a history of the breakfast industry, *Cerealizing America*, write. This was a high-class spa, attended by actresses, musicians, writers, intellectuals, businessmen, and politicians.

They would come to eat the vegetarian food, including a meat analogue made from nuts, called Protose, as well as stewed prunes, wheat gluten mush, oatmeal crackers, graham rolls, and dyspeptic wafers. (After meals, attendants would brush and polish the guests' teeth.) This diet was aimed at cleansing the digestive tract, the root of all happiness, according to Dr. Kellogg, who ate bran and enjoyed a daily enema (though he avoided sex). He despised spices and vinegar, thought coffee crippled the liver, and called cola drinks an "insidious poison." But he also prescribed fresh air and sunshine for tuberculosis (and was labeled a heretic for this by the medical establishment), discussed the link between smoking and lung cancer, and listed proteins, fats, and carbohydrates on the sanatorium's menu once such measurement became possible in 1904. Granula was served for breakfast, though when Jackson sued him over using the name, Kellogg changed it to Granola.

Concerned about the digestive qualities of bread, Kellogg asked his younger brother Will to experiment with wheat paste, which mimicked the action of saliva in breaking down wheat as the first step in the digestive process. Will accidentally let a batch of the paste stand overnight, and it dried out. He ran the substance through a set of rollers and ended up with flaked wheat and thus another breakfast cereal, which the Kelloggs named Granose. Following Jackson's lead, the sanatorium set up the Battle Creek Sanitarium Health Food Company to market the breakfast cereals and a coffee substitute made of burned bread crusts, bran, and molasses, called caramel coffee. It was one of the sanatorium's popular drinks, along with tea made from South African Kaffir grass.

C. W. Post was thirty-seven when he arrived at the sanatorium, emaciated and in a wheelchair, having suffered various business setbacks. He stayed for several months but didn't recover under Dr. Kellogg's regimen. He took refuge at the home of a relative, a Christian Scientist who believed sickness was nothing more than a state of mind. Post soon got better and began to capitalize on Kellogg's innovations—creating the coffee substitute Postum, coming up with the cereal Grape-Nuts, and even opening a rival sanatorium that had a meatcentric diet (and undercut Kellogg on price). Sounding positively New Age, he preached about "the power within" to heal the body. By the turn of the century, Grape-Nuts had rung up millions in sales and left Post with a fortune. "Never had anyone got so rich so fast from selling a consumer product," the authors of *Cerealizing America* write.

Battle Creek turned into a health-food boomtown, as more than a few former Kellogg sanatorium employees absconded with the formulae for various products. By 1904, more than forty companies sold cereal, with names like Lucky Boy, Corn-O-Plenty, and HoneyMoon Brand. They tasted like celery, were made from beans, or could "raise the dead." Onetime auto mechanics, cowboys, and tire manufacturers went into the business, driving up rents in the city and even producing their food-stuffs in tents. Battle Creek was promoted as the "World's Cereal Bowl," the "Health City," and the "Cornflake Capital of the World," but when the boom died because of over-production, only the strongest survived. Mainstream America simply wasn't ready to give up eggs and bacon for cold cereal.

The competition had been enough to destroy Granose, which Will K. Kellogg was determined not to let happen again when he came up with toasted cornflakes. When John Harvey was away in Europe and could not object, Will added sugar to the cornflakes formula.

The epilogue to this story is better known than these origins. Kellogg became the number-one breakfast cereal company, expanding on the back of consumer advertising for sugary cereals such as Frosted Flakes, introduced in the 1950s. Post grew, too, under the founder's daughter, Marjorie Merriweather Post, who bought two dozen companies in the 1920s and created the nation's first food conglomerate.

By then, cereal's roots in Seventh-Day Adventism, wheat bran and fiber, a clear digestive tract, and vegetarianism were long forgotten. The product was tailored to meet the mass market, not the ideals that surrounded its founding.

Curiously, though, the marketing of health regained its footing at Kellogg in 1984, when the company became the first to display a health claim on product packaging. Wording on its boxes of All-Bran cereal linked the consumption of the high-fiber food to a reduced cancer risk—a claim endorsed by the National Cancer Institute, despite initial misgivings by its sister agency, the Food and Drug Administration. In the business-friendly climate of the Reagan administration, however, the claim was approved, resulting in a 47 percent jump in the market share of All-Bran in six months. "The message to the food industry was clear: Health claims sold products," writes Marion Nestle, professor of nutrition at New York University, in her book *Food Politics: How the Food Industry Influences Nutrition and Health.*

Health and natural food rose on the back of the now-aging baby boom generation. By 2000, $7-billion Kellogg had taken notice of this niche and bought Kashi, which had sales of $25 million and was growing 100 percent annually. Kellogg kept its name off Kashi, however, since that would have sullied the brand, which, the smaller company said, meant "food for spiritual enlightenment" in Sanskrit.

The cereal business had come full circle. What was once part of a nineteenth-century alternative vision of nutrition had evolved so far into the mainstream that Kellogg had to buy another company to rediscover its roots. In this new incarnation, Kellogg brought organic food to my breakfast table, with the claims of goodness—or "truth," as the packaging called it—an echo of the spiritual and nutritional ethos that inspired cereal's invention a century ago. Within the broader health-conscious market, the white-flour alternatives have gained so much steam that General Mills—the maker of Wheaties, Cheerios, Trix, Cocoa Puffs, and Lucky Charms—now makes all its cereals with whole grains.

In the evolution of breakfast cereal, the marketplace trumped the founding ideals as the product moved into the mainstream. Might organic food, with its resounding success, fall prey to the same fate: losing touch with its roots, becoming nothing more than a profit center for Big Food, and reinventing itself with each market shift? By the late 1990s, as pioneering organic food companies were acquired by larger corporations, this became a prevalent question.

How odd this would have seemed thirty years earlier, when organic food was first gaining traction and the aim was to spread the word, turn people on to the cause, so that farming, human health, and the environment would be set right again. J. I. Rodale was one of the earliest mission-driven entrepreneurs in organic food, promoting the vision in his magazines; the Keene family in central Pennsylvania were among the first in the organic food business, establishing Walnut Acres in the 1940s and selling by mail-order catalog. Business was the vehicle that brought the message—and the food—to the people. By the mid-1970s, organic food entrepreneurs presented the ideal in bulk-grains bins and tofu buckets, with wilting vegetables, and snack foods to sate the munchies. It was an offbeat, loose revolution led by artisans and small-scale operatives. Counter-culture rags played up the subversive nature of communal gardens and subsistence living, but the juice bars, health-food restaurants, and co-ops made up the Main Street of this alternative world. Yet, what would happen if this vision actually succeeded in any meaningful way? Would the artisans—and their concoctions—survive their own success?

I was staring at one answer in my cereal bowl, for soy milk had run through every phase of the movement, from the artisan to the industrial. The product—specifically the Silk brand, made by White Wave in Boulder, Colorado—had hit the proverbial home run, remarkable not only among organic food products but in the annals of the contemporary food industry. Silk was the number-one organic packaged-goods brand in 2003, reaching $270 million in sales. It was the number-one brand in the dairy case, among all milk and soy milk brands until Horizon Organic milk overtook Silk in 2005. Sales were growing by one-third annually as overall milk consumption steadily declined.

Silk's makers had achieved this feat by answering a fundamental question: How do you create a health food Americans actually want to eat?

If you wanted to stay in the alternative-food ghetto, serving soy to tofu-loving vegans, that was one thing. But if your aim was to reach the mass market, that was something else again. And getting big was the point, because then you would convince people to eat this *superior* food, edging humanity up a notch. While not a universal thrust in the organic food movement, it was as powerful a line of thought as the goal of local, alternative-food networks pursued by small-scale organic farmers.

Achieving this with soy, though, was especially difficult due to one big hurdle: Americans hated tofu. For most, the bold frontier of soy ended with soy sauce. The big challenge, then, wasn't getting people to try something new, or something slightly different, which is what most companies face when rolling out new food products. No, if the organic soy-food revolution was going to get anywhere, you had to get Americans to try a product they already knew they hated and then to buy it in increasing numbers—a losing proposition for any sane entrepreneur.

So why even try?

Because the world would be better off. Everyone would be healthier. It was the same proposition that propelled organic foods in the first place, the same idealistic streak that prompted Kellogg a century before. It wasn't a million-dollar-business idea that led you down this road, because as businesses went, this one looked like a flop. It was *belief* that kept you going. And you would keep at it, even if it took twenty years, so that the middle-of-the-road consumer would pour soy milk over cereal in the morning, drink it up, and actually enjoy it.

Toiling over a big vat of tofu in 1977, Steve Demos did envision a time when soybeans would be consumed in the average American household. He just had no idea how it would come to pass.

Speaking to me in his modest corner office, in a business park outside of Boulder, Demos said he first had this vision during a seventy-six-day Buddhist meditation retreat in California. He would arise at 3:00 A.M. to make tofu for the day's meals, before the first of several daily meditation sessions. He was enamored of tofu, which westerners tend to view as bland, mushy, or simply disgusting. In Asia, where it has been eaten for thousands of years, from Indonesia to Japan, it's prized for its subtle, nutty flavor, ineffable texture, high protein, and versatility. Plus, it's a fast meal. Tofu can be braised, grilled, fried, or sautéed, and dished up with an endless number of sweet, salty, or spicy sauces, or even eaten on its own chilled on ice with a bit of scallion, ginger, shoyu, and bonito fish flakes—as Hiyayakko—an everyday dish in Japan.

"You're supposed to be focused on other things during these meditations but I started getting into business visions, because I came up with the company name, the products I wanted to make, what I was going to do, and how I was going to do it," Demos told me. "When I left the course, it was very clear: I was going to start a tofu company called White Wave. And it would have this wave logo and it would make these products and it was going to be an artisan shop, and we were going to change the world. We absolutely were going to change the world! One bite at a time!"

Demos has told this story often—it was in the company's PR materials—and relishes it. Clutching an ever-present coffee mug and casually dressed in a muted earth-tone shirt and dark slacks, with a bushy mustache and blond hair, Demos spoke intensely. He had found a purpose, a direction, over that vat of tofu, and it had set the course for the rest of his life. It came after a few years wandering in the wilderness—or, more precisely, vagabonding through India with his first wife, Pat Calhoun, while in his twenties. Now a millionaire many times over, Demos waxed on, nostalgic for his days on the "guru trail."

To get to India in those days, you flew to Europe, then hitchhiked to Istanbul. From there, you made your way east through Iran, Afghanistan, and Pakistan and dropped down into India. Demos and Calhoun followed this trail and ended up north of Delhi in Rishikesh, a holy center near the foothills of the Himilayas, along with other westerners. (Maharishi Mahesh Yogi, the Beatles's guru, was based there.) They eventually settled in caves near the Ganges River—gathering wood for their fires; making dal, lentils, chapatis, and yogurt; practicing yoga and meditation; and bathing in pools carved out by generations of nomadic ascetics. Wild peacocks and monkeys meandered about.

"We were livin' the life," Demos mused.

A boatman on the Ganges asked if they belonged to the new "hippie caste."

"We did, and it was a badge of honor," said Demos.

The couple exported hand-embroidered shawls and Afghan shirts, then sold their belongings when the money ran out. Locals gave them food. When they returned to the States, their only aim was to make enough money to go back to India. In the meantime, they learned *vipassana* meditation—an ancient Buddhist practice of concentration—from Satya Narayan Goenka, a Burmese industrialist turned meditation instructor who has since spread his teaching worldwide.

Demos eventually came to view his life as an ascetic in India as hypocritical, since he was taking handouts from people who had nothing. He had been born into a wealthy family outside of Philadelphia. His father, Anthony, was a chemical engineer who had started a business, Chemalloy Company Incorporated, with revenues of about $100 million. Demos thought his father defied the counterculture stereotype—"that big was bad, profit was ugly, and everything was wrong about business"—because he had worked hard. Countering the prevalent leftist rhetoric, Demos said he came to realize "the basic problem with America had nothing to do with free enterprise or capitalism. It had to do with humans making bad decisions, exploitive decisions, [with] lack of vision." There was hope in a kind of values-based Horatio Alger model that could counter the pillaging capitalists of the world.

Business could be *good*, in other words, if it were practiced with "right livelihood"—a concept Goenka explained in meditation retreats. One of Buddhism's precepts on the eightfold path, right livelihood is a vow to avoid harming other humans, animals, or the earth.

As with any religion, these concepts are open to interpretation, but right livelihood can be understood less as a rigid list of acceptable professions or practices than as a vow to be conscious about one's work. A policeman with a gun might be in conflict with the essence of the precept to avoid harming any living thing; but if the cop acts with compassion and reduces abuse and suffering, he might not. This gray area would be highly relevant in the business world, where a practitioner might justify an ethically questionable act as ultimately reducing suffering. As American Zen priest Roshi Bernard Glassman writes, "Some people feel that right livelihood is livelihood that eliminates suffering completely. But every business causes *some* suffering or damage . . . Right livelihood is livelihood that *minimizes* suffering or damage." These are highly personal decisions, rooted in Buddhist concepts of awareness and inquiry, rather than in the universal commandments of a religious hierarchy. In a sense, each practitioner must find his own way, which was particularly apt for an entrepreneur such as Demos. "Do no harm to anything that touches the economic stream," Demos said, summarizing his view of the precept. "And that was you, me, and everybody who consumes, supplies, and derives any part of their livelihood from what we're doing. They have to be treated with respect and find benefit."

Leaving India, Demos didn't want to fight capitalism, but to try his hand at it. "I wanted to prove to the profit-makers that I had a better model, based on values," he said. But he was also ambitious and wanted to make money. He didn't deny that aspect of his personality—he was refreshingly open about the subject of greed—but wanted to feed it ethically, creating what he termed "wealth without guilt." This amounted, he said, to "enlightened selfishness, if such a thing exists."

There followed a few forays, including an ashram in New

Hampshire, where he first learned how to make tofu by following a recipe in the *Ten Talents* cookbook. (Demos and Calhoun had sworn off meat after seeing insect-ridden meat carcasses in a market in Kandahar, Afghanistan.) The book, self-published by Frank and Rosalie Hurd, in 1968, was an early guide for counterculture vegetarians, before the *Moosewood Cookbook, Laurel's Kitchen,* the *Tassajara Bread Book,* and other influential cookbooks were published. The Hurds were Seventh-Day Adventists following the prescriptions of their sect's nineteenth-century founder, E. G. White: "Vegetables, fruits and grains should compose our diet. Not an ounce of flesh meat should enter our stomachs. The eating of flesh is unnatural. We are to return to God's original purpose in the creation of man." *Ten Talents* was replete with recipes for whole-grain dishes as well as soy foods such as tofu. As with cereal, the early history of soy foods in America was propelled by the Adventists, who made soy infant formula, soy milk, and, later, meat analogues such as soy hot dogs long before the counterculture and then mainstream food companies discovered them.

Though Buddhists like Demos jettisoned the book's Christian underpinnings, tofu fit the bill for right livelihood, because it could theoretically replace meat and benefit the world. *The Book of Tofu,* a bestseller in 1975, laid out this argument in the opening chapter. Its author, William Shurtleff, had lived and traveled in Japan, where he met his wife, illustrator Akiko Aoyagi. Shurtleff had been a student of Shunryu Suzuki Roshi, a Zen priest and founder of the San Francisco Zen Center, and lived for a time at the Tassajara Zen Mountain Center, the order's remote monestary in the Santa Lucia Mountains near Big Sur. (The Zen Center's Green Gulch Farm, in Marin County, and Greens Restaurant in San Francisco later became influential in the organic movement. Chefs who worked at the

restaurant included Deborah Madison, author of the voluminous *Vegetarian Cooking for Everyone,* and Edward Brown, a
Zen priest and the *Tassajara Bread Book* author.)

Shurtleff argued that soy could produce a third more protein per acre than any other known crop and twenty times the
protein as could be raised on land given over to cattle grazing or
grain growing. The forty-seven-million-ton soybean harvest of
1973 was enough to provide every person in the United States
with 165 pounds of pure, high-quality protein. "If all this protein were used directly as food—in the form of tofu, for example—it would be sufficient to fulfill the average adult protein
requirement of every American for about 3 years!" he wrote.
Shurtleff cited Lappé's argument in *Diet for a Small Planet*:
Since it took seven pounds of grain and soybeans to produce one
pound of meat, meat production was "a protein factory in reverse." Lappé's recommendations for the kinds of vegetarian
proteins and grains needed to achieve a balanced meal were digested by a generation of college kids, including me. Living in
a semivegetarian student house in Portland, Oregon, in the late
1970s, my friends and I ate copious amounts of brown rice,
grains, and beans bought in bulk sacks at the local food co-op.
These foodstuffs were filling but ultimately unsatisfying, and
without the faith of counterculture zealots, we pursued the
Small Planet diet for only a year.

Shurtleff said the "tragedy" of American agriculture was
that nearly all its soybeans ended up in factories where oil was
extracted and the remaining high-protein pulp processed into
animal feed. With America's meatcentric diet, only 1.5 percent
of all soy protein became soy foods such as tofu, and only 13
percent provided indirect human sustenance in meat and dairy
products. "These losses, creating the appearance of scarcity in
the midst of actual plenty, are a direct result of our failure to

understand and make use of the soybean's great potential as food. For if the total protein available from these crops were utilized directly by human beings, it could make up an estimated 90 percent of the world's protein deficiency," he wrote.

Since Americans consumed five times as much protein as those in developing countries—by eating meat, poultry, and eggs from grain-fed animals—they were in effect stealing protein from poor people's mouths. One clear way to reverse this trend and more evenly distribute the world supply of protein, the book argued, was to eat less meat. "By rediscovering the wisdom inherent in traditional dietary patterns that make use of non-protein sources, we can free millions of tons of high-quality soy and grain protein to be used directly as food," the book stated. Soy was a direct means of overcoming rampant starvation in the world—if you could get it to starving people. The book also presented tofu shops as a potential model "for decentralized enterprises using technology on a human scale" in both the developed and undeveloped world.

This wasn't an esoteric Buddhist argument about the virtues of vegetarianism, but a case made by food scientists, development experts, government agencies, and the myriad interests involved in growing, selling, and exporting soy around the world. The International Soy Program at the University of Illinois Urbana-Champaign was one effort, founded in 1973 and backed by government and industry funds. Three decades later, its Web site still emphasizes the potential markets for soy protein in Asia, Africa, and Latin America. The soybean, after all, is the second-largest U.S. crop after corn, worth $15 billion, with nearly every other row bound for export.

But whereas Shurtleff envisioned artisan tofu shops around the world, the food industry had something else in mind: refining soy into a highly concentrated form of protein that could be spun into ever more profitable synthesized foods, since vegetable oil and animal feed were low-margin commodities in the best of times.

The late 1960s saw the appearance of these synthesized meat replacements, none of which were very eagerly consumed. Two decades later, the more palatable veggie burgers showed up, their primary ingredient soy protein. More recently, soy-based energy bars have become the largest and fastest-growing segment of the industry.

But the starting point of all these soy protein foods is low-margin animal feed, more or less. When the soybean is crushed at the factory, it is soaked in hexane, a highly toxic petroleum derivative that leaches the oil from the bean. The mixture is then heated so that the hexane evaporates. The remaining substance is distilled, leaving crude soybean oil. This crude oil is degummed, extracting soy lecithin—an emulsifier found in many baked goods. What's left is then further refined, bleached, and deodorized, creating twenty million pounds of oil—80 percent of all oil consumed in the United States—used in everything from french fries to salad dressing. Vitamin E supplements are also a by-product of this process. Once the oil is refined, it is often hydrogenated, thickening it so that it can be spread at room temperature in products such as margarine and shortening. This creates trans-fatty acids that contribute to heart disease by raising LDL cholesterol (the bad type) and lowering HDL (the good type). The soybean industry has bred soybeans that reduce the need for hydrogenation, but this development is still in its infancy.

These oils contain about 2 parts per million of hexane, which is too low a dose to have an effect on humans. Gasoline contains 1 to 3 percent hexane (you can breathe it when pumping gas), and the solvent is also found in rubber cement, cleaning agents, roofing materials, and floor coverings. The main risk is to those who work with it and breathe it regularly, according to the Agency for Toxic Substances and Disease Registry. Workers who breathed it at exposures of 500 to 2,500 parts per million ended up with nerve disorders, but they recovered. American and European teenagers who sniffed glues containing hexane have suffered paralysis of their limbs. One petroleum research facility using hexane was shut down in 1996 after six employees contracted a deadly form of brain cancer. But the EPA has not listed the substance as a carcinogen because of a lack of studies, although the agency last looked at the issue in 1991. Of the several hundred million pounds of hexane produced annually, about 30 percent is used for vegetable oil extraction.

Hexane is not the only way to leach oil from the bean, just the most prevalent and cost-effective. In organic food production, hexane and other extraction solvents are banned, so the beans must be crushed to remove the oil. The "expeller pressed" method is less efficient and one reason that organic oils are more expensive.

Vegetable oil, though, is a by-product that makes up only 20 percent of the soybean. The bigger source of revenue are the defatted flakes that remain after oil is extracted. These are toasted and ground, with 90 percent going to animal feed. The remaining 10 percent of the flakes are processed to remove the flatulent-inducing sugars, creating soy protein concentrate, the mainstay of veggie burgers. The substance can then be further refined to remove the remaining fiber, creating soy protein isolate. The stuff is malleable, tasteless, and filling (it's pure protein after all), which means it can be added to just about anything. It is the basis for protein drinks, sports bars, and other soy protein foods. Most likely sourced from genetically engineered soy (which is now 80 percent of the U.S. soybean crop), processed with the petroleum solvent, and chemically treated with acid and alkaline washes, these soy derivatives are about as far from organic and "natural" food as you can get.

"It's the dirty little secret of the natural-foods business," Demos told me. He, like many other organic soy foods entrepreneurs, entirely avoided these processed ingredients to focus on whole soy foods.

Even with all this dazzling food science to create soy-based "value-added" and vegetarian foods, the mundane reality is that animals still consume nine out of every ten bushels. "Demand for animal production is what pushes growers to plant more soybeans," said Peter Golbitz, president of the market research firm Soyatech Incorporated.

With three decades' hindsight, shifting soy protein from animals to humans to solve third-world hunger now seems naive, since it didn't address indigenous food cultures and the multiple causes of malnutrition—among them, ownership and control of land, complexities of food distribution, the impact of regional conflicts, and the price of food. Even if you could transfer soy foods to the third world, how would you convince people to eat this stuff? Affordable soy could provide protein to the 850 million people in the world who are malnourished, but if these people had enough money to buy or grow soy foods, they might rather spend it on foods they'd prefer.

Vegetarian proponents never triumphed with soy the way they had hoped. Even with food shortages in the third world, meat consumption in developing countries rose by 150 percent from the mid-1960s to the late 1990s. Soy, as a hunger-fighting food, was a seventies-era solution. Now, in the continuing search for wonder foods to feed the world, genetically engineered crops have taken center stage. These crops have lowered the price of animal feed, prompting ever-larger industrial farms to boost meat production—a process underway most dramatically in China. But for the malnourished, meat from grain-fed animals remains a luxury, not a solution to hunger.

Still, in the 1970s, soy was an altruistic food alluring enough to spur counterculture artisans to get into the business and to motivate those like Demos to stay in it for the long haul. "Today, we're the largest-selling organic food [product], certainly in the United States," Demos told me in 2003. "And whenever anybody says that, I usually say, 'Well, that's great. Am I the largest soy company?' Because that's what our mission is: to drive people low on the food chain to eating soy or vegetable protein."

By the mid-1970s, Demos had moved to Boulder, Colorado, which turned out to be the perfect place for a tofu-making practitioner of Eastern religion. Nestled next to the idyllic Rocky Mountains, Boulder had become a center for metaphysical pursuits—yoga, tai chi chuan, various Buddhist sects—and, not coincidentally, natural-foods businesses like tofu, which wasn't hard to get into.

He borrowed $500 from a neighbor, bought a pot, blender, and small stove, then opened a shop on Pearl Street in downtown Boulder. (His father didn't invest, viewing him as too much of a risk.) Although he and Calhoun had split up after returning home—things apparently went sour in the New Hampshire yoga ashram—he called her up in northern California, where she was working as a waitress, and she agreed to join him in the business, after a meditation retreat. "We were artisans," Demos said. "Remember, we're in the mid-seventies: Small is beautiful. We forgot the highly impossible part. But it was very beautiful." Working six and a half days a week, they joked they should have named the company White Slave.

By now, Calhoun had remarried and was pregnant with her first child. (Demos had remarried, too.) One of her many jobs was sitting on a tofu press to form the blocks of bean curd, becoming a spectacle to people passing by the store window at night. "We were like the local TV show at two o'clock in the morning for Boulder," she said. Calhoun eventually became White Wave's chief financial officer, serving as the nuts-and-bolts pragmatist who kept the visionary in check.

To make soy milk, dried soy beans are soaked overnight, then ground up with hot water. The puree is strained to remove the fibrous bean pulp, known as *okara*. The remaining liquid is soy milk, or what the soy industry calls "base extract." This is a traditional Asian food. In Japan, people used to store their personal bottles at neighborhood tofu shops and pick up hot soy milk in the morning for breakfast. In China, soy milk (*dou jiang*) dates back nearly two thousand years.

The Book of Tofu shows how soy milk base can be made at home with a blender, pot, and cheese cloth as Demos did when he started out. Once you have the milk, you can easily make tofu. In a process similar to the way cheese is curdled with rennet, a coagulant such as *nigari*, made from mineral salts in sea water, is added to the soy milk to form curds. The liquid whey is then drained off and the remaining curds placed in molds and pressed into square blocks of tofu.

In developing this process, the Chinese overcame a major obstacle to digesting the beans. Like other beans, soybeans contain sugars (oligosaccharides) that pass undigested into the intestine and feed bacteria. This can create bloating, gas, and, in extreme cases, diarrhea. Tofu solves this problem by concentrating the soy proteins, leaving the bulk of the sugars in the remaining whey. (Since soy milk contains the whey, and thus the sugars, some have a harder time digesting it.) Cooking or fermenting overcomes a second drawback of the beans—trypsin inhibitors, which obstruct an enzyme critical for digestion—which is why Asians invented fermented foods such as soy sauce, miso (a condiment and soup base), and tempeh (a loaf-like soy product).

In the early days, Demos's Good Belly Deli, as it was then called, sold Japanese foods such as miso, *umeboshi* (salted pickled plums), and seaweed for the macrobiotic set, but these weren't the items that had people lining up outside the door. Familiar American foods were the big sellers. Demos and Calhoun created marinated tofu sandwiches, served up soy milk in a juice machine, and sold "soysage" (soy sausage) and granola made out of the *okara*. Also on the menu: tofu pizza, eggless egg salad, and a faux tuna salad made with soy mayonnaise, along with a line of pies, cakes, and muffins with soy fillings.

Like other soy foods entrepreneurs, Demos bought organic soybeans from the start, often creating markets where none existed and convincing farmers to go organic to ensure a supply. He and other pioneers in the soy foods trade also got farmers to plant high-protein beans, which were better suited for tofu than those used in oil production. This also created a commodity source for Japan, which by the 1980s had became a dominant buyer of American organic soybeans.

Within a couple of years, White Wave outgrew its three-hundred-square-foot deli and moved production to a larger factory, where the company made more than 200,000 pounds of tofu a year. White Wave got its first big break when Demos showed up at King Soopers supermarket with blocks of tofu in Chinese food containers with labels slapped on their sides. "The buyer laughed so hard he nearly fell out of his chair," Demos said. "Then he told me, 'If you give me a package, we'll give you a shot.'"

Demos returned a few months later with a sealed plastic container, which the chain stocked in two stores for a test run. Each day, Demos sent a couple of employees to buy the tofu, then he and others would purchase it after work. "And sure enough when we went back to King Soopers, the buyer said, 'God, these numbers are great! This stuff's really selling!' I said, 'I'm telling you, we can barely keep up.'" White Wave won the account, which paved the way for Safeway and other supermarkets to stock White Wave tofu.

By 1980, Demos had shut down the popular deli to focus on tofu manufacturing. He also experimented with other soy products, searching for one that would be a major hit. White Wave made, at one time or another, nearly every soy food now on the market: "Hotdogs, hamburgers, pocket sandwiches, ice creams, ice-cream sandwiches, soy cheese. That was Soy Melt and Super Melt. Dips, dressings—there's a dressing picture around here somewhere," Demos said, fumbling through a stack of brochures. "It just went on and on; we had it all," he said. "We couldn't find the contact point."

Each product had a drawback. Though he tried meat analogues, Demos decided not to go up against major food companies that were testing soy burgers. And while he made low-fat, cholesterol-free soy ice creams, healthy desserts seemed an oxymoron. He wasn't about to outrun Ben & Jerry's.

"They were a politically correct vehicle for saturated fat, and with Cherry Garcia, bingo, they rang the bell. What are you going to say, 'I've got the [soy] alternative to Cherry Garcia?' Not a chance," he said.

Even tofu wasn't easy. Packaging equipment failed and expenses ballooned. In the mid-1980s, losses ran into the six figures even as sales hit $6 million. For the first time, Demos turned to his father, who gave him $25,000 and advised him to take "a meat cleaver" to costs. His brother Jack, a Pittsburgh plastic surgeon, became his biggest backer, taking out a second mortgage on his home. Demos fired managers and cut salaries, then he and Calhoun negotiated with creditors to delay payments on their debts. He also won a timely boost from a soy ice-cream maker who paid him for his recipes. Demos, who admits to falling off the meditation cushion with regularity, redoubled his Buddhist practice. White Wave narrowly avoided bankruptcy.

I asked Demos what compelled him to keep pursuing new soy foods instead of sticking with tofu.

"Well, I believed I was headed to a billion dollars."

"Okay, but, I mean, what were the signs?"

"Oh, inherent in the business? Nothing was successful. No, no, no, nothing. But I knew without any question in my mind that the human was going to move down the food chain to meet their needs going forward because it was absolutely inevitable that we were going to either fish up, farm out, or somehow pollute our food supply. And I suppose that was the one hook that said, 'Don't stop.'

"There is an inevitability to the need for this product," he continued. "It was a full protein. It could feed people. And it was environmentally better than all the other models out there. So it was *me* making a mistake. The concept was clean."

Soy milk wasn't an obvious candidate for the breakthrough Demos sought, because it can have a beany, grassy, or chalky taste unacceptable to many consumers.

I discovered this firsthand when I bought a pound of organic soybeans for seventy-nine cents and tried to make soy milk, following the recipe in *The Book of Tofu*. I soaked the beans overnight, then added them to boiling water in a blender.

When I strained the soy puree through a thin cotton towel, all that remained was the fibrous pulp, the *okara*, which looked like fine grains of couscous. The milk flowed into a pot underneath, which I heated to a boil, and then simmered for several minutes. I added a few tablespoons of honey and some vanilla (the stalwart flavors of the counterculture) but the milk still had a strong beany taste, so I threw in a half cup of sugar.

I tested the concoction on Ellen, who dubiously sipped it and made a horrid face.

"It tastes like beans!" she said.

No amount of sweetener would mask the damage wrought by the enzyme lipoxygenase, which is released when the bean is crushed, destroying oil molecules and creating an almost rancid taste.

For years, the counterculture ate foods like this, because "if it tasted bad, that meant it was probably good for you," as Demos put it. The equation did not prove enduring. The hippies became boomers, moved back from the land, got jobs, and gave this up, which is why companies such as White Wave had to alter the flavor. Stonyfield Farm achieved something similar with yogurt, creating a mild version of the tart food and adding sweetener to make it more acceptable in the mass market. I tested my homemade soy milk against Silk, which had only a hint of beans and was obviously superior.

I still had a quart of the homemade stuff and wondered what to do.

"Put it on the compost pile!" Ellen said. (The backyard compost bin was another spin-off of this book project, consuming all manner of kitchen detritus.)

Heating should have killed the bad flavor. I may have failed in following the recipe, stumbled on bad beans, or simply been tripped up by a problem that bedeviled Demos and his colleagues for two decades. It took all of a half hour to make soy milk, but making it drinkable—that seemed like pure alchemy.

By the late 1960s, food scientists at Cornell University had come up with a method to neutralize the dreaded lipoxygenase enzyme by heating the milk in a precise fashion. The Cornell method was applied first in Asia, where soy milk began to be mass produced after World War II. Vitasoy, the top brand, even overtook Coca-Cola to become the bestselling beverage in Hong Kong at one time and still ranks among its top-ten food products. One reason soy milk is so popular in Asia is that lactose intolerance—the inability to digest milk sugars, or lactose—approaches 100 percent. This is actually the norm for the human race, with rates reaching about 75 percent globally. The lactose-digesting enzyme, *lactase,* peaks after birth, then declines between age two and five, the exception being northern Europeans who evolved the ability to digest milk throughout life because they were dependent on dairy for protein. If you lack the enzyme, the reactions differ. Some people can digest a bowl of ice cream, others get bloated and uncomfortable. A cup of milk may be fine for some but not for others. (Cheese doesn't produce the effect, since it contains little lactose.) For those with the condition, numbering thirty million to fifty million people in the United States, a milk alternative makes sense.

The soy milk market began in earnest in the mid-1980s, when Eden Foods, an organic foods company founded as a co-op in Ann Arbor, Michigan, began importing soy milk from Japan with enormous success. Other natural-food companies soon followed. In a mind-boggling example of high-energy food transport, organic soybeans were exported from the Midwest to Japan, made into soy milk, and then shipped back to the United States. The product could travel this distance because it was "shelf-stable," meaning it had been processed at a high enough

temperature to kill food-spoiling bacteria, then packaged in special containers that could be stored at room temperature for up
to six months. This became the way soy milk was sold, sitting
on the grocery shelf.

White Wave, which was pumping out tofu and dozens of
other soy foods experiments, missed this development. But this
was a blessing, since it meant Demos had to take a different
path to crack the market once he woke up to its potential in the
late 1980s. His solution: to sell a refrigerated product in a familiar gable-top milk carton right in the dairy case. This would
transform the perception of soy milk from a natural-food product to a true milk alternative—a revolutionary breakthrough in
marketing.

"Your perception is that it's fresher," Demos said.

Demos wasn't alone in this thinking. The Soy Crafters Association, a group Demos cofounded in 1978, openly talked
about applying a dairy model to soy because the manufacturing
process was identical.

"We always shared the idea that all these products could be
made in a dairy facility with dairy distributors," said Jeremiah
Ridenour, president of Wildwood Natural Foods, an early soy
company based in Watsonville, California. "Our strategy was, if
we grow up, we need to find a dairy partner and get involved in
their manufacturing and distribution."

Ridenour, a Buddhist and vegetarian who had spent summers on his family's soybean farm in Illinois, was a pioneer in
this development. He had started out making tempeh in his
garage. By 1985, he had joined Wildwood Foods, run by a
gospel-singing chef and a few partners. Wildwood was highly
successful on the West Coast, building regional sales rivaling
White Wave's nationally. Ridenour, like Demos, saw a greater
potential and thought dairy analogues such as soy milk and soy

cheese would bring wider acceptance. And like so many others, his foray into the business came upon reading *The Book of Tofu*.

Soy milk's nutritional profile is similar to milk's, though it has more protein, fewer carbohydrates, and no cholesterol. The raw material, base extract, could be shipped to a dairy plant by truck, just as raw milk is from farms. It could then be pasteurized, packaged in a carton, and sent out on a dairy route. It could also be made into yogurt and cheese, though these products still leave a lot to be desired.

Processing soy in a dairy plant would amount to a big cost advantage, because you could merely pay a "tolling fee" for a soy milk run, rather than invest millions in building a factory. Eden Foods had gone down the latter path with Japanese partners, setting up a soy milk plant in Saline, Michigan. This saved the expense of carting soy milk across the ocean, but it locked Eden into a big investment. Eden wasn't alone. Every major soy milk company either imported the product from Asia or made it in proprietary plants. No one had partnered with a mainstream dairy company, in part because the gulf between the conventional and natural-foods business was still so great. The dairy industry viewed soy milk either with disdain or as a competitive threat.

Although Wildwood had sold a "fresh" refrigerated soy milk since 1982 (in honey-vanilla, chocolate, and banana flavors), Ridenour knew he had to overcome two issues to go mainstream: reduce the beany flavor, even more than the Asian manufacturers, and link up with a dairy company to produce the stuff on a massive scale.

He solved part of this problem by finding a California dairy processor, Morningstar, which made a nondairy soy creamer, so was familiar with the process. It agreed to make soy milk and distribute the product in its trucks. Ridenour then enlisted another soy foods maker who had been influenced by *The Book of Tofu*, Ted Nordquist, a Californian of Swedish descent who many credit with perfecting soy ice cream. Nordquist had built Sweden's first tofu plant and had run several soy businesses in the country—curious, since Swedes have among the lowest rate of lactose intolerance in the world—but returned to the Bay Area in 1994 with his family, agreeing to work with Ridenour.

Huddled in the dairy's R & D lab in Gustine, California, Nordquist came up with the precise ultrahigh heat process needed to reduce sharply the beany flavor. This was tricky, since the milk is flavored and sweetened before it is subjected to high heat, potentially throwing the taste out of kilter. By 1995, though, Nordquist had developed a flavor profile that proved acceptable. He ran a test batch through the full-scale dairy and got the thumbs-up from Ridenour's taste panel. Ridenour and Nordquist were ready to make the first refrigerated soy milk in the market.

Nordquist—who now runs WholeSoy & Company in San Francisco, making soy-based yogurts, smoothies, and ice cream—was eager to hit the streets with the product. But at that moment, Wildwood was stretched thin. Ridenour had tied up a lot of money in an organic farm in Mexico and planned to plow the cash from a coming harvest into the new soy milk.

"It was a matter of two months," Ridenour said.

But Nordquist was impatient. He began shopping the formula around, eventually taking it to Demos. "I put an enormous amount of time and money into the project—I had to go somewhere," Nordquist told me.

Although White Wave has long gotten a lot of press for "inventing" refrigerated soy milk, Demos confirmed to me that

Nordquist approached him with the formula. He said he tried it and it tasted "great."

"We had been already working on it in R & D," Demos said. "So I called him up and said, 'You know, what you'll do is accelerate the R & D process here. You'll bring me to market a year faster.'" He said he did not learn until a year later that Nordquist had been working with Ridenour.

Ridenour talked to a lawyer about suing over the loss of the formula, but was advised the partnership with Nordquist had not been ironclad. All he could do was follow Silk to the market six months later. But it was too late. Wildwood Foods never caught up with what became the top soy milk brand.

Ridenour, who is Zen-like about the episode, has seen Nordquist at trade shows, where Wildwood and WholeSoy are dwarfed by White Wave's huge display. "We stand at the shows tickling each other: 'We could have the big soy milk display Steve has over there. That could be you and I!' And we laugh at it, but at the same time . . ." His voice trailed off.

Demos immediately ramped up production in January 1996, flooding natural-food markets with the first refrigerated soy milk in the familiar gable-topped carton. After nineteen years of throwing every permutation of soy at the market, he thought he'd finally hit on a winner. "We believed that it was just going to take off like a rocket ship," he said.

This proved a costly miscalculation. Customers had no idea what to make of refrigerated soy milk and looked right past it as they reached for milk. The unsold cartons were returned to White Wave. Losses rose quickly, bringing the company to the edge of bankruptcy for the second time.

Demos slashed expenses to buy time, then worked to get

sales back on track. The company began offering free samples as people left stores, with a coupon to buy a carton of Silk. "We said, 'It's vanilla, try it on cereal. Silk is for cereal." He realized he had a breakthrough when people tried it and said, "That isn't bad." Given the prevalent view—that soy was disgusting—even this guarded opinion amounted to an endorsement.

"It's all you needed to hear, because you just broke down the mental barrier about soy," he said. "If I challenge your premise about something and prove you wrong about it, you're open to me."

Free samples and an edible product weren't the only things changing the mental barrier to soy. In 1995, the *New England Journal of Medicine* published an assessment of thirty-eight clinical trials that found soy protein significantly lowered total cholesterol, LDL cholesterol, and triglycerides—all factors in heart disease. Many of the studies were funded by the United Soybean Board (the growers' main lobby), various state soybean associations, and soy food companies, to build the case for soy foods. Then, in May 1998, Protein Technologies International, which made soy protein isolate, petitioned the FDA for approval of a claim that soy reduced the risk of heart disease. In 1999, the FDA approved a claim that "25 grams of soy protein, combined with a diet low in saturated fat and cholesterol, may reduce the risk of coronary heart disease." A serving of food had to contain at least 6.25 grams, or about a teaspoon, of soy protein to qualify for the label.

The FDA decision was like rocket fuel for the soy foods industry. Soy milk wasn't just for the lactose intolerant, macrobiotic, or vegetarian any longer. It was packaged as a way to avoid the leading cause of death in the United States. On the back of other highly publicized studies, people also believed soy would relieve menopause, fight cancer, and cut their waistlines. In 2000, more than 300 soy foods were introduced. Grocery products featured labels that said NOW WITH SOY, even if the foods contained less than 6.25 grams of soy per serving and couldn't carry the FDA health claim. One Cargill official called soy as important as vitamin C as a food additive. By 2004, there were 5,137 products in the $4 billion soyfoods market, including over 1,000 energy bars, 463 soymilk drinks, 431 meat alternatives, and 343 tofu products. After taking nineteen years to hit $6 million in sales, White Wave had topped $10 million the first year Silk was on the market. By 1999, when the FDA claim appeared, sales had reached $70 million. By 2003, they clocked in at $300 million.

The hype around soy led to a backlash, with the most extreme, antivegetarian opponents likening it to a toxic substance. Others simply cautioned against viewing soy as a magic bullet. Since the early studies, for example, researchers have found only a modest effect in lowering cholesterol, though this cannot be dismissed as insignificant compared with the saturated fats and cholesterol in meat.

There are also questions about the phytoestrogens in soy, which mimic estrogens in the body responsible for breast cancer. Some researchers suggest these plant estrogens are protective; by attaching to estrogen receptors and blocking the uptake of much more powerful human estrogen, they prevent the growth of breast cancer. Others say these phytoestrogens promote cancerous growth by acting like human estrogen after all. There is no definitive answer, which is why some physicians advise breast cancer survivors to limit or avoid soy foods. Soy does appear to be beneficial for men, since a number of animal and epidemiological studies suggest it may cut the risk of prostate cancer. When scientists study people who consume large amounts of soy, such as the Japanese, they find lower rates of breast cancer, prostate cancer, and heart disease, but these observations are less than conclusive since other factors might play a role. The Okinawa Centenarian Study, a twenty-five-year study of the remarkable number of Okinawans over one hundred, attributed their longevity to low caloric intake, high consumption of vegetables and fruits, intake of good fats (omega-3, mono-unsaturated fat), a high-fiber diet, low body-fat, physical activity—and soy foods.

While Silk was soaring, it wasn't because of Howard's pioneering equation linking soil, food, and health. People were buying Silk because of the health claims linked to soybeans, not because it was organic. When I pointed out that White Wave had ridden the coattails of the conventional food industry's publicity campaign, Demos replied, "That's exactly right. Funny who your allies become."

While White Wave could have earned more with a *non-organic* soy milk product (since conventional soybeans are cheaper), it stuck with organic soy because that was its mission. The upshot is that the vast majority of soy milk on store shelves is organically produced, while other organic categories fight to get 2 percent of market share.

Even so, White Wave's organic soy milk managed to become extremely profitable. When it first appeared, Demos set the price higher than milk, though Silk costs far less to produce. It takes about a pound and a half of soybeans costing $0.45 to make a gallon of soy milk that wholesales for about $4.75; a gallon of organic milk for a dairy plant costs about $1.90, then wholesales for about $4.25.

Demos set this fat margin to fund expansion, because Silk had no competition in the dairy case. Once sales grew, revenues flowed right to the bottom line, giving White Wave cash to fund more free samples and build still more sales.

To his chagrin, Demos lost slices of those hefty profits on the way to the supermarket—first by buying soy base-extract from which to make the milk, then to the shippers who transported the base by truck, and then to the regional dairies who processed, packaged, and distributed the soy milk. Supermarket companies also sought "slotting fees" in the millions of dollars just to place the soy cartons in the dairy case. To protect his profit margin, Demos began to look for a dairy partner who could bring plants, distribution channels, and capital. His goal was to set up soy extraction plants next to dairies and pump the soy base material right through the wall, to be processed and packaged, cutting both his raw material and transport costs. While circling venture capitalists sought to make an investment, too, they could only offer money, not access, so he kept his focus on the dairy industry.

In June 1998, Demos walked into a meeting with top executives of Dean Foods Company, the nation's second-largest dairy company, carrying an aluminum attaché case. Inside was a carton of Silk and a few shot glasses. After offering a taste of the milk and giving a quick verbal pitch on the business, Demos asked for $5 million. Dean officials agreed, eventually buying a third of the company for $15 million—enough to launch Silk into mainstream supermarkets.

But the cost proved high. Demos felt Dean didn't deliver all that it promised and yet it still had an option to buy the remainder of White Wave at a big discount. When Dean Foods then sold out to its bigger rival, Suiza, Demos sued the new parent company. He wanted out of the deal. As the suit dragged on, Demos called the executives at the merged company—which kept the Dean name—to seek a resolution.

He met with Gregg Engles, the Yale-educated lawyer who had founded Suiza and built it into the number-one dairy company by buying up smaller companies around the nation. Engles had become familiar with the organic market through his earlier purchase of a stake in Horizon Organic, the Boulder-based milk company. He liked the market, especially its growth prospects in comparison with the stagnant food business. In the meeting, Demos told him his beef, and Engles agreed to scratch the provision allowing Dean to buy the rest of White Wave at a discount. "We want you to stick with it, run it, grow it, make it bigger—we'll make a whopping deal to help you do this," Engles told him.

Engles then offered to pay full value for White Wave (an extra $30 million to Demos alone) to keep him on board.

It was an offer Demos couldn't refuse. He wanted to push Silk's expansion and cash out after thirty years in the business. As for Engles, he later said, "This was an underappreciated business."

The original investors in White Wave—mostly Demos's family and Calhoun's—split the $192.8 million Dean Foods paid for the remainder of the company in 2002.

But even with the backing of the $9 billion dairy giant, Demos could not let go of his old canard, that soy was the *future.* Driving his new boss to the airport after they cut the deal, Demos said, "You do realize that my job is to outdate your product."

"What's wrong with my product?" Engles replied.

"There's nothing wrong with milk. I just have a better product."

Engles, though, had something else in mind.

He bought the rest of Horizon Organic in 2004, and put Demos in charge of the top two brands in the organic food industry. Dean siphoned a few more brands to the division, which had about $1.1 billion in sales and was the fastest-growing unit of Dean Foods. As the *Wall Street Journal* later wrote, these mergers "helped transform Dean Foods from a low-margin milk producer into a Wall Street stand-out with a growing stable of high-margin brands."

Demos had always wanted to play on the big stage. Now was his chance. He told me this was the only thing that kept him working. After all, he had a big hunk of cash and a nice ranch in Boulder with 160 organic fruit trees and a thriving organic vegetable garden. Soy milk was widespread. "We had integrated this into the culture," he said. "Our mission was done."

But now he was after bigger prey, figuring out how to bring what he saw as his values-based approach to a wider corporate stage.

"That was the entire mission going all the way back to why we all got in business—to influence the way the world works," he said. "Not only the way we eat, but the way we derive our livelihoods and exist in our culture. We'll end up with a billion-dollar consumer packaged goods company based on social responsibility! Unheard of! What a dazzler!"

He wasn't selling out. Dean was buying in.

Demos wasn't naive about Dean's intentions, but thought he could influence the company once it learned that the strength of the organic food business derived from its values, from its mission. It was never just food.

"I said, 'You know, we're all about green.' And Gregg said, 'So am I. Mine just has dead presidents on it.' And I said, 'Well, I'm going to prove that my green makes your green grow.'"

That was how we left things when I talked with Demos in a two-day interview in 2003. A year and a half later, the *Wall*

Street Journal ran a long, front-page article about how the merger of White Wave and Dean Foods had brought together this unlikely pair, the Buddhist and the mainstream CEO, and how it had proven a success. "We all gave each other high-fives when it came out," Demos told me.

But a few weeks later, lunching at Demos's home in Boulder, Engles told the soy milk guru he wanted him to move into a nonexecutive role. "He wanted me to be Colonel Sanders or the company mascot, and I looked at him and laughed," Demos said. "They were going to pay me a lot of money, give me a company jet, but that didn't interest me. I already had money. He simply did not get what I was about." When Engles then asked for his resignation, Demos refused and said Engles would have to fire him. So Engles did. (The Dean Foods press release, however, said Demos "resigned.")

Soon after, Calhoun resigned, and many of the managers at White Wave left, too. The mission—or this stage of it—was over, "shot in the head," as Demos put it.

It was a good lesson in the Buddhist concept of non-attachment, of letting go of any material or egocentric endeavor. Demos had tried the middle way. For him at least, it turned out to be a dead end.

What Dean was ultimately buying was Silk, not Steve Demos. As in the annals of conventional start-ups, the organic food industry is littered with founders who built companies, then cashed out to mainstream food giants. One of the few who has managed to survive is Gary Hirshberg, who sold a majority interest of his yogurt company Stonyfield Farm to France's Groupe Danone (which also owns Dannon yogurt) in an unusual deal that allowed him to keep control of Stonyfield's board. "The fact that we achieved this negotiation with Gary . . . shows

Danone is a multinational corporation with a special spirit. We are driven by social values similar to Gary's," Franck Riboud, Danone's chairman and CEO told one reporter. Echoing Demos, Hirshberg told me his mission now was "to change the way the big players make and sell food." But he had influence at Danone because of the deal he had struck. Faced with a fast-growing product, Demos was forced to cede control and ended up as roadkill.

Within a few months of Demos's ouster, White Wave launched two new soy products, a light soy milk and a soy smoothie drink. Dean Foods was taking the organic brand and extending it further. I bought Silk Light to try it, but only after I got home and looked at the carton closely did I notice that the word *organic* was nowhere to be found. The only organic ingredient was evaporated cane juice, a sweetener. Conventional soybeans cost about two-thirds less than organic ones, so using them would only swell the already robust profit margin on the product, without affecting the health claim. Dean Foods also brought in an executive from Gillette to run the company. Was Silk growing into just another supermarket brand, divorced from the organic food values responsible for its birth?

As we shall see, a contingent of the organic movement believed this type of development had become so rampant that it sullied the entire concept of organic food. Principles at the heart of the movement had been lost in the surge to the mainstream. But others thought tight regulations were the armor for the organic idea; keep them strong and even big companies would have to manufacture organic food with true integrity. This would be the equivalent of the agroecological ideals followed by a large-scale farm. Regulations thus became the battleground for the future control of organic food, the place where each faction in the organic community tried to craft rules that reflected their worldview. Without the rules, organic food would be meaningless—just another grocery product—but with them, one could try to create a particular vision of the way agriculture, industry, food, and the world should be.

6. Backlash

The Meaning of Organic

*Hard as I try, I cannot think of another
private-sector group being regulated that continually demands
tougher regulations be inflicted on themselves.*
—JIM PIERCE, CERTIFICATION CZAR, ORGANIC VALLEY

On February 28, 2004, a farmer from upstate New York, Elizabeth Henderson, addressed the Upper Midwest Organic Farming Conference in a talk entitled, "Who SHOULD own Organic?"

"We need to make a decision," she told the fifteen hundred people in the audience. "Are we an industry? Or are we a movement?"

She listed the disturbing trends: Half of all organic sales in California came from the twenty-seven largest farms, 2 percent of the total farms; eight of the top food corporations owned the thirty-eight largest organic businesses; Archer Daniels Midland, Cadbury Schweppes, Coca-Cola, ConAgra, Dean Foods, Dole, General Mills, Groupe Danone, H. J. Heinz, Kellogg, Mars, Parmalat, Kraft, Sara Lee, and Tyson Foods had all "formed partnerships with organic companies or developed their own organic lines."

The organic food companies had sold out. The retail sector, consolidated. United Natural Foods, a distributor, was now a billion-dollar public company, having snapped up smaller distributors around the country. Its purchase of the last two natural-food-distribution cooperatives, Blooming Prairie in the Midwest, and Northeast Cooperatives in New England, marked the end of any alternative distribution network. Henderson could have included Whole Foods in the talk, since it had grown through acquisitions to establish itself as the predominant natural and organic retailer in the United States.

Henderson sketched a futuristic picture of giant organic farms filled with migrant farmworkers who outnumbered independent organic farmers; Cargill undercutting American farmers with cheap organic grain from South America; companies such as Tyson, Horizon, and Heinz setting the regulations for organic food; and, quite possibly, a Monsanto executive with a soft spot for genetically engineered crops heading up the National Organic Program at the USDA.

"Is this what you want?" she asked. "Let's have a show of hands."

She paused. If any hand had gone up, she told the audience, she would have packed up and left.

"Okay, so we agree that we want a *movement.* What does that mean?" she asked.

Henderson then presented another vision tied closely to the organic movement's radical roots, to "indigenous farmers," and to the peasant model of farming that inspired Howard, Rodale, Steiner, and other pioneers. It would be a movement based on "local food sovereignty," built on the right of people to grow their own food and save their own seeds rather than being forced to buy patented versions from seed conglomerates, of farmworker rights, and fair pricing for small farmers.

She held up Organic Valley, the nation's largest farmer-owned organic cooperative, as an example. But she also warned that "members would be well-advised to cherish its democratic foundations and keep a close watch on its management," lest the cooperative end up as just another giant. For Henderson, and many like her, the growth of organic food had come at an awful price, compromising standards, undercutting small farms, diluting healthy food, ignoring social justice—polluting the very ideals embodied in the word *organic*.

Her talk was similar in tone to one given by agrarian essayist Wendell Berry thirty years earlier at a conference called "Agriculture for a Small Planet," at the birth of the organic movement in the Pacific Northwest. Berry, who later expanded the talk in his seminal work *The Unsettling of America: Culture and Agriculture*, spoke of the dangers of industrial farms and their effect on the small community where he grew up in Henry County, Kentucky.

When he was a boy, Berry said, the fields had been plowed with horses and mules, and "a prevalent pride in workmanship and thrift was still a social ideal." But with the rise of "modern agriculture," farms became increasingly larger and mechanized, the owners fewer, the land "falling more and more into the hands of speculators and professional people from cities." "Those who could not get big got out—not just in my community but in farm communities all over the country," he said. What was left was the "monomania of bigness," totalitarianism. The fabric of the farm community unraveled under this industrial onslaught. Leisure, comfort, and entertainment eroded the values of workmanship and thrift, and the community's inherent wisdom about the land gave way to an avaricious culture of environmental exploitation.

Modern culture—city life; having a home, a job, and commuting to work; relying on food grown in distant places, all of which divorced people from nature—would need to change to prevent this degradation. "Nowhere that I know is there a mar-

ket for a hen or a bucket of cream or a few dozen eggs. Those
markets were done away with in the name of sanitation," he
said. "It is, of course, one of the miracles of science that the
germs that used to be in our food have been replaced by poisons." In a culture premised on mass production and consumption, knowledge of how to work with nature, and of nature
itself, was lost. And this loss would spell humanity's doom.

Berry wove a radical critique of capitalism with a highly
conservative plea for a vanishing agrarian way of life. He sought
a cultural solution that amounted to capitalism without capital,
of exchange without large-scale trade; of small-scale business—
conducted by artisans, farmers, and self-sufficient landowners—
without the competition, avarice, exploitation, and creative
destruction that accompanies the ruthless free market.

This message, and the iconography of the small farmer, still
resonates in a culture that romanticizes agrarian life. Charles
Frazier's bestselling novel *Cold Mountain,* published in 1997,
was perhaps the most recent popular expression of the ethos.
The book tells the story of Inman, a Southern soldier wounded
in the Civil War, who journeys through a treacherous landscape
back to his home. There, nestled in the Blue Ridge Mountains,
is Inman's love, Ada. A city-bred woman, she repairs her father's
dilapidated farm with the aid of a self-taught, mountain-wise
woman, Ruby, who gradually imparts her knowledge of nature
and the telltale signs of planting and harvest. Ruby—true to the
agrarian ideal—views "money with a great deal of suspicion
even in the best of times, especially when she contrasted it in
her mind with the solidity of hunting and gathering, planting
and harvesting." The land holds a mystical appeal with secrets
that must be conjured. Ruby can spot wild edible plants, cure
ham, harvest tobacco, and create all they need from the small
and bountiful farm by tapping into nature. This oasis is ever

under threat by the nearby ravages of war, by the ignorance and failure of society at large—akin to abuse of nature in our time brought about by industry, consumption, global markets, agribusiness, and the culture of greed that Berry had spelled out.

By the time Henderson and other agrarians brought Berry's arguments forward, the target of the critique had evolved. For the path that agrarian idealists had taken in the 1970s—to farm in concert with nature and sell organic food outside the dominant food system—became compromised by its success. Organic food had become too popular to remain in a backwoods niche, morphing into yet another food industry profit center.

Writer Michael Pollan called this the "organic-industrial complex" in an influential article in the *New York Times Magazine* in 2001. Articulating the view of a number of organic farmers and activists, he argued it was time to move "beyond organic" because entrepreneurs and mainstream food companies had co-opted and compromised the vision of the organic pioneers and the quality of organic food. Eugene Kahn, a well-known figure in the organic food industry, was Pollan's poster boy for this corruption. Kahn had started out as a back-to-the-lander at Cascadian Farm, in Washington state; had created an organic food company, Small Planet Foods; and, by the time Pollan talked with him, had sold out to General Mills, and was making organic TV dinners. Kahn had also helped write the regulations that defined organic food, which the agrarian critics said cleared the way for Big Food to get into the market and compromise its meaning.

Whether Kahn sold out organic or played a crucial role in building the market—well, that depended on what you meant by "organic" and what you wanted "organic" to be. Pollan sided with the agrarians. (I could not get Kahn's view, for after a brief, tense conversation, with questions about my slant, he did not return calls or e-mails. It seemed he didn't want to risk being a symbol once again.)

Kahn, though, did not have the power to skew the regulations all by himself. As the record shows, all but the staunchest purists worked on the regulations, participated in decisions, bought in to compromises, and voted with Kahn many times— including those who later regretted it. While there may have been agreement on the need for regulations to help the nascent organic market, a singular conception of what that market was or should be never evolved; the regulations reflected a difficult consensus, not fiat.

Agrarians, such as Henderson, advocated a limited approach, constructing an organic sector outside of mainstream agriculture, food manufacturing, and distribution, as Berry had envisioned. Fred Kirschenmann, former director of the Leopold Center for Sustainable Agriculture at Iowa State University and a longtime organic grain farmer, put it this way: "An ecological-based system is not willing to sacrifice philosophic principles to increase sales." But the agrarians represented only the most articulate strand of an extremely diverse coalition, which continually evolved as more businesses, farmers, and consumers came into the fold.

On the other end of the spectrum, processors such as Kahn wanted to take organic food mainstream, so Americans could buy it where they already shopped. He and the rest of the entrepreneurial crowd didn't see selling out to food companies as a compromise, but as a way to raise organic consumption and get more farmers into the sector. "I've always been a scale freak. I've always had an obsession to be big," Kahn told one reporter. Whole grains and honey sold at the local food co-op weren't going to cut it.

This diversity of opinion and approach underscored the movement's greatest strength, akin to the various, competing, and interdependent components of any ecosystem. Agrarians honed the organic ideal. Environmental groups, which since the 1970s had pressed for clean-water and clean-air laws and stringent regulations over pesticides, raised awareness about the value of organic food. Consumer groups mobilized grassroots campaigns to protect the organic sector whenever it was threatened. Organic certifiers helped define standards. Nutritionists kept an eye on the health implications of the food; chefs popularized the organic concept; farmers grew the crops; and entrepreneurs, wholesalers, and retailers built the businesses and distribution channels to take the products to consumers. These interests did not see eye-to-eye, because they had different agendas, but that was the point. In its diversity, the organic coalition enlarged itself and avoided a stagnant monoculture.

But this diversity proved to be the movement's greatest weakness, since it could easily devolve into conflict. These conflicts tended to play out in the arena of regulations, in defining organic production practices and in the very meaning of "organic" food. Agrarians had a more purist vision of what organic practices should be—a vision of small farms, whole food, and local distribution, not factory farms, highly processed food, and national sales. Compromise with the growth advocates, who sought a more expansive definition to bring more consumers into the fold, became elusive, because principles and profits were at stake. After three decades of growth, the coalition showed signs of hemorrhaging after the organic regulations took effect in 2002 and then thoroughly fragmenting in a way that threatened the entire industry. By then, the bedrock vision of a common enemy—conventional agribusiness, or chemical farming—couldn't keep all the factions in line because agribusiness had gotten in the organic game, too. The enemy was now within.

———

Senator Patrick Leahy—Vermont Democrat, supporter of sustainable agriculture, and sponsor of the Organic Foods Production Act (OFPA) of 1990—recognized that these interest groups were rife with conflict. So his staffer Kathleen Merrigan tried to give them each a voice when writing the law.

By all accounts, it was a vociferous group, with farmers, certifiers, consumer advocates, organic food entrepreneurs, and retailers pushing for different emphases in the law. The varying certification regimes of California Certified Organic Farmers and Oregon and Washington Tilth on the West Coast, the Northeast Organic Farming Association on the East Coast, Farm Verified Organic in the Midwest, and many others complicated matters. "It was very, very difficult, if not impossible, to get groups to sit down together and agree that there was one common cause that was called *organic,* or even that there was some benefit to us agreeing with each other," Katherine DiMatteo, the executive director of the Organic Trade Association, told me. At least twenty-two state laws were on the books. Certifiers did not recognize one another's standards. California had instituted a one-year period to transition fields until the mid-1990s, while others had a three-year period. Would fruit certified as organic in California qualify as organic where the three-year transition was in place?

"We fought about that for years," Joe Smillie, longtime Vermont-based certifier with the private group Quality Assurance International, told me. In 1986, he helped craft national standards for the forerunner to the Organic Trade Association, but while they were accepted by his group, they never got traction and became just one approach among a patchwork of standards. (A similar regulatory mishmash around the world now significantly inhibits trade by forcing export-oriented organic growers in developing countries to seek certification from multiple bodies in Europe, Japan, and the United States.)

Soon events took over. In the Alar apple scare of 1989, DON'T PANIC, BUY ORGANIC headlines led to a sharp rise in demand, followed by commodity shortages. Concerns about integrity quickly surfaced, since wholesalers and retailers slapped ORGANIC labels on food to get higher prices. Packaged foods carried ORGANIC labels even if they contained as little as 20 percent organic ingredients, because national standards and sanctions did not exist. In 1988, workers at a California produce company were photographed taking carrots out of conventional bags and placing them in packaging marked ORGANIC. The Great Carrot Caper made headlines around the state. Nine years later, a food wholesaler in Minnesota was convicted of defrauding customers up to $700,000 for selling conventional grains and beans labeled CERTIFIED ORGANIC. This type of fraud is not uncommon in the food industry, and continues—at an unknown level—today. In 2002, the year the national organic law finally took effect, the USDA detected pesticide residues on 15 percent of the "organic" foods it sampled (compared with 43 percent of conventional foods). A report by the Organic Center for Education and Promotion, the nonprofit organic think tank, said only a third of these residues on organic food might be explained by drift from conventional fields or irrigation lines. "Clearly, some organic samples tested . . . were actually intensively sprayed conventional samples," the report stated. This could stem from fraud by the grower or seller, or a mix-up at the USDA testing facilities. In a different sector of the food industry, New York City food retailers were caught in 2005 selling farm-raised salmon as "wild" to get a premium price.

"If a labeling concept works in the marketplace and provides an economic reward, somebody will try to rip it off," said Mark Lipson, who worked on California's organic law at California Certified Organic Farmers (CCOF), then pushed for a national law as policy director of its offshoot, the Organic Farming Research Foundation (OFRF). He believed to maintain "consumers' faith" in the ORGANIC label, the industry needed regulatory oversight. "We've always had a hard time cleaning up our messes and imposing sanctions on those who don't live up to the standards," he said.

With the market threatened by fraud, the factions put aside their differences, sat down in Washington, and crafted the OFPA with Merrigan.

To keep this unruly alliance in line, the law set up a National Organic Standards Board (NOSB), an advisory panel of fifteen members appointed by the secretary of agriculture. The board—which must include farmers, retailers, processors, consumer and environmental interests, a scientist, and a certifier—was designed to represent *all* constituents, so that each would have to buy into the regulatory regime before it came to pass. No one interest group could control the standards or claim victim status.

The NOSB would, in effect, be the high priests in the organic world, determining which organic methods to accept and then passing those recommendations on to the National Organic Program at the USDA, which oversees the rules. The NOP would write the regulatory language and send it to the secretary of agriculture for final approval.

There were weak links in this chain, and the advisory body and the USDA clashed even before the NOSB had issued its first set of recommendations. Many believed the USDA had a conflict of interest, since it represents, as one organic farmer put it, "the Big Boys," or conventional-farming-and-food interests. And while writing and implementing any regulation is complex and fraught with missteps, the USDA has done little at key junctures to disabuse critics of this conclusion. As early as 1994, NOP officials declared in meetings with the NOSB that the department would "lead" the program, since it had the "expertise and experience." Board members objected to remaining in a "subservient" advisory capacity, and argued they should have a primary role in regulatory decision making.

Then, in 1995, after three years of deliberation, the NOSB finished its recommendations and submitted them to the USDA. Covering everything from crop rotations to animal husbandry, from the specific natural pesticides that could be used on an organic farm to the acceptable way of making organic tofu, this broad coalition had decided what organic farming and organic food processing should be.

The USDA took two years to digest these standards, but when the department issued its preliminary rules for public comment in December 1997, they were barely recognizable. Most galling, the USDA had rewritten the rules to consider allowing what became known as the Big Three—genetically modified crops, sewage sludge fertilizer, and food irradiation—all of which the NOSB had rejected as incompatible with organic food production. Organic activists were livid. It was a "train-wreck of massive proportions," one organic policy advocate said. The department chartered with insuring the integrity of organic food appeared set on undermining it.

The USDA, however, hadn't come up with this bastardized plan on its own. At the time, the Clinton administration was engaged in trade talks to pry open European markets to genetically modified food. Banning this food from the U.S. organic program would have undercut Washington's argument that these crops were safe. The U.S. Trade Representative and the Office of Science and Technology Policy had pushed to allow genetically modified crops in the organic regulations, even though USDA officials knew "few if any existing (organic) standards permit GMOs (genetically modified organisms)." The government also promoted food irradiation as a new method to combat tainted meat and sought to channel sewage sludge to farms, because of ocean dumping restrictions. These policy aims extended to the organic program, too.

The organic community had one powerful card to play in response, its ability to mobilize the growing number of organic consumers. The USDA was flooded with a record 275,603 comments criticizing the rule. Working Assets, a phone company with an advocacy mission, alerted its customers, who sent in nearly thirty-six thousand letters. The USDA was "succumbing to pressure from biotechnology, agribusiness and other industry giants that want to weaken the regulation of organic food production," the form letter said. Others wrote that the USDA rules "completely disregard the long established meaning of organic agriculture," and could "fatally undermine consumer confidence in the organic label." The USDA rules were an "insult to truthfulness and freedom." On Capitol Hill, Senator Leahy and Representative Peter DeFazio (the Oregon Democrat who had brought the 1990 law to a vote on the House floor after it had been voted down in a committee) whipped up support for the NOSB standards as originally proposed.

In the face of public outcry, strong opposition of consumer and environmental groups, and media attention, the USDA did a U-turn. When the final regulations were reissued in 2000, the Big Three had been removed and the pendulum of power had swung back to the NOSB. Organic consumers had won.

Challenges to the "organic" label continued over the years, since, as Lipson pointed out, the price premium of the food invited abuse. In 2003, Representative Nathan Deal, a Georgia Republican, sought to undo rules requiring organic feed for organic livestock. His measure on behalf of a Georgia poultry processor was tacked on as a rider to a congressional spending bill and passed in the dead of night. Once it came to light, Senators Leahy and Olympia Snow, a Maine Republican, and Representative Sam Farr, a California Democrat, won widespread congressional support in overturning the measure.

Then, in April 2004, the USDA published three "guidance statements" and an "enforcement directive" on its Web site that appeared to redefine organic rules once again, contravening the NOSB. Although viewed as a power grab, a more generous—and perhaps more accurate—reading was that the NOP was trying to iron out conundrums in regulatory text and define the limits of its regulatory powers vis-à-vis other government agencies. But the move only enraged the NOSB and the organic community by making a number of highly controversial and unilateral decisions.

One measure would have allowed organic cows to be treated with antibiotics, as long as the drugs were administered at least a year before organic milk was produced. This was a hot-button issue since consumers paid more for milk produced on organic farms that didn't use antibiotics. The labels of Horizon Organic and Organic Valley, the biggest organic milk producers, said as much. Antibiotics in milk aren't the concern, since samples are tested for antibiotic residues. Rather, the use of antibiotics on conventional farms raises concerns about growing antibiotic resistance, which could render drugs impotent in humans. And now the USDA was allowing antibiotics on organic farms without consulting anyone?

Although highly controversial, this decision was not without support. Two years earlier, the Organic Trade Association's livestock committee had unanimously recommended allowing the use, at least twelve months before the animal's milk was sold, of "medications deemed necessary for the animal's health and survival." The drugs could be targeted to fight specific diseases rather than administered in feed in constant low doses, as with antibiotics on conventional farms. Plus, as Hubert Karreman—a widely regarded Pennsylvania veterinarian for organic farmers who sits on the NOSB—has argued, withholding antibiotics can amount to animal cruelty. The rules banning antibiotics force the organic farmer to choose between administering the drug or letting the cow fight disease naturally. If the drug is given, the animal must be sent to a conventional farm after she recovers; if withheld, the cow may suffer more but she can stay on the farm. Karreman thought this forced farmers to make a terrible choice, especially at 3:00 A.M., with a cow withering in pain. But limited antibiotic use wouldn't play well with consumers used to paying for organic milk from "antibiotic-free farms" and Karreman's view was by no means the consensus. Organic activists rose up, saying the NOP compromised organic milk.

In another hotly contested decision, the NOP said certain products—such as pet food, cosmetics, and seafood—could use the ORGANIC label without meeting any standards. This applied to garden products, too, since James Riddle, chairman of the NOSB, once held up a package of "organic herbicide" at a board meeting. (In chemistry, *organic* means only that the substance contains carbon.) Depending on the aisle of the grocery store or garden center you shopped in, the meaning of *organic* could change from a regulated standard to a nonexistent one, which didn't help consumers understand what *organic* meant.

Why would anyone care about organic pet food? Organic milk was one of the industry's bestsellers, because parents wanted their kids to drink it. Since people tend to view their pets as children, too, organic pet food has become one of the fastest-growing organic product categories. As for organic shampoo, if you believed in eating chemical-free food, why douse your body with chemicals?

At the semiannual meeting of the NOSB in April 2004, a

parade of commentators chastised the USDA officials who attended. In the media, articles charged the officials with selling out organic consumers. The USDA argued that its statements had reflected *existing* regulations, not new ones, but that meant either the rules were deficient or the department was trying to lead the industry to a place it did not want to go, undermining the NOSB in the process.

In May, in the midst of the 2004 presidential election, Secretary of Agriculture Veneman abruptly withdrew the measures, to the great relief of the organic community. A year later, facing a lawsuit by a personal care products company, the USDA clarified its position further and said that *any* agricultural product could carry the ORGANIC label so long as it conformed with the USDA regulations—which is what the industry believed all along. So lip balm and cat food were back under the regime once again and a committee met to draw up organic seafood regulations. This regulatory seesaw raised questions about the USDA's intentions, doing little to nurture a sense of trust in the government's ability to oversee the industry.

These conflicts with the USDA could almost be seen as a blessing, since they unified the otherwise fractious organic coalition. Internal fissures appeared regularly, and no more so than in 2005, at the conclusion of the lawsuit brought by the seventy-two-year-old organic blueberry farmer from Maine, Arthur Harvey. He had filed suit against Secretary of Agriculture Veneman on October 23, 2002, just two days after the national organic program took effect. He argued that the regulations circumvented the underlying Organic Foods Production Act by allowing practices the act expressly forbid.

An organic certifier and a member of the Organic Trade Association, Harvey submitted twenty-seven comments when the

USDA issued its first set of proposed rules in 1987, then another sixteen after the final rule in 2000. "He's been doing this for twenty years," said Bob Scowcroft, executive director of the Organic Farming Research Foundation. "He won't give an inch!"

Many participants compromised in writing the organic rules, but Harvey felt core principles had been sold out. "I had to do this," he said, "otherwise the government could get away with anything it wanted."

Appearing before the NOSB, five months before he filed suit, Harvey used his allotted five-minute public-comment period to run through the main problems with the regulations. He noted in a separate three-page handwritten comment—"my final blast," he called it—that the regulations were "likely to be invalidated by a court if this Board and the NOP do not come to their senses."

He got just one question—from George Siemon, the NOSB board member and CEO of Organic Valley, the milk cooperative.

"You want us to start all over again. Right?"

"I'm afraid you'll have to do quite a bit of that, yes," Harvey replied.

Although he might have been viewed at the time as just another ranting purist, Harvey pursued the case, acting as his own lawyer at a cost of $10,000—far below the $250,000 a lawyer had estimated it would cost.

He lost in a lower court but appealed to the First Circuit Court in Boston. By then, his case was on the radar screen and he gained the support of several environmental groups and individuals, who filed amici briefs with the court. A Washington lawyer agreed to represent him for a reduced fee.

Harvey's most far-reaching objection—with enormous consequences for the industry—targeted "synthetic" substances in processed organic food. The use of synthetic ingredients might be surprising, since organic food is often thought of as "natural" or "whole"—foods such as grains, dairy, and produce, or packaged goods free of "artificial" ingredients. The law supports this by banning "synthetic" substances, such as chemical fertilizers, pesticides, and artificial food additives, and conceiving of organic food as "natural."

But over the years, the NOSB considered and approved use of thirty-eight synthetic ingredients and processing aids sought by food manufacturers. They were placed on the so-called National List, which the law had established for these exceptions. Once an otherwise prohibited substance was added to the list, it could be used freely. The purity of organic food thus rested on the integrity of this list, which was the reason Senator Leahy gave the NOSB—and not the USDA—explicit control over it. Lobbyists would not be able to push a synthetic through a back door of the USDA; the substance would have to be considered by the NOSB in public hearings.

Organic processors argued that packaged foods would be impossible to make without some key exemptions, which is how the thirty-eight came to be approved. They included ammonium carbonate (baking powder), tocopherols (vitamin E, a preservative), ascorbic acid (vitamin C, which prevents the oxidation of canned tomatoes and preserves fruit juices), calcium hydroxide (a clarifying agent in sugar refining), and xanthum gum (a thickening agent). These synthetics may be derived from natural agricultural ingredients, but are chemically processed to such a degree that they are deemed synthetics under the law. Bleached lecithin, the emulsifier made from hexane-extracted soy oil, is one example. A type of pectin, the gelling agent made from citrus peels and used to make jelly and jam, is another. (A nonsynthetic version of pectin requires more sugar to set.)

The NOSB wasn't alone in allowing synthetic substances in

organic food production. Various bodies with organic standards, such as the International Federation of Organic Agriculture Movements, the European Community, the Soil Association of Britain, the Japanese Ministry of Agriculture, and the United Nations standards body, Codex Alimentarious, have approved a limited number of synthetic additives in organic food, though specifics differ. Still, these exemptions have been controversial. The debate has always been whether to ban additives and forgo packaged organic goods—keeping organic food a pristine oasis in a world of industrialized food production, as Harvey and his supports sought—or to sell organic cookies and TV dinners in order to reach more consumers. The debate has pitted purists against growth advocates, with all the standards bodies cited above tilting toward growth. Britain's Soil Association explains its thinking: "Organic foods in the form of familiar processed foods increases the market for crops while making the benefits of organic products available to the widest possible number of consumers."

Plus, under U.S. law, nonorganic ingredients may make up no more than 5 percent of an organic product, excluding water and salt. Ninety-five percent of the ingredients *must* be organic. If you wanted to make an organic blueberry muffin, organic flour, organic sugar, organic milk, and organic blueberries would make up 95 percent of the ingredients. Since baking powder was an approved synthetic ingredient, it could be used. You could also add natural and nonorganic flavorings, but these ingredients plus the baking powder could total no more than 5 percent of the muffin. If you could not meet the 95 percent hurdle because you found organic sugar too expensive, you could drop down to the next labeling category and stamp your blueberry muffin MADE WITH ORGANIC INGREDIENTS. In this category, you would need only 70 percent organic ingredients. But you couldn't include just anything in the remaining 30 percent—only natural ingredients such as nonorganic sugar. Artificial flavors, colors, and other synthetics would still be out of bounds, if not specifically exempted on the National List.

Harvey never had an issue with the MADE WITH ORGANIC INGREDIENTS label, only with ORGANIC. In essence, he was fighting over what went into the 5 percent.

He felt synthetics compromised organic integrity, confused consumers, and contributed to the industrialization of organic food. He wasn't questioning any particular noxious substance, since the National List would "sunset" every five years, with each substance subject to review and reapproval. What he found objectionable was the existence of a National List of synthetic food ingredients at all, for that was the first step down a slippery slope. In his written remarks, Harvey said: "The NOSB is bogged down with endless applications by large manufacturers who want to add synthetic (and eventually proprietary) chemicals to the list." The thirty-eight were just the first ones conventional food giants would use to pry open the organic food market. Ban the synthetics in food processing—as Harvey argued the law clearly intended—and you would keep organic food pure, uphold the OFPA, and prevent a takeover by Big Food.

But if Harvey was gunning for Big Food, his weapon was less a sniper's rifle than an atomic bomb. It wasn't just Campbell's Soup or General Mills that relied on these substances, but Newman's Own Organics, the philanthropic venture; Amy's Kitchen, the fifth-largest organic brand and an independent company; and small organic farmers selling homemade jam. By 2004, multi-ingredient organic packaged goods, snack foods, drinks, and sauces accounted for about a third of the $11 billion organic food industry.

But the impact wouldn't end at manufactured goods, since the synthetics included processing aids such as carbon dioxide,

used for grain storage, and chlorine, a common produce disin-
fectant used in highly diluted form in the salad mix industry.
Even Jim Crawford, on his modest farm in Pennsylvania, applied
a chlorine solution to wash down food preparation surfaces. In
an internal poll, the Organic Trade Association found 70 percent
of its members relied on at least one synthetic substance. No one
really knew the total number of organic food products that could
be affected, but DiMatteo, the OTA's executive director, thought
the figure could be as high as 90 percent, whittling the $11 bil-
lion industry down to $1.1 billion in size. (Others suggested
$2–4 billion of organic products would be at risk.)

The Boston appellate court's ruling in January 2005 in favor
of Harvey sent the organic food industry into a panic. Products
would have to be reformulated to keep the organic seal, or relabeled MADE WITH ORGANIC INGREDIENTS, which could force
changes up the supply chain: Why would a manufacturer maintain organic ingredients at 95 percent if they only needed 70
percent under the lesser label? Spelling out its remedy in June,
the court gave the USDA twelve months to write new rules and
conform with the law; noncompliant products would have to be
removed within two years of the ruling.

I wondered why a desire for organic purity in the law had given
way to a more liberal reading a few years later, when the NOSB
approved these substances. And now, with the Harvey case, why
had the pendulum swung back and whacked the fast-growth
industry?

With organic food, the aim was always to remain as close as
possible to a natural system, avoiding additives of any sort. Sir Albert Howard's dictum had been that artificial fertilizers created
artificial food, which in turn created artificial people. California's
first organic law, in 1978, defined organic processed foods as

consisting of 100 percent organic ingredients, with no additives besides water and salt. Washington and Oregon state laws allowed 1 to 2 percent, so baking powder could be used. But these laws came out at a time when organic food processing barely existed.

Organic proponents had far more experience with synthetics in farming than in food processing. Organic farmers laid down plastic sheeting as a mulch. They relied on chemical pheromones to disrupt the mating cycles of insects. They applied soaps, oils, fish emulsions, insect traps, copper, and sulfur—all less toxic than conventional pesticides, yet all synthetic. In an organic system defined as "natural" rather than simply "benign," these would need legal exemptions.

"The key was whether they could be used with what we called 'agronomic responsibility,'" said Lynn Coody, a cofounder of the certification body Oregon Tilth, and one of the participants in national legislation.

As organic farming methods developed, these materials could be phased out. In the meantime, farmers could use the synthetics after fully evaluating their impact on health and the environment, and only as a last line of attack, not the first. If that meant using petroleum-based plastics to prevent weeds, so be it. Still, conflicts flared over many of these materials, and certification bodies addressed them in different ways.

By the time participants gathered to work on the OFPA, organic farmers had a wealth of practical knowledge about agricultural synthetics and listed those they viewed as indispensable. The same could not be said for organic food processing, still in its infancy. (As late as 1993, NOSB board members could identify only one organic manufacturing plant in the entire country, owned by Walnut Acres in Pennsylvania.) Ironically, while Coody, representing the Organic Farmers Associations Council, pressed to include the limited number of substances farmers wanted, a group of the natural-food brokers, processors, retailers, and distributors who would later benefit from processed organic food opposed all synthetics.

"I thought at that time, if you took away all the synthetics, people would find alternatives," said Mark Retzloff, then a retailer who led this group, the Organic Food Alliance, in the Washington talks.

Several times Merrigan, Leahy's staffer, raised the issue of allowing synthetics in processed food. "I thought some synthetic processing aids were probably being used in food and I urged the group to come up with a universe of categories that would be acceptable," she told me.

But since no one made a list similar to the one Coody had drafted for crops, Merrigan wrote the law to conform to the wishes of Retzloff's group, banning synthetics in processed food. This was accepted by Senator Leahy. As the OFPA stated: "For a handling operation to be certified under this title, each person on such handling operation shall not . . . add any synthetic ingredient during the processing or any post harvest handling of the product."

Coody recalls saying, "This will lead to the first lawsuit we will face."

It took twelve years, but she was right.

The broad prohibition against synthetics in processed organic food proved too restrictive for the quickly evolving industry, forcing a blatant contravention of the law. The reversal began in 1993, a year after the NOSB began meeting to craft the organic regulations. Some viewed the law's stance as ambiguous. USDA staffers offered the legal opinion that the law allowed the secretary of agriculture to approve "essential synthetic" substances in food manufacturing.

The board continued on that tack, debating, reviewing, and voting in a number of synthetics. Some were unfamiliar, even unknown, to board members. Even after the mandated reviews by technical advisory panels, which looked at the synthetics' impact on health and the environment and their consistency with organic principles, gray areas remained. The board voted first to determine whether a substance qualified as synthetic and then whether it should be allowed in processed organic foods.

Kahn, of Cascadian Farm, pushed for use of synthetics, arguing that "the realities of food manufacturing requires many of these synthetic materials in order to produce food expected by consumers," according to NOSB minutes. Craig Weakley of Muir Glen, who later worked for Kahn, was in his camp. They won the day, despite heated discussions. Founding NOSB chairman Michael Sligh, of Rural Advancement Foundation International, a small-farm advocacy group, voted for many synthetics (though he later supported Harvey's suit). Sligh said these were bitter battles, but he sought consensus. "I was trying to find a way forward and not be deadlocked," he told me. Kirschenmann told me he figured he had lost on this issue, so he went along, too, focusing on other battles he might win. Margaret Wittenberg of Whole Foods also joined in, since consumers were "primarily concerned about pesticide use in food, and not synthetic materials used to process them," according to the NOSB meeting minutes. So did Merrigan, who had left Leahy's office and was now on the NOSB. "I bought into this process," Merrigan told me, "but in my heart of hearts, did I know someone would challenge it? Yes."

Only one NOSB member, an organic cattle rancher from Wisconsin, Merrill Clark, consistently voted against synthetics. She brought a motion that they only be allowed in the "made with organic ingredients" category, but it was voted down, eleven to two. A decade later, she supported Harvey in his suit, which pursued the same formula.

While Kahn may have been obsessed with producing an organic TV dinner, he had not hijacked organic regulations. His position became the *consensus,* reached by a board groping its way on new ground. As Sligh later stated, the regulations the board sought were not perfect, nor comprehensive, but a stab at a difficult task. The recommendations reflected the "best thinking of a broad base" of constituents.

Soon, however, the NOSB came under attack. Joan Dye Gussow, a Columbia University nutritionist, educator, and avid organic gardener, wrote an article entitled "Can an Organic Twinkie Be Certified?" (a question the NOSB actually debated). Her conclusion, based on the proposed organic regulations, was yes. All the ingredients of the dreaded Twinkie could be sourced from organic suppliers, with natural flavors and colors replacing artificial ones. This was akin to the "input substitution" model of organic agriculture, in which a farmer looked for the organic equivalents of pesticides and fertilizers rather than taking the more difficult but fundamental step of creating an entirely new agroecological farming system. Instead of pursuing that kind of comprehensive change in food manufacturing, Kahn and his allies were, Gussow wrote, "working toward a parallel food supply where a certified organic Twinkie or its equivalent would not be beyond imagining." This meant organic food would be nutritionally no different from the food it was supposed to replace. While the organic Twinkie has not come to pass, near equivalents certainly have—soda, salty snacks, salsa, cookies, crackers, and the tasty organic chocolate truffles, imported from France and loaded with organic saturated fat, that I occasionally pick up at Whole Foods.

In another essay, Kate Clancy, a nutritionist, and Kirschenmann, the NOSB board member, argued that food processing that changed the "original wholeness and complex ecological character" of organic ingredients should not be labeled ORGANIC. Such highly processed foods should use the less stringent MADE WITH ORGANIC INGREDIENTS label. At the extreme, this could mean only raw food would be organic, since even cooking alters food. But few, including the authors, were moved to such extremes. If you accepted that cooking could create an organic food product, what about other processes or ingredients? "Minimal" processing, and basic chemicals—such as salt, baking soda, baking powder, and natural flavors that had been used for hundreds of years—were acceptable. "In essence, the commercially processed foods that [should] carry a 'natural' or 'organic' label are, in the main, those that would be prepared by cooks in home kitchens, using the equipment and food ingredients available in retail markets," they wrote. "This means honey as sweetener, whole grain flours, cold pressed oils, and only natural colors or flavors." They also accepted traditional fermented foods, and a limited number of natural preservatives. In short, the essay provided an elegant justification for creating a firewall against many packaged organic foods. Organic food would be kept whole and nutritious, without exception.

In a reply, Kahn, Weakley, and Steven Harper, an NOSB board member and Cascadian Farm food scientist, said Clancy's and Kirschenmann's "logic and supporting arguments are severely flawed and would, if adopted, cause a major decline in the growth of the organic industry and our ability to change the world of agriculture." (Growth advocates made the same response to the Harvey ruling.) They had a number of good points but their arguments were reactive; they never articulated as clear a position as their adversaries. Perhaps they didn't have to, since they were building the de facto market. Even a pragmatist like Demos told me he didn't have time to participate in organic policy. He was too busy turning organic soy milk into a mainstream product. While the processors might not have had the intellectual muscle of the purists, they more than made up for it in market weight. For they—and not the whole-grain-and-honey set—largely became the organic marketplace by the late 1990s, as more consumers came aboard.

The question of synthetics finally came to a head at an NOSB board meeting in February 1999. At that time, a deal was brokered between the factions and a compromise rule written by Gussow, the Columbia University nutritionist, who was now on the board.

Synthetics would be allowed only if they met stringent criteria: The synthetic could not be used as a substitute for an organic ingredient, nor have any adverse impact on the environment, health, or the nutritional quality of the food; its primary use could not be as a preservative, nor could it be used to improve flavors or colors. And it could only be used if truly essential to making the organic food product. The NOSB approved this rule in a unanimous vote on February 10, 1999.

Even so, Gussow and Kirschenmann had doubts. The following day, Gussow brought another motion, seconded by Kirschenmann, "to prohibit synthetics in the processing of food labeled CERTIFIED ORGANIC." (When I asked Gussow why she had second thoughts, she told me the pressure from critics had been enormous.) On this vote, the board split. Five voted to ban all synthetics in processed food and six favored them. The synthetics slid in by a single vote.

DiMatteo, executive director of the OTA, thought this settled the issue. "We had an agreement," DiMatteo told me. "We supported a strict review of these materials, and I thought everyone was on board."

But not everyone was. Two organizations that later supported Harvey in his suit—Beyond Pesticides, a pesticide watchdog group, and the environmental group Sierra Club—objected.

The National Organic Program didn't help matters when it issued a statement in late 2002 granting a blanket exemption to a class of more than three hundred chemicals—so-called Food Contact Substances. These substances, which are overseen by the FDA and used in processing and packaging, are deemed "not present" in the final food product and therefore not classified as "ingredients." To use one of these chemicals in organic food, all a manufacturer had to do was document to its certifier that it was a "Food Contact Substance" rather than an "ingredient." Processors could thus make organic food with chemicals that did not "exist" in the food and avoid mentioning them on the ingredients label.

Urvashi Rangan, an environmental health scientist at Consumers Union, one of the consumer groups active in organic regulations, was livid about this decision because one Food Contact Substance, styrene-divinylbenzene, is used to make high-fructose corn syrup. This is the central sweetener in soft drinks and snack foods implicated in the childhood obesity epidemic. With a blanket allowance of this class of processing aids, cheap organic soda—and organic food-induced obesity—was a possibility. Although one small company became interested in making organic high-fructose corn syrup, I heard the effort fizzled due to lack of demand. Still, that organic foods could now be made with more than three hundred chemicals, some of which had been reviewed by the NOSB and *rejected,* was an idea few could stomach.

The Organic Materials Review Institute (OMRI), a nonprofit formed jointly by Oregon Tilth and California Certified Organic Farmers to review substances used in organic production, laid out the objections in a memo to the National Organic Program. These materials should be submitted for NOSB review just like any other synthetic, the institute said.

"Just as the use of a synthetic fertilizer or pesticide disqualifies crops [from carrying the organic label] . . . this principle applies as well to the use of a non-organic processing aid that does not appear on the National List," OMRI staff wrote. "This is true regardless of whether or not the prohibited substance leaves detectable residual contamination."

By now, many organic proponents had had enough. The industry had gone too far, allowed too many substances, sacrificed too many principles for growth, and avoided the hard work of seeking organic alternatives. Under NOP rules, organic food would not only become the mirror image of conventional packaged goods, as Gussow predicted, but would also use the same loathsome processing chemicals. With the identity of organic food at stake, the tenuous balance struck in 1999 over synthetics evaporated with the Harvey suit.

As a solution, though, the Harvey ruling looked like a potential disaster. The door had been open for too long; now relabeling or reformulating every organic packaged good that contained a synthetic could potentially wreak havoc with sales. Plus, if consumers saw organic goods relabeled as something less-than-organic, the confusion might cause them to question the integrity of the entire category.

But Harvey's supporters thought the ruling would protect the industry by reinforcing its unique identity, creating a more solid foundation for future growth.

Still they worried about the impact of the ruling, saying in a statement that their aim was not to destroy the $11 billion organic food industry. The groups—including Beyond Pesticides, Center for Food Safety, Greenpeace, the National Cooperative Grocers Association, Organic Consumers Association, and Sierra Club—said they sought to have a voice in its outcome and to limit the USDA's power grab. "This was precedent setting," Sligh said. They were willing to sit down and "consider the limited allowance of some synthetic substances" in organic food as long as the NOSB review process was improved. But products continuing to use the rest of the synthetics would have to drop down into the "made with organic ingredients" category.

Although the two sides met periodically, each viewed the other as intransigent. "We now find ourselves in a time of unprecedented division," Riddle, the NOSB board member, said in a widely circulated e-mail. The OTA took matters into its own hands by lobbying Congress to rewrite the OFPA to return to "the status quo"—that is, what existed before the Harvey ruling. But opponents said this was hardly the case, since the OTA not only wanted the thirty-eight synthetics to remain, but also sought to freely use food contact substances, potentially without any NOSB review. The OTA did not help matters when it came up with language to rewrite the law but did not disclose it; the changes only came to light when a congressional staffer leaked them. Senator Leahy made clear all sides should try to reach a consensus before Congress rewrote the underlying legislation, but this did not suit the OTA's timetable. DiMatteo told me the industry needed a change quickly because future investments would be scrapped without it; others would drop out of the industry altogether. "Our first job is to protect our members," she said.

Although the OTA sought to change the OFPA through a rider to the annual agriculture appropriations bill, its language failed to make it into either the House or Senate version. But the group made headway when the bill went into conference in October 2005 to reconcile the House and Senate bills. Although the organic rider was never openly discussed, the Republican leadership quietly inserted it in the final bill after meetings had ended. The OTA got its way, though only by resorting to the same backroom congressional tactics it previously had criticized others for using. This incensed many long-standing participants in the organic industry who felt action was taken without consensus or transparency.

"It was a secretive process," Scowcroft, executive director of the Organic Farming Research Foundation, said to me. "Now what actions are they (the OTA) going to take to reach out, or are they going to continue to keep us at arm's length at best or attack us at worst?"

The consensus—the diversity—that was always at the heart of the organic movement had evaporated. And in the heated rhetoric and maneuvering, the central issue about these substances got lost. Wasn't the basic question whether synthetics harmed people or the environment and could be used responsibly in organic food? By 2005, the organic community could not answer that question because synthetics were not really the issue. The real issue was whether organic food should become a kind of agrarian niche in the food system, with natural, whole food, or whether it should expand to include the industrial food complex that it was created to replace. The thirty-eight synthetics had become the proxy for this conflict and so economically crucial to the industry that the OTA felt it necessary to take the decision-making process into their own hands and craft a solution. This wasn't biodiversity at work in the organic community, but the exertion of power by one segment that could no longer work with the others. Both the OTA and Harvey had acted unilaterally to protect their own interests, their own definition of *organic food*; whether these actions would nurture organic foods or undermine their future remained an open question.

Synthetics wasn't the only battleground for the future of organic food. Just as the purists and growth advocates split vehemently over processing organic food, they also clashed over producing organic milk. The factions split down the lines Henderson had laid out: small farmers against big ones, the family against the corporation, and pasture-based cows against those in feedlots.

This wasn't a quaint philosophical battle, since, like so much in the organic industry, a lot of money was at stake. Organic milk had grown 20 percent a year, becoming one of the most lucrative segments of the market, worth $1.39 billion in 2003. "When people look for organic food choices, they often look at the foods they consume the most," a marketing executive at Horizon Organic, the biggest organic milk company, explained. Parents paid at least 50 percent more to ensure that hormones, antibiotics, and pesticides were banned in the production of milk their children drank. By 2005, demand had swamped supply, sending prices still higher.

What makes milk organic? The cows need to be fed organic or transitioning pasture and forages for at least a year before producing milk; they cannot be given antibiotics, hormones, or synthetic drugs (with a few exceptions) while on an organic farm; they can't be fed other animals, or plastic pellets for roughage; they must be tracked throughout their life; and they need "access to pasture," to eat fresh grass.

No one disputed this definition. The issue was how much grass a cow should eat, since the answer implied radically different approaches to dairy farming. Small organic farms largely depend on pasture, while big farms tend to rely on centralized, open-air grain feedlots close to their milking barns. Small farmers thought that by tightening the pasture requirement and mandating a specific amount of grass, the NOSB could clearly define "organic" milk as "pasture-based" and prevent lower-cost, feedlot operations from taking control of the organic milk market.

Cows like to graze, maybe not when the sun beats down or snow covers the fields, but in the spring, when the grasses return, farmers will swear cows prefer pasture. "Cows run out to pasture when you open up the gate," said Nathaniel Bacon, Northeast Organic Farming Association (Vermont) dairy and livestock advisor. Kathie Arnold, whose family runs Twin Oaks Dairy in Truxton, New York, said their 120 organic cows start "bawling and get restless" if she doesn't let them out to fresh grass. "Out on pasture, they settle down," she told me.

If pasturing fits neatly into the image of a farming family tending its cows, it also derives from a practical reality: It is easier and cheaper on a small-scale farm to let animals feed on grasses than to harvest the forages or buy grain rations for the animals. Most farms practice a combination of these feeding approaches, but small farms located primarily in the upper Midwest and the East tend to graze cows on pasture several months of the year. Farmers divide the pasture into sections, known as paddocks, so the cows can graze in a defined area. After the cows mow down the grass, the farmers herd the animals to a fresh section so the former one can grow back. This system of "rotational grazing" protects against overgrazing and soil erosion, reduces the cost of harvesting feed, cuts veterinary bills (because the cows are outdoors, breathing fresh air and exercising), and allows the cows to eat what they want—grass. With manure as the principal source of the land's fertility, the nutrient cycle becomes a closed loop—plants feeding animals feeding plants—the ecological ideal. During the winter, when the pastures grow dormant, the cows may eat grains or forages raised on the farm, such as corn and hay, as well as purchased feed. Come spring, when the rye, clover, alfalfa, and fescue grasses sprout up, the cows return to the land.

This age-old farming model still exists in dairy regions, though on a diminished scale because so many farms have gone bust over the past two decades. I visited a few organic dairy farms in the southwest region of Wisconsin, on back roads that cut through fields, pastures, and rolling forested hills, with picture-perfect grain silos sitting beside old red barns. Cows milled about the fields. Dan Volden, who had recently transitioned fifty-six cows to organic production, got off his tractor one warm day and spoke to me about the benefits of going organic. "The main motivator was we didn't like paying feed bills and the vet bills," he said, sitting in the shade beside his fields. Both costs fell, which is why in the 1990s in Wisconsin, grazing operations have tripled while 44 percent of its dairy farms have shut down. Volden joined CROPP (Cooperative Regions of Organic Producer Pools), the nation's largest organic co-op, which sells under the ORGANIC VALLEY label.

Nationally, only 5 to 15 percent of all dairy farms graze their animals. Most others use some combination of pasture, barn, and feedlot, or rely on a confinement model. At the extreme, this consists of a warehouse containing hundreds if not thousands of cows that may never go outside, let alone eat fresh grass. The EPA designates these large farms as Concentrated Animal Feeding Operations (CAFOs), mandating plans to deal with their manure. Since one cow voids eighty pounds of manure a day, a five-thousand-cow farm will yield four hundred thousand pounds, which if not properly dealt with, can foul streams and groundwater. Since confined cows eat a high-caloric grain diet and don't walk far, they can devote much more energy to producing milk—the yield-based rationale for this model. Confined animals, however, face risk of udder infections, such as mastitis, and lameness from walking on concrete. If the grain rations contain too little fiber (since fiber cuts milk output) the cow can suffer from subacute rumen acidosis, a not uncommon condition of high acidity in the first of the cow's four stomachs. The condition has been called "a silent thief," because it lowers immunity and can lead to a host of other diseases, reducing profits. Antibiotics help keep diseases in check and production on track. Recombinant bovine growth hormone (rBGH)—a genetically engineered hormone—extends lactation cycles, boosting output. Once a cow's production sags, after as little as one or two lactation cycles, she is sent off for slaughter and processed into hamburger meat.

"The main paradigm is to get every last drop of milk out of the animals by taking them off the land," said Karreman, the veterinarian and NOSB member based in Lancaster County, Pennsylvania.

In the capital-intensive CAFO model, the farmer spends money on feed, medicines, replacement heifers (young cows), and facilities, covering costs with high production. In the land-intensive grazing model, the farmer conserves cash by maximizing fresh grass, reducing medicines, and keeping cows in the herd. (Organic farmers told me they kept their cows for three to four lactation cycles, and some for as many as twelve.) While pasture produces less milk per cow—forty pounds of milk a day on grass vs. seventy-five pounds on grain—the lower costs that come with pasture more than offset the decline, and the farmer can end up making more money. Hence, the increase in grazing in places like Wisconsin.

The pasture-based regime also has a salutary benefit in more nutritious milk. A 1999 study found that grazing cows produced milk with 500 percent more conjugated linoleic acid (a beneficial fatty acid with anticarcinogenic properties) and vitamin E, compared with cows fed grain diets. Whole milk was higher in omega fatty acids and had a higher proportion of unsaturated fat—a benefit to heart health. A 2004 study by the Danish Institute of Agricultural Sciences found that organic milk from pastured cows had 50 percent more vitamin E, 75 percent more beta-carotene (vitamin A), and two to three times more antioxidants than conventional milk, though the absolute levels were still quite small. Still, "When you go to pasture, we know that . . . the nutritional value of the milk is higher," said Tilak Dhiman, a professor of dairy science at Utah State University and a principal researcher in this field. He said if you fed a cow a diet of organic grain, you would not get the same benefit as fresh grass.

The national organic regulations codified the pasture-based system, recognizing the importance of ensuring the "*health* and *natural behavior* of animals" through "access to the outdoors, shade, shelter, exercise areas, fresh air, and direct sunlight suitable to the species, its stage of production, the climate and the environment." This meant "*access to pasture* for ruminants" (emphasis added).

Kirschenmann, the NOSB member who chaired the board's livestock committee in the late 1990s, told me the intent of the rule was for cows to express their true nature. "They evolved on the savannah, eating grass," he said. "'Access to pasture' meant they should be out on grass."

But what constituted "access to pasture" on an organic farm, and how long should it last? The rules didn't spell this out because the number of days a cow can graze differs between seasonal Vermont and arid Colorado. If too rigid, some farms would be knocked out of organic certification. But if they were too loose, their loopholes could be exploited by farms using a minimal-pasture, high-grain, high-production model. Balancing restrictions with a recognition of regional and farm variation proved exceedingly tough. The result was vague language requiring "access."

The pasturing requirement, however, favored smaller producers, since it becomes progressively harder to graze larger herds on fresh fields and get the cows back to the barn to be milked two or three times a day. Kathy Soder, an animal scientist at the USDA's Pasture Systems and Watershed Management Research Unit, in University Park, Pennsylvania, explains: "The larger the herd, the more pasture acreage is required, and at some point in rotational grazing, the cows have to walk a long ways from the milk parlor to get to fresh grass. This requires energy that could otherwise be used to produce milk. It also takes time. Cows don't walk that fast, especially in hot weather!"

Soder said she knew of no dairy farm in Pennsylvania that grazed more than 275 cows, though the average was 75 to 100. Pennsylvania's landholdings tend to be much smaller than out West, where one may find exceptions to this grazing rule—though not many.

Blake Alexandre, a fourth-generation dairy farmer, runs one with 1,350 cows, most organic, in Del Norte County, on the northern coast of California. When he and his wife, Stephanie, bought the two-thousand-acre farm in the mid-1990s, it was a confinement dairy. They followed the standard regime, feeding the animals indoors and milking them three times a day, using "all that hooey," he said, meaning drugs.

"We harvested the grasses and the cows didn't go outside at all, but we felt like we were fighting the natural system," he told me. "It didn't feel right."

The couple converted the farm to grazing, the norm in this part of the state, then to organic production, by certifying the fields and cows. Since Del Norte gets eighty to one hundred inches of rain annually, the cows graze every day of the year. In the summer, the grass grows back within two weeks, meaning the animals can rotate through the paddocks repeatedly. In the winter, when the grass grows slowly, the cows visit the pasture once a day. The pastures are about two thousand feet from the milking barn—or a fifteen-minute walk for a cow. I imagined Alexandre herding the cows with horses, but he told me they use four-wheelers or mountain bikes, if the ground is dry. Alexandre Family Eco-Dairy Farms, which sells to the Humboldt Creamery and Clover Stornetta Farms in California, has two additional farms in Ferndale, where he grew up, with about 650 cows each. This puts the operation at 2,650 cows total, making it the largest organic grazing dairy farm I heard about. The topography of the land, quality of pasture, and abundant rainfall made it possible, even on this large scale, to adhere to the regulations' intent of "access to pasture for ruminants." Alexandre, a conservative Republican, also supported a strict pasture requirement to protect the market for organic milk.

Another production model appeared in 1994, only a few years after the organic dairy sector started up. Horizon Organic took over an abandoned Idaho dairy farm once owned by Boulder-based Aurora Dairy Corporation, one of the largest dairy farm companies in the nation, with properties in Colorado, Florida, Georgia, and Texas. Horizon spent $24 million on the organic conversion of the Twin Falls farm, which eventually housed four thousand cows. While the Idaho farm did not confine the animals indoors, they were fed primarily grain and hay in outdoor feedlots rather than on fresh pasture. As early as 1993, Horizon cofounder Mark Retzloff had described mandated pasture as a hardship on organic dairy producers.

Retzloff told me the main impetus for acquiring this farm was to ensure a supply of organic milk. Retzloff had already been in the organic food industry for two decades, having launched Eden Foods with two college roommates at the University of Michigan, in 1969. Like many others, he moved to Boulder (where his guru was based) and ran a couple of natural-foods retail chains. One of them, Alfalfas, was sold to Wild Oats. He also chaired the Organic Food Alliance when it lobbied to keep synthetics out of processed organic food. Retzloff had first looked into the organic dairy business in the late 1980s, but couldn't find many suppliers and was unsure about demand. After the OFPA passed, Retzloff, through his business partner, Paul Repetto, learned that CROPP, the Organic Valley co-op, had supplies in the upper Midwest. With a source assured, the two launched Horizon Organic in 1992.

CROPP—which had only fifty-nine members at the time and probably fewer than three thousand cows in its entire pool—made cheese from the butterfat and sold the leftover skim milk to Horizon, which began making organic nonfat yogurt. ("Our goal was to get into milk, but there wasn't enough milk and it was located in one part of the country," Retzloff said.) Two years later, Horizon opened the four-thousand-cow Idaho farm, which was far closer to its key West Coast market. In 1997, it added a five-hundred-cow farm on the eastern shore of Maryland, feeding the East Coast. It became the leader in the organic milk market, followed by Organic Valley.

The timing could not have been better, since the FDA approved rBGH for use in cows in 1994. Although the FDA deemed rBGH safe, critics worried about studies that showed the genetically engineered hormone produced higher levels of a naturally occurring protein, insulin-dependent growth factor-1, linked with breast cancer risk in women. Cornell University's Program on Breast Cancer and Environmental Risk Factors says the level of risk is unknown: "It is too early to study the breast cancer risk of women who drink milk and eat milk products from hormone-treated animals." As with Alar on apples, attention on the controversy boosted demand for an organic alternative, which Horizon helped supply from its large farm.

"From day one, we said, 'That's not where it's at,'" Siemon, the long-haired CEO of Organic Valley, told me in his office in an old creamery in the two-street town of La Farge, Wisconsin. "There was plenty of milk, but they really believed they were going to produce milk cheaper . . . and they got a lot of flack for it, a lot of disrespect in the industry for doing that." Siemon and Retzloff, or Organic Valley and Horizon, might be thought of as the yin and yang of the organic dairy industry. Both were as aware of their contributions in building the organic milk market as their stark differences. "We're very different companies but have worked together as best we could over the years," Siemon said. Yet, as in much of the organic industry, the differences became harder to ignore as the market grew.

The Idaho farm was the first of several large-scale organic dairy operations that appeared over the next decade, capturing about 20 percent of the organic milk market. Retzloff, who then left Horizon, pursued the model again when he cofounded Aurora Organic Dairy in 2003. As with Horizon's Idaho property, he transitioned Aurora Dairy's conventional dairy farm in Platteville, Colorado, with 5,200 cows, to organic production, and then another, in Texas.

Aurora's Colorado ranch had what sounded like a lot of pasture—2,900 acres of irrigated fields and 12,000 acres of native grassland—but in this dry region of the state, that appeared to fall short of levels recommended by the USDA's Natural Resource Conservation Service. With little rain, the grasses grow slowly and the land is vulnerable to overgrazing and erosion. Jon Wicke, NRCS district conservationist in Weld County, where Aurora is located, advises farmers on the number of animals the land can support, by studying grasses, soil type, rainfall, and the amount of grain feed rations. Generally, he said, he has recommended five to ten acres of irrigated pasture per cow. On native grassland, the rate was twenty-five to forty acres per cow. "It's all related to a lack of rainfall," he said.

If his figures were right, then Aurora's land would support 600 to 1,100 cows—not 5,200. If only a portion of the herd were pastured, or pastured for a portion of the year, or fed largely in a feedlot, the density could be increased. This appeared to be Aurora's approach. While its Web site showed cows lazily eating grass, Aurora said its cattle grazed "on organic pasture during the times of the year when that pasture is nutritionally optimal." Even if it had enough pasture, it would be difficult to graze thousands of lactating cows and get them back to the milking barn three times a day, since fresh grass would be progressively farther away. I wasn't too surprised when Wicke said: "I can't think of any organic grazing operations out here. (Grazing) would definitely be a drawback."

While Aurora officials argued its system of sheltered outdoor pens was best for animal health in the dry region, critics only saw a "factory farm" making money by skirting organic pasture rules.

Aurora was quite plain about its goal: "We make organic goodness affordable." The company put a dairy plant on the farm to centralize production and eliminate the cost of hauling milk. Since it sold milk to the private-label market, it had no need to build a brand and thus avoided marketing expenses. These two factors, along with its production model, cut costs. "If we're not the lowest [priced], we'll be one of the lowest in the organic milk industry," Retzloff told one reporter. With this business model in place, Aurora raised $18.5 million in venture capital from Charlesbank Capital Partners, a Boston firm backed by Harvard University's endowment fund. "With consumer demand for organic foods continuing to grow at double-digit rates, we believe that organic dairy production on a large scale, which Aurora Organic Dairy will offer, will provide superior return on capital," said Tim Palmer, a managing director at Charlesbank.

Retzloff told me his motivation in scaling up has always been to take pesticides out of agriculture. "Whether it's air, water, antibiotics in cows . . . the more acres that we can get in sustainable production, the more we eliminate this source of degradation," he said. Aurora purchased organic grain and hay from farms totaling fifty thousand acres. It also shipped its voluminous composted manure out to those farms, providing soil fertility.

But its model put Aurora squarely on the radar screens of small dairy farmers, who worried that it would cheapen the image of pasture-based organic milk and undercut them in the market. One group, the Northeast Organic Dairy Producer Alliance (NODPA), with a membership of 179 certified organic dairy farms, wrote about Aurora in its August 2004 newsletter and discussed the issue at its annual field day in Vermont the same month. It came out that Aurora had researched opening a farm in New York state—NODPA's backyard. The northeast—Maine, Vermont, New Hampshire, Massachusetts, New York, Connecticut, and Pennsylvania—has around four hundred small organic dairy farms.

"Can anyone who really understands organic dairy conclude that Aurora Dairy and the Northeast family organic dairy farmer are producing the same product?" Greg Jackmauh wrote in the NODPA's newsletter. "Aurora Dairy and its ilk have a right to exist . . . But they do NOT have the RIGHT to be a member of a society of producers whose dedication is to the animals and the land before it is to profit. The Auroras of the industry benefit from their association with OUR values, never will we benefit from our association with theirs."

Although Aurora officials tried to assure the NODPA that big and small producers could coexist in a world of rising demand and short supply, the farmers would have none of it. They saw brute competition, with Aurora pursuing a lax organic model to pump out more milk. They feared that as supply caught up with demand, small producers would be picked off one by one by the low-cost, large-scale farms. Organic milk would no longer derive from small farms and pastured herds, but concentrated feedlot operations. Once undercut on price, the smaller farmers wouldn't have many alternatives. They couldn't, like vegetable farmers, go "beyond organic" and sell to high-end restaurants, because that market was so small. They couldn't easily sell direct to consumers because of milk regulations. "I will be very surprised if organic dairy producers are not in the same leaky boat as conventional milk producers by around 2010," Joel McNair wrote in *The Milkweed,* a milk marketing newsletter.

This worry had a subtext that might be thought of as the posttraumatic stress disorder of American dairy farmers. Production by large confinement farms had grown as demand declined, sending conventional milk prices to their lowest level in twenty-five years, in 2003. (Demand for milk has fallen for half a century, dropping 18 percent since the early 1980s alone.) Dairy farmers who couldn't compete during the price drops resorted to eating their cows, or selling them for hamburger meat when the Atkins diet pushed up meat prices. Brenda Cochran, a Pennsylvania farmer, ran a crisis hotline for dairy farmers: "The farmers calling me . . . are numb with desperation, some near emotional collapse," she wrote in late 2002, after a decade in which 41 percent of the nation's dairy farms shut down. "A farmer from Wisconsin with young children has no money for his family's groceries. A farmer in Pennsylvania cannot cover pay for his hired help. Many callers can no longer afford vet care for their cattle or even medical insurance." While prices came back in 2004—in part because the supply of cows had declined so sharply with the previous fall in prices—farm closures continued.

While one wing of the organic dairy industry was willing

to ignore this uncomfortable reality while busily creating new markets, another wing tried explicitly to address it. Indeed, saving small dairy farms was the principal motivation for creating the organic dairy industry. CROPP was founded in the mid-1980s in response to the failure of government programs to help small farmers. The members were primarily small Midwest family farmers seeking to survive, not back-to-the-landers propelled by idealism. "One of our objectives was a fair marketing system so that farmers could be rewarded for being who they are," Siemon told me.

Instead of being conventional price takers, they would be price makers in organic milk. The farmers set the price high enough to cover production costs and to make a moderate living. "One of our sacred cows is to keep that pay price where it ought to be," Siemon said. The co-op chose early on to dump excess organic milk in the conventional market rather than cut organic milk prices, figuring rightly that consumers would eventually catch up with its supply.

Organic Valley also adopted measures—some controversial—to ensure it had a market for its farmers. It introduced high-heat ultra-pasteurization to extend the shelf life of organic milk; it shipped to distant markets, rather than just locally; it supplied Wal-Mart, after a divisive internal debate, but then cancelled the contract when the retailer pushed for a lower price. Like any other mission-driven business, the co-op made compromises to survive. Companies that shared the mission made a point of supporting the co-op, which is why Stonyfield Farm buys the bulk of its milk from Organic Valley to make yogurt. In all these decisions, the goal was to ensure the small farmer got a fair price *and* a place in the supermarket dairy case.

The vision proved successful. Organic Valley grew from 7 farms in 1988 to 689 farms in 2004, with revenues of $206 million, becoming the fourth-largest organic brand. Horizon kept in step, adding to the milk from its own two farms by bringing more than three hundred small farmers into its network. With this supply, Horizon controlled 70 percent of the organic milk market and was the number-one brand.

Even so, organic dairy farmers were not raking in cash. A 2005 study by the Northeast Organic Farming Association (Vermont) found that a farm with thirty to eighty cows would have to get at least $28 per hundred pounds (the standard measure, equal to 11.7 gallons) to earn $35,000 a year. Though prices vary depending on quality, organic milk runs about $22—a 50 percent premium over conventional milk. "Organic farmers are covering their costs, but they are not making much money," said Bacon, the dairy specialist at NOFA (Vermont) who carried out the study.

On January 10, 2005, a small-farm-advocacy and corporate-watchdog group based in Wisconsin, the Cornucopia Institute, filed a complaint against Aurora Organic with the National Organic Program. "Climatic conditions—such as arid climate, which makes pasture impractical or not cost-effective—cannot be used to justify year-round noncompliance with the pasture rule," the complaint read. Cornucopia also launched a media offensive about organic "factory farms." The NOP responded by asking the NOSB to clarify what "access to pasture" meant.

Six weeks later, dozens of farmers from New York, Pennsylvania, California, Wisconsin, and Vermont came to the Washington Terrace Hotel in D.C. to attend an NOSB meeting. Wearing baseball caps and work pants, each farmer made the same plea in an allotted five minutes: The pasture standard must be tightened. They had more than five thousand letters from consumers and other supporters.

Aurora's officials made the counterargument, saying the company was in compliance with organic regulations "as currently interpreted." They argued pasture rules should be based on scientific studies of animal diet and health in various climates of the United States, taking into account pathogens lurking in pastures. Only then could regulators determine what "access to pasture" should mean. "The full set of data has not yet been assembled, nor has it been studied by experts in dairy science, veterinary science, and agronomics to make firm and final conclusions regarding an optimum organic system," their statement said. One can only guess where the corpus of organic regulations—and the organic food industry—would be if such a scientific standard were applied across the board.

The company also raised questions about dairy farmers in the Northeast and Upper Midwest who confined cows indoors during the winter months. To Aurora, these small farms appeared less than upstanding when it came to the health of their animals. At least, the matter was open to scientific inquiry. Aurora argued that pasturing reflected regional tradition, not science or health, and the company shouldn't be held to that arbitrary standard. Aurora officials also felt the bias against big farms was misguided, for how could you otherwise feed organic consumers?

Though some view the National Organic Program as the handmaiden of corporate farming, Richard Mathews, then its deputy administrator, made sure each farmer who signed up to speak got a chance at the podium. He also went out of his way to thank the farmers for testifying, saying, "All too often people show up to speak on behalf of farmers and it's very rare that we actually hear from farmers." He also made clear to the board that if it did not come up with a well-defined pasture standard, he would have little power of enforcement.

"You do have people out there who undoubtedly are taking

advantage of the wording as it is," he said. "You have to write your regulations to prevent the bad guys from taking advantage of it. And I'm not talking in terms of dairy, I'm talking in terms of all animals that are supposed to be provided with access to the outdoors."

After hours of testimony, the NOSB voted to rewrite section 205.239, paragraph A, subsection 2 of the pasture regulation. Instead of "access to pasture," the regulation would now call for "grazing on pasture during the growing season." The only exceptions were for cows birthing, calves up to six months of age, and beef cattle during the final four months of "finishing," when they may be fed grain in feedlots. The wording made clear: "lactation of dairy animals is not a stage of life under which animals may be denied pasture for grazing." If you were milking cows, they still had to eat fresh grass. The measure passed thirteen to one, including an affirmative vote from the Horizon Organic representative who sat on the board. (The company later announced plans to modify the Idaho farm, adding another 1,400 acres and improving its existing pasture.)

In a separate proposed "guidance" document, the NOSB suggested that the goal of each farm should be to pasture its cows at least 120 days a year. Cows should only be confined in "inclement weather," to protect the health or safety of the animals, or to preserve soil and water quality. In a direct swipe at large farms, it stated: "In no case shall temporary confinement be allowed as a *continuous production system*" (emphasis added). While the guidance document did not have the force of regulation, it made the spirit of the proposed rule clear.

Although the NOSB sent the recommendations on to the USDA, it got a rude surprise a couple of months later. The National Organic Program office kicked the changes back, requiring more clarification—a typical course of events. Even the

234 · Samuel Fromartz

USDA Office of Inspector General found the NOP's relationship with the NOSB dysfunctional, saying in an audit that it had not "established protocols for working with the NOSB or resolving conflicts with them." Pasture could now be added to at least twenty-six other NOSB recommendations left in regulatory limbo by the NOP.

When I spoke with Retzloff, he said Aurora would abide by any new regulations, whenever they appeared. "We'll be in compliance no matter what happens," he said.

Did that mean Aurora could graze its five thousand cows and still get them back to the barn three times a day to be milked?

"Yeah, it will be difficult. We don't think it's the healthiest thing for the animals, to be walking that far, but we'll be able to do whatever the standard is out there," he said. "It's not a problem."

Aurora was trying to disabuse small dairy farmers of the idea that regulations would limit scale. Throw enough capital at the problem, even in arid Colorado, the company seemed to say, and it could be solved.

Where did this leave consumers?

Demos, who briefly ran both Horizon Organic and White Wave under Dean Foods, told me Horizon was able to fill only 70 percent of its milk orders because of shortages in supply. In the absence of more big farms like Aurora, small farms would need to convert to organic production in increasing numbers. Retzloff figured there were seventy-five thousand organic cows in the country. If milk demand grew 20 percent annually, the number of organic cows would need to increase at a commensurate rate. That would mean adding fifteen thousand cows in one year, which would require converting 150 to 300 new farms—a quarter to a half as many as Organic Valley had converted in fifteen years. With supplies short, retail prices had jumped 10 percent in the summer of 2005 (to around $5.50 per gallon in the Washington area). Stonyfield Farm even sought to import organic milk powder from a New Zealand dairy cooperative, to keep pace with demand. The very popularity of organic milk was overwhelming the ability of the industry—big and small—to produce enough of it.

"That could be the case," said David Carter, executive director of the American Bison Association and a member of the NOSB, when I brought it up. "But that doesn't mean you should start compromising the regulations." Plus, if the market worked, higher prices would entice more farmers to raise supplies—not immediately, but eventually. Carter, who is based in Colorado, viewed pasture as the alternative to the conventional farm model; that's what consumers wanted. "By default, that will favor the small producer," he said, "but if a larger player can figure out how to do it, well, then, more power to them."

One warm spring day, I met Sligh, the soft-spoken founding chairman of the NOSB, for coffee on Capitol Hill in Washington. He had participated in organic policy for more than three decades, directing the sustainable agriculture program at Rural Advancement Foundation International USA. "I had planned to leave my farm for a little while and work on policy issues, but haven't found a chance yet to get back," he said.

For Sligh, small farmers were at the root of the organic movement. "Part of what drove family farmers into organic farming was that conventional agriculture drove them out," he said. "And for many of us, that was the main constituency we were concerned about." As organic moved out of its niche and grew, those farmers faced increasing competition. The organic movement had morphed into an industry, abetted by regulations that had defined the method in a way that any farm, big or small, could follow. The vague "access to pasture" language was just one example.

He thought that the key element that set organic food apart—differentiation—was being sacrificed in a world of processed foods, and, now, mass market milk. Interpret the regulations in a lax or expansive way and consumers lost a primary element that made organic food different.

Looking back over a decade, Sligh thought many of the conflicts might have been avoided if the movement and industry had chosen a more "sustainable" and slower growth path, one that ensured a place for small producers. In essence, what Sligh sought was protection of a niche. But, as his opponents continually have replied, this would leave many new consumers, producers, and acres of land behind.

While growth and ideals often ended up in conflict, they were not mutually exclusive. The same forces leading organic food into the mainstream supermarket industry also propelled farmers' markets—if only because the consumer in both venues was often the same. Like the entire food industry, the sector had split into niche and mass-market categories. This represented a larger shift in the way Americans shopped, wreaking havoc in the supermarket industry and leading to the ascendancy of venues as varied as Whole Foods and Wal-Mart. Whether organic food could maintain its identity across all these channels remained an open question, not only for its meaning but—as Henderson put it—its ownership.

7. Consuming Organic

Why We Buy

We all need only purchase a $4 latte at the airport
to realize that "Things aren't as they used to be."
—HARVEY HARTMAN, THE HARTMAN GROUP

Walking though the sliding glass doors into the Whole Foods
Market on P Street recently, I perked up upon seeing the bright
displays of produce, but noticed that the early romance I felt toward the store had mellowed. I had acquired the slightly jaded
mien of the seasoned shopper who could find exactly what he
wanted and get out, leaving the more expensive enticements for
novices. Since I owned only five shares of Whole Foods stock
(I kept them to receive the annual reports), my rationalization
that buying whatever I wanted would swell the company's bottom line and thus my own no longer held water. Now more
knowledgeable and with a young child, I had become more
price conscious and my shopping venues had splintered.

My voluminous purchases of Whole Foods's fresh produce
slowed between May and October, when I bought at the local
farmers' market; in the winter, I shopped for Earthbound organic salad mix at Costco, which priced it about a third less than
Whole Foods. I heard about a smaller local supermarket, My
Organic Market (MOM's), which stocked a lot of organic

goods and had a business model largely premised on undercutting the prices of its bigger rival. ("We don't mark prices up from wholesale, we mark them down from Whole Foods," Scott Nash, MOM's CEO, told me.) Employees also carried your grocery bags to the car—a big plus with a child in tow. Occasionally, I shopped at Trader Joe's, the cheaper, smaller, eclectic food chain. I largely avoided Whole Foods's artisan bread and sprung instead for superior loaves from local bakers and didn't buy much of their high-end cheese, since I discovered a far better artisan shop in nearby Alexandria. But, as Ellen said one day, "We can't shop at a hundred stores!" Whole Foods still ranked as our main supermarket, since it stocked the most of what we wanted in one venue. I also found if I shopped smart and bought its private-label products, I could avoid emptying my wallet. Still, compared with the giddiness I felt a few years back, my loyalty had diminished.

Whole Foods initially hooked me by satisfying two primal impulses articulated by William Grimes in a *New York Times* review of Whole Foods's mammoth supermarket in Columbus Circle, which opened in 2004. Whole Foods, he wrote, "subscribes to a religion that might be called moralistic hedonism. With an eye to pleasing presentation and attractive packaging, it offers a Venusberg of gustatory temptations, often rarefied, and all guaranteed to be good for you." These two traits—pleasure and health—for too long stood in opposition to one another in the same way that desire clashes with restraint.

Health food historically meant bug-eaten organic produce, hardy beans and grains, and badly prepared tofu—their health quotient rising as palatability declined. On the other extreme, gourmands consumed, say, a milk-braised pork loin, butter-whipped potatoes, and yet another plate of chocolate truffles—delicious, but full of cardio-challenging saturated fat and calories. Instead of viewing these camps as opposed and static and choosing one, Whole Foods saw a dialectic and came up with the synthesis; it made healthy food delicious and marketed the perfect meal. Foods with artificial preservatives, colors, flavors, sweeteners, and hydrogenated oils were verboten; so, too, were the agro-industrial brands like Kraft, General Mills, and Coca-Cola. They were replaced with offbeat natural and organic producers like Hain, Eden Foods, Spectrum, and Amy's Kitchen; natural and organic brands like Boca, Cascadian Farm, and Odwalla, owned by the agro-industrial giants; and artisan fare that could run the full gamut of possibilities. Customers could find tofu or a cheeseburger in this world because it was up to them to find the balance, but as retailing consultant Willard Bishop Jr. told me, Whole Foods "did the editing," setting the boundaries of feel-good food.

Whole Foods was hardly alone in this marriage of health and taste, since chefs such as Alice Waters repositioned organic food to emphasize its high quality. Others, like Deborah Madison, showed how spices, fresh herbs, and ethnic techniques could make a vegetarian dish the center of a fabulous meal. The restaurant movement had by the mid-1980s rebelled against stuffy, elite, saucy French fare, coming up with simple dishes made with the freshest ingredients often bought at the farmers' market. Service at the most popular fine-dining restaurants became friendly, rather than haughty, in the same way that Whole Foods's high-end comestibles enticed rather than excluded the customer. At the same time, the organic movement's historic antipathy to artificial and highly processed food dovetailed with a broader perception that "fresh" meant "healthy." The long-winded arguments about soil biology and organic agriculture could never match the visceral appeal of a perfect tomato or peach. Simply presenting organic produce in an attractive setting became a slam dunk against tough, bland supermarket fare, creating the largest segment of the organic marketplace and, not accidentally, the entryway to Whole Foods. A twenty-foot stroll through the pampered produce section convinces the customer of the high quality of organic food and articulates the values of the store, even if only a portion of what it sells is organic.

Bishop told me Whole Foods's merger of quality goods with a concept of health created a niche in the grocery industry. "One of the reasons they've been so successful is that they are quite clear and consistent about who they are and what they deliver to the customer," he said.

The timing was right because health had become increasingly important to shoppers, even if they had trouble following any consistent regime. Fifty-five percent of Americans cited health as a key motivation in food purchases in 2004 (up from 45 percent in 2000), and 59 percent said they tried to eat healthy food to avoid illness later in life. These consumers weren't looking at food as medicine but as a way to avoid medicine, doctors, and hospitals in the future, just as J. I. Rodale had in the 1940s. Even among those on a diet (six in ten Americans), the biggest motivation was health (cited by 77 percent). Pesticides, antibiotics, and hormones also played a role in these decisions, since seven in ten Americans report they are "somewhat concerned" about the risk posed by these substances in the food supply. The 28 percent who view them as a "high risk" roughly mirrors the percentage of people who buy organic food regularly.

With this backdrop, it should not be surprising that health and nutrition motivate 70 to 80 percent of all organic shoppers, reaching 90 percent among frequent buyers. Freshness, taste, environmental benefits, and helping small farms are also cited, with those reasons becoming more important as purchases increase.

But ordinary consumers wouldn't begin to care about these

benefits if organic food remained unpalatable, unavailable, or too closely associated with a fringe diet. Indeed, organic food persisted and grew precisely because the movement defined *organic* as a production method rather than a prescriptive diet such as Atkins, South Beach, the Zone, or Weight Watchers. The benefit came from eating the food, not from avoiding foods or counting calories. In this way, organic food became associated with a "healthy lifestyle," which meant you ultimately decided what made you feel good. Whole Foods's organic chocolate truffles epitomize this for me; they taste good because they contain chocolate, sugar, and saturated fat—not the healthiest mix. Yet by making them organically, Whole Foods tempered the "bad" quotient and transformed them into something "good."

"For years, people said, 'Consumers don't know what organic means,'" said Harvey Hartman, head of the Hartman Group marketing firm, whose clients include Whole Foods. "We knew that. But we also knew that consumers didn't care! They just wanted to feel good that they were doing the right thing."

When the cofounder and CEO of Whole Foods, John Mackey, opened the original store, called Safer Way, in Austin, Texas, in 1978, it was a typical counterculture venue that sold only vegetarian fare. But then Mackey and his friends realized if they wanted to grow, they had to loosen their grip on granola and sell meat, seafood, beer, wine, and coffee. "We didn't think they were particularly healthy products, but we were a whole food store, not a 'holy food' store," he told one interviewer.

This brought in consumers of various persuasions beyond the company's core market. Now vegetarians are just one small segment of a wide base that includes health-and-nutrition devotees, fitness fanatics, foodies, environmentalists, and core organic consumers. Since their concerns overlap to a degree, Whole Foods can feed them all, so long as its message remains consistent. Selling meat, for example, might alienate vegans and vegetarians, but Whole Foods is now developing a program to ensure its meat, which is free of antibiotics and hormones, will be raised to "animal-compassionate" standards. While Mackey publicly dismissed the animal-rights activists who initially pressured the company on this issue, he also looked into their arguments, switched from a vegetarian to a vegan diet, and then began a dialogue. He was not about to ban meat in Whole Foods stores, but he decided if animals must be eaten, the ones the company sold would at least be raised humanely. This would further differentiate Whole Foods's meat from the factory-farm fare in conventional supermarkets, and create a common ground for consumers as divergent as vegans and high-protein dieters. The company won the endorsement of People for the Ethical Treatment of Animals (PETA) in 2004, giving the meat, in effect, a vegetarian seal of approval.

The company's broader success lay in selling this enhanced food in an enticing setting, with a lot of customer coddling— adding another dimension to the idea that healthy food could be pleasurable rather than puritanical. Mackey has said that Whole Foods capitalized on a paradox: Americans loved food and loved shopping, but hated shopping for food. So the stores, in retailing lingo, became "an experience," wowing customers who had long associated grocery shopping with a loathsome task. As it has grown, Whole Foods has continued to improve the customer's experience. In the late 1990s, when the company gobbled up regional natural-food chains such as Fresh Fields on the East Coast, Mrs. Gooch's Natural Foods Markets in Los Angeles, and Bread & Circus in New England, each of these acquisitions brought much more than real estate; they brought expertise— which was given a chance to flourish in a culture of autonomy.

Mackey allowed each region and store to make decisions and

compete so that the best ideas would win. Bonuses reflected a team's performance in the store, so that all had a stake in making the model hum at the ground floor. Mackey envisioned a company that took care of customers first and employees second; then shareholders, the community, and the wider environment. Profit, in short, was the result of a highly competitive and localized customer focus, not the dictates of a control freak at the top.

When I popped into stores in Berkeley, Seattle, Portland, Denver, Boulder, western Massachusetts, New York, and Washington, they looked similar but never alike. Unique offerings at one would later appear at another. Boulder had a stunning Eden-like fresh flower display at the entrance that I soon saw replicated in other stores, even if they did not quite hone theirs to the same effect. Seattle, a top store, boasted a highly theatrical prepared-foods area all abuzz at dinnertime, with customers mingling as cooks worked an open grill. Whole Foods's store in Columbus Circle took this to the extreme, rolling out Asian, Latino, and Indian food; brick-oven pizza; and sushi. In the mid-Atlantic region, I noticed the company renovated and reconfigured often, expanding meat sections and playing up thick cuts of aged beef once high-protein diets took off. This refinement demanded engagement, which made the stores fun.

Whole Foods soared high and dove low to capture more varied customers. Its lower-priced 365 brand of natural and organic food products sold alongside premium artisan fare. This made eminent sense since few brands dominated the organic and natural-food marketplace, leaving it to Whole Foods to, in effect, become a top brand. Reaching high, it slapped an Authentic Food Artisan (AFA) seal on products deemed worthy of discriminating customers. A shopper seeking value might snap up the perfectly acceptable 365 pasta ($0.79) or choose the organic version ($1.29); if less concerned about price, she could reach for the Montebello brand ($2.99), made from wheat grown on the grounds of a former hilltop Italian monastery that has been farmed free of chemicals since 1388, earning the AFA seal. Or, if she sought an even more rarefied plate of spaghetti, she could buy the Rustichella d'Abruzzo offering ($5.29), crafted by a third-generation Italian master using stone-ground, local organic wheat extruded through handmade bronze dies and dried exceedingly slowly. Each product has a slightly different appeal for a particular occasion, such as feeding the kids or impressing a date.

Mackey has described this work as marrying love and creativity, which might translate to passion and innovation in a more traditional business context. Whole Foods has no employees, only team members; no managers, but team leaders. The company believes the communal character of the tribe gives its workers more than a union ever could, which is why it trumpets a 100 percent union-free shop (a plus on Wall Street). When an organizing drive at its Madison, Wisconsin, store succeeded in 2002, Mackey e-mailed employees that "the temptation to contract into fear and anger is very powerful. Love and forgiveness are the more difficult choices to make." A year later, two organizers said they were unfairly fired and a pro-union Web site claimed Whole Foods played hardball, but the union was out. Perhaps this was tough love, for Mackey's libertarian, New Age vision—as in much of the organic food industry—never included a place for industrial-era unions. In his view, they impeded the team. To dismiss this as corporate greed would be simplistic, however, since the company also limits salaries and bonuses of the highest paid to no more than fourteen times the average and donates 5 percent of after-tax profits to charity, both of which are unusual in corporate America, union shop or not.

If you were an organic or local food purist, vegan funda-
mentalist, or union agitator, the store might irk you, but for
Mackey, losing these customers was the price of success. "What
if we only sold organic stuff? We'd . . . cease to exist because not
enough of our customers want us to just sell organic," Mackey
said in one interview. "They would find it would be too expensive for them; they wouldn't be willing to buy it." To succeed,
the business had to connect with an audience beyond the core
by offering a wider palate of attributes.

Again, this wasn't unique in the organic food market. Salad
mix and soy milk didn't win in the marketplace solely because
they carried an ORGANIC label, or any other single attribute. The
appeal of salad mix derived from the trendy taste of baby greens,
the cleanliness of triple washing, the convenient package; for
soy milk, it came from the health benefits and improved palatability of soy and a chilled-shelf placement that implied "fresh."
As with Whole Foods, an array of overlapping attributes and
connotations—along with the ORGANIC label—made these products attractive to a broad customer base. It was the only way to
prevail in the marketplace.

Picture an organic shopper: a thirty-something, upper-middle-
income, Volvo-driving, Pilates-practicing, latté-swilling, suburban white woman or soccer mom. Right? Well, not entirely.
While this demographic profile may be in the organic market,
she is not alone—for income, race, and age aren't overriding
factors in plucking an organic shopper out of the populace.
(Gender is, if only because most food shoppers are women.)

When the Hartman Group surveyed more than twenty-six
thousand households in 1999, it found organic food consumption closely reflected the breakdown of society, with slight but
meaningful differences. Most significant? Single women with

children, consumers with at least a college education, and elderly and younger shoppers reported slightly higher rates of consumption. Organic food sales were stronger on the West Coast than in the Midwest, though this appeared to reflect availability. Surprisingly, more than half of self-defined "heavy" buyers of organic food earned less than $30,000 a year.

"When we do organic studies, income is about the only thing that doesn't skew at all by user and nonuser," said Laurie Demeritt, president of the Hartman Group. "You get little skews in age, little skews in geography, little skews in education, but there's nothing at all for income, so we don't even look anymore." She said organic shoppers' median income—that is, the figure at which half the incomes fell above and half below—was usually within $2,000 of the national median. "It's not something we can use to pinpoint whether someone's an organic user or not."

The Food Marketing Institute reported similar findings in a 2004 survey. "Shoppers who buy organic foods, even those who buy foods from three or more categories of organic products, look pretty much the same as other shoppers," the survey said, attributing this to the increasing availability of the food.

Even those at the very bottom of the economic ladder will buy organic produce if it's available. In Washington, D.C., a local nonprofit, the Capital Area Food Bank, set up a farmers' market to bring fresh, local, and mostly organic produce to Ward 8, a section of the city whose seventy thousand residents earn an average of $12,000 a year and have not had a grocery store since 1998. "It's great for me because there's nowhere else to go for fruits and vegetables like this," one resident told the *Washington Post*. The same dynamic has unfolded in West Oakland, California, a low-income area that has one supermarket for twenty-five thousand people but thirty-six convenience and liquor stores, only three of which sell any fresh produce. There, the nonprofit People's Grocery has provided fresh, organic produce from local farms and community gardens. Just Food has done the same in New York City, connecting rural farmers with low-income consumers through CSAs. Poor diet, stemming from a dearth of food options in these communities, has led to increased heart disease and diabetes. Food markets—organic or otherwise—are what's missing, not demand.

While Whole Foods and Wild Oats (the two biggest natural-food retailers) clearly cater to higher-income and better-educated shoppers—Whole Foods has even been nicknamed "Whole Paycheck" because of its prices—these stores don't provide a good sample of organic shoppers. Only 11 percent of organic food shoppers polled by the Food Marketing Institute bought organics at a natural-food supermarket. Including smaller natural-food stores, the number rose to 26 percent. However, the shoppers who frequent these stores buy a disproportionately higher amount of organic food, accounting for about 43 percent of organic food sales. Meanwhile, 57 percent of all organic shoppers bought at mainstream grocery stores and discounters. There are more of these shoppers, but they buy fewer organic goods—primarily milk, soy milk, baby food, and salad mix—and tend to skew to a lower-income profile in discount stores.

This selective buying pattern for premium-priced goods fits into a larger trend, as shoppers pay up for products they care about—whether golf clubs, big-screen television sets, Nike basketball sneakers, body-care products, iPods, SUVs, or organic food—and buy at rock-bottom prices for everything else. It's the only way you can afford a premium good if you aren't rich. Retailing has bifurcated between value outlets where price rules and premium niches "driven more by cultural and lifestyle patterns than abject utility," Hartman points out.

Michael Silverstein, a retailing consultant at the Boston Consulting Group, and Neil Fiske, CEO of Bath & Body Works, dubbed this phenomenon (and their book on the subject) *Trading Up*. They call these premium products "new luxury" goods, because in contrast to "old luxury" goods, which are sold on status, class, and exclusivity, they are widely available. Consumers "trade up to the premium new luxury product if the category is important to them," the authors write. "If it isn't, they trade down to the low-cost or private-label brand, or even go without. They scrimp and save across a broad swatch of spending in order to afford their new luxury purchases—polarizing the household budget. Almost every American engages in this practice of 'rocketing'—spending a disproportionate amount of his income in a category of great meaning."

There's a flip side to rocketing—not only do middle-income shoppers buy premium goods but high-income shoppers buy at discount retailers. The goods you choose to buy depend more on what you value than on how much you make.

In this polarized retail world, why buy a product that has neither a fabulous price nor a special attribute? That defines the middle market, which has lured customers with sales and then made up the losses on higher priced goods. Now shoppers who want low prices buy at low-price venues, decimating traditional retailers such as supermarkets. They sold 81 percent of all groceries in 1994, but a decade later had only 52 percent of the market. Wal-Mart, dollar stores, and other discounters jumped from 9 percent to 32 percent in the same period. Whole Foods thrived, too, not by competing on price but by offering a unique product mix, shopping experience, and health focus. As one Whole Foods shopper told the *New York Times*: "Anyway, I make up some of the difference at Wal-Mart."

On the premium end, policemen and high school kids line up with white-collar workers for $3 to $4 coffee drinks at Starbucks. Starbucks isn't just selling a cup of coffee, but, with unique lingo to describe the size, blend, and flavors of the offerings, a culture. The more language you know, the more connected you become, and with nineteen thousand different combinations to choose from, your order becomes personal, fast. Plus, Starbucks has infused values into its product line, whether through a small selection of fair trade and organic coffees or its recently launched Ethos line of spring water that funds clean drinking water in the third world. All create an emotional bond with the customer that can justify a premium.

In organic food purchases, the Hartman Group—by trailing and interviewing subjects and then looking into their cupboards—found consumers didn't simply switch to organic goods, but selected foods they most strongly associated with the ORGANIC label. So a consumer would buy organic milk or strawberries, but also his usual conventional pasta sauce and cookies. The organic idea usually began to flounder in processed food, sold at the center of the store, away from the chilled perishables on the perimeter. The notable exceptions: cereals and children's food. In order to keep spending under control, consumers most commonly traded up only for products in which they perceived a clear value or benefit.

"We're not saying, 'No one cares about the price differences,'" Demeritt, of the Hartman Group, said. "But we've definitely found, within those categories that consumers ascribe a high organic value to, such as organic milk for their children, it doesn't matter what your income level is. If you think that's an important value, you're willing to pay more for it. But that very same person might say, 'Well, but rice doesn't matter for me, I don't see the value there, so I'm just going to buy the cheapest rice I can.'"

So, while the core customer might buy as much organic food as possible, the much more prevalent mid-level consumer fills far less than half her shopping cart with organics. Her choices aren't only parsed by product, but by who consumes it. A mother may buy organic milk for her children and conventional half-and-half for herself, but if fifteen other kids are due over for a birthday party she may decide organic milk is too pricey and serve conventional milk instead. "The [buying] decision is based not only on the product category, but the individual product, who is going to use it, and the specific occasion," Demeritt said.

Given these buying patterns, the debate about the organic Twinkie and a "parallel food system" made with organic ingredients was misguided. Organic-growth advocates argued that making an organic Twinkie would "Grow the market! Convert more land!" The purists said, "No! Organic food should be kept pure and the Twinkie banned!" What neither side imagined was that consumers might buy conventional Twinkies and wash them down with organic milk, or that such mixed consumption might be preferable.

This also explained a paradox that had bothered me throughout my research: If nearly a third of consumers bought organic food regularly, why did organic sales amount to barely 2 percent of food sales? Because consumers, it turned out, were messy, inconsistent, and buying very discretely—as would be expected with a premium good.

Trading up explained the long lines and full parking lots at Whole Foods, even while most shoppers appeared to fill small baskets with perishables such as meat, produce, dairy, fish, and takeout. They were rocketing in fresh and ready-to-eat foods. Though virtually none of the latter were organic, the convenience of prepared food trumped the desire to eat organically.

But trading up didn't always mean high prices, as Whole Foods's value line established. Trader Joe's also bridged the high-low gap, by selling about two thousand specialty items at competitive prices. The retailer could still make money because sales velocity increased—these items flew out of the store much faster than in a conventional supermarket that stocked twenty times as many products. These premium-type products required knowledge and interest, and in turn a commitment, which is a distinct quality in goods that matter. Whole Foods seeks out locations with a lot of college graduates. At Trader Joe's, the underpaid but well-educated shopper has become such a distinct customer base that a Seattle store morphed into a way for young people to meet each other, according to the *Seattle Post-Intelligencer.* "It's mostly like a different bracket of society there," a twenty-four-year-old woman who organized a singles gathering of Trader Joe's devotees said. "I often find myself pondering the domestic microbrews section and realizing I'm inadvertently checking out the guy next to me, only to realize later that he's there with his girlfriend, or something, after she rounds the corner with a bag of frozen shrimp pot stickers and a potted orchid or whatever." A man who attended the singles event said, "I'm looking for people who have at least a somewhat similar overall personality, and the folks that shop at TJ's seem to share a certain sort of character. Flavor, even."

Products were not, in other words, the only way to parse a marketplace. People could have flavors, too.

I, like most consumers, am messy. I buy organic salad mix at Costco in the winter, though shipping it from California burns up fossil fuel. I eat meat, too, though it takes far more calories, energy, and water to produce than soybeans. In general, I find the debate about whether local is better than organic tiresome because each represents such a small portion (1 to 2 percent) of the food supply. It's like two people in a room of one hundred arguing about who has the most righteous alternative to what the other ninety-eight are doing. Both are right for different reasons and can thrive simultaneously.

Within this inconsistent pattern, I also decided to try growing food as this book progressed, though my sole experience in agriculture consisted of planting trees in northeast Washington state the summer I graduated from college. Each night, by the light of a campfire in the middle of the Colville National Forest, my co-op partners and I argued over how to divvy up the $25,000 contract pay. Finally, in a kind of democratic-socialist approach, we split half the pay communally and divided the other half based upon how many trees each of us planted. After waking at four each morning to plant the seedlings on steep hillsides of clear-cut forest, we spent the last day getting high and hiking up a mountain to see our newly installed Douglas firs, returning later to a sweat lodge we had built by a creek. Then I returned to city life and stayed for good. Now, twenty-five years later, I joined an organic community garden, and in the shadow of an elevated highway a half mile from the nation's capitol, grew lettuce, tomatoes, cucumbers, beans, basil, peppers, and greens. Jim Crawford and Heinz Thomet gave me advice, but my results were mixed, which meant Heinz and Jim still got a fair share of my business. In homage to the organic-salad-mix pioneers, I grew spring mix to four inches, then cut off the tiny heads and rushed them home to a cold-water bath and the refrigerator. I left the baby heads whole until we ate them, assuring freshness, just as Weber advised.

In my evolution as an organic consumer, an interest in food had brought me into this world, but I had kept moving. From Whole Foods, I branched out, buying direct from farmers, seeking more affordable products, then growing a small portion of my household's food supply. I didn't imagine myself a prototypical organic consumer, and yet I was. I parsed my consumption into venues high and low and off the grid, driven by freshness, idealism, personal relationships, shopping experience, price, quality, and convenience all at once. My choices, like most shoppers', lacked consistency and were not static, which is why retailers like Whole Foods had to keep shifting to keep my attention.

Given this consumer behavior, two things need to happen if the original organic vision of "changing agriculture" is going to play out. First, consumers unconvinced of the benefits of organic food will have to come into the fold. Second, those already buying organic food will have to buy more. Whether either development will take hold is an open question at this point.

The Food Marketing Institute found the number of consumers buying organic food has held steady for two years. Another market research outfit, the Natural Marketing Institute, reported the number of consumers *declined* in 2004, while industry revenues rose, suggesting core users offset customers lost at the fringe. Moreover, the FMI found about 70 percent of the population doesn't buy organic—about the same who cite price as a barrier—none of which is very promising news for the organic food revolution. Even within the core, the Hartman Group found that many consumers usually hit a wall and wouldn't buy endless amounts of new organic products.

This kind of finding is ammunition for the organic-growth camp, which wants to make organic food as accessible as possible to consumers. Its members thought this might mean making more familiar products—like an organic Twinkie. It didn't. They now think it means low prices. But this won't help, either, if the prices result from a diluted organic method that undermines the public's perception of the food. Clearing small farms out of the organic sector, rather than supporting them, would be ill-advised, too, since no one likes a bully pounding away at a founding segment of the movement. Survival-of-the-fittest tactics have led some consumers to question organic food—and could prompt them to look for a new label. The alternative, however, isn't simply small-scale purity, since shackling the food to a prescribed niche could lead to stagnation and even decline in an elitist or fringe market.

Both approaches, growth and purity, are necessary for the organic food industry to thrive. Growth cannot occur if the ideals become compromised, but the ideals can't come to fruition without growth. The approaches must be melded and balanced, perhaps in the way that Whole Foods meets its customers' conflicted needs, in the way that certain products merge a variety of attributes, or in the way that Senator Leahy envisioned the functioning of the NOSB. It's all about diversity, not monoculture. When the recent disputes engulfed the organic food industry George Siemon, the CEO of Organic Valley, said in a widely circulated e-mail, "I feel that it is crucial to all sit down and work through this and to let our love of organics be our guide, and not allow factions and sensationalism blur our past commitment to consensus." *Organic*, he said, was "about the parts making a whole." What he did not discuss was the alternative—a final splintering of the organic coalition—which could wreak more damage than the work of any supposed demons in the USDA or agribusiness.

The organic industry will grow, perhaps dramatically, if these disputes get worked out, organic food prices inch down, and aging baby boomers and young families raise consumption—all possibilities. Growing awareness of the risks of factory farming, along with studies on pesticides and nutrition, could have an impact. The expansion of suburbs into farming areas could be another factor, as conflicts flare over the environmental consequences of farming practices. Plus, organic food has barely entered the restaurant business, which accounts for nearly half of all food spending. Three regional natural and organic dining chains, Real Food Daily in Los Angeles, Organic To Go in Seattle, and O'Naturals in the Northeast, are just getting started. Will an aggregator similar to Whole Foods appear in a decade and gobble them up and go national? Who knows, there could even be another wild crossover success like organic soy milk in the industry's future.

The consumer research may look a bit bearish at the moment, but had the organic pioneers followed conventional wisdom, they would have never created the industry that exists today. Whole Foods never thought it would be as big as it is now, yet it currently aims to reach $10 billion in sales by 2010 (two and a half times bigger than in 2004). In Europe, where Whole Foods now has a beachhead, organic food accounts for 5 percent of food sales and there's a far higher awareness of issues such as humane animal treatment. As Europe's devastating experience with mad cow disease shows, food scares can rapidly modify buying patterns—which hasn't happened in the United States since the Alar scare in 1989.

Still, it's hard to imagine that organic food will ever become a "parallel food system," rather than a discrete set of products that people buy—more of a model of how farming and business can put values at the core of a mission, rather than a wholesale solution to all the ills of conventional agriculture.

Perhaps that's enough, because this model might motivate conventional growers to get into the game, like Tom Jones in his strawberry fields, Stan Pura in the lettuce patch, and an ever growing number of farmers seeking an alternative answer to their continuing economic plight. In 2005, to support a fading rural community, Woodbury County, Iowa, in the corn belt, even rolled out tax rebates to farmers transitioning to organic methods. As this kind of measure gains traction, organic farming could move well beyond a niche. The result might not be what the pioneers envisioned, or rigorous enough for the purists, or expansive enough for the growth camp, or motivated by all the right ideals, but maybe that's all right.

It's not a revolution, but it'll do.

Acknowledgments

Narratives begin with conversations, going over old ground, filling in gaps, hearing stories, and then following up on details that seem curious and that open up new worlds. This book would not have been possible without the participation of Jim Cochran, Jim and Moie Crawford, Drew and Myra Goodman, and Steve Demos in that conversation. They answered all my questions about their businesses, on the record, over a period of two years. I thank them. Others proved crucial, especially Tom Jones and Steven Gliessman in organic strawberries; Jack Hedin and Chris Fullerton on local food networks and small farms; Dale Coke, Warren Weber, Todd Koons, Stan Pura, and Amigo Bob Cantisano in organic spring mix; and in soy foods, Jeremiah Ridenour, Ted Nordquist, and Peter Golbitz.

I would not have been able to navigate the thicket of organic regulations without the help of Katherine DiMatteo of the Organic Trade Association, and Arthur Harvey, both of whom talked with me extensively. Lynn Coody, Kathleen Merrigan, Fred Kirschenmann, Michael Sligh, Bob Scowcroft, Mark Lipson, Urvashi Rangan, George Siemon, Gary Hirshberg, Dr. Hubert Karreman, Mark Retzloff, and the Northeast Organic Dairy Producers Alliance also helped immensely.

Harvey Hartman sent me volumes of consumer research; Michael Straus provided a sounding board on the organic food industry. Anne and Eric Nordell helped me to understand the complexity of an organic farm. Anthony Rodale, Joan Gussow, Brian Halweil, Judith Redmond, Paul Muller, Tim Mueller, Andy Powning, Laura Tourte, Karen Klonsky, John Dunaway, Isaac Cronin, Jim Wedeberg, Theresa Marquez, Joe Pedretti, William Brinton, Emily Brown Rosen, Rick Christianson, Edward Brown, Susan Kegley, Peggy Miars, Sonja Tuitele, Heinz Thomet, Ann Yonkers, Bernadine Prince, Nora Pouillon, Georgeanne Brennan, and Sibella Kraus helped out too. At the USDA, Frank Martin, Thomas Trout, Carolee Bull, Mark Bolda, Jon Wicke, and Kathy Soder educated me on everything from soil diseases to range conservation.

Max Holland, Gene Santoro, and Stephen Hall offered advice and suggestions throughout, as did former Reuters colleagues Roger Fillion, Roger Atwood, Dick Satran, and Dan Grebler. Michael Pollan and Eric Schlosser provided the models, Mas Masumoto the wisdom, and Ken Auletta the spark to get going.

Amigo Bob, Lynn Coody, Barbara Graham, Josh Hyatt, Kathleen Merrigan, Natan Margalit, Sean Swezey, Stephen Hall, and Bob Scowcroft reviewed chapters. James Riddle helped with my descriptions of the organic regulations. I owe them all a debt, though any remaining errors are my own.

I would not have been able to accomplish my reporting on the central coast of California if not for Katherine Beiers, who graciously opened her Santa Cruz home to me for several long visits. Tom Bruenig and Tomi Obayashi let me stay at their house in Berkeley; their son Toby gave me his room. Jack Hedin and Jenni McHugh, and Charles and Jane Niemeyer, put me up in Minnesota; so did Jody, Ann, and Henry Chafee in Seattle; and the Crawfords on their farm.

Among the many people I interviewed but who do not appear in this book is Dan Barber of New York's Blue Hill. He offered a chef's view of sustainable agriculture, waxed poetic about his pigs and the organic vegetable gardens at the Stone Barns Center for Food and Agriculture, and tossed off a few cooking tips while serving me a superlative dinner in his busy restaurant kitchen. I thank him and the many others who spent time with me.

The themes in this book began with discussions with my friend John Sheehy, though I had no clue that they would lead to this book. John also read every chapter closely, providing helpful suggestions. My agent, Denise Shannon, helped shape the idea for this book out of a half-baked proposal, then hustled like mad to sell it. Rebecca Saletan, my editor at Harcourt, got the idea instantly, then waited patiently as the deadline passed, finally marshaling the manuscript to completion. Her assistant, Stacia Decker, marked up an early draft with prescient questions, no doubt informed by her formative years on a Kansas wheat farm.

A special thanks to my family and supporters throughout this project—especially Mitzi Sawada and Pat Vidil, Lisa Fromartz and Ron Hunnings, the Chafees, Sarah Neimeyer and Joe Warren, Jovi Munoz, and Sean Jones and Kristen Beiers-Jones, who helped out in more ways than they know. My father Bernard Fromartz passed away before the book was done but his influence, I hope, is evident in its pages. Finally, I could not imagine having written this book without my wife, Ellen, who prodded me on, read through many drafts, provided much-needed perspective, and ran our life when I was in way too deep. In the final stages, she and our daughter Nina always reminded me how to laugh.

Notes

When I began researching this book, several works proved indispensable for my understanding of American agricultural history. Although they do not all show up in the body of the book, they helped to frame it. These include Allan Kulikoff's *From British Peasants to Colonial American Farmers*, Steven Stoll's *Fruits Of Natural Advantage: Making the Industrial Countryside in California* and his more recent *Larding the Lean Earth: Soil and Society in Nineteenth-Century America*, John Fraser Hart's *The Land That Feeds Us*, Henry Nash Smith's *Virgin Land: The American West as Symbol and Myth*, Carolyn Merchant's *Major Problems in American Environmental History*, Jack McLaughlin's *Jefferson and Monticello: The Biography of a Builder*, and Thomas Jefferson's *Notes on the State of Virginia*.

A thorough history of organic food and farming has yet to be written, but a number of works help fill in the gap, such as Philip Conford's *The Origins of the Organic Movement*, primarily focusing on the British roots of the movement. Major source works I turned to are E. B. Balfour's *The Living Soil and the Haughley Experiment*, Albert Howard's *An Agricultural Testament*, Robert McCarrisson's "The Cantor Lectures," and various works by J. I. Rodale. Julie Guthman's *Agrarian Dreams: The Paradox of Organic Farming in California* is the most thorough work on organic farming in America, seen through the lens of the California experience. Michael Pollan's article "Naturally: Behind the Organic-Industrial Complex" in the *New York Times Magazine* (May 13, 2001) framed the current conflicts, and Warren James Belasco's *Appetite for Change: How the Counterculture Took on the Food Industry* located their roots in the 1960s and 1970s. Three other sources proved indispensable:

the California Certified Organic Farmers' *Certified Organic* magazine, *Natural Food Merchandiser*, and Rodale Institute's NewFarm.org Web site.

Andrew Kimbrell's *The Fatal Harvest Reader: The Tragedy of Industrial Agriculture* proved useful as an overview of the critique of conventional agriculture, as did Wendell Berry's classic *The Unsettling of America: Culture and Agriculture*. My understanding of pesticides and regulations was helped immensely by John Wargo's *Our Children's Toxic Legacy: How Science and Law Fail to Protect Us from Pesticides*.

I interviewed the main subjects in this book on multiple occasions, in person or on the telephone and by e-mail. The reader can assume quotes and narrative histories of the main profile subjects came from my interviews with the subjects, unless otherwise noted. When I rely on a quote that appeared in a published book or article, I provide the source. The Web links for documents in these notes were accurate as of mid-2005. The financial information from the private companies in the book were provided by the company owners.

Introduction

x **As a tax resister** . . . For Harvey's IRS fight, see Aaron Falbel, "War Tax Resistance and Blueberry Fields Forever," *Nonviolent Activist*, September–October 1996, and Aaron Gallegos and Julienne Gage, "Between the Lines: The Blueberry Tax," *Sojourners*, September–October 1996.

xii **Craig Weakley** . . . Weakley's comments at National Organic Standards Board meeting, March 1, 2005, Washington, D.C.

"If this goes through . . ." DiMatteo quoted in Lisa Everitt, "Plot Thickens in NOP Challenge," *Natural Food Merchandiser*, April 1, 2005.

xvii **reaching $11 billion** . . . the Organic Trade Association, "The OTA 2004 Manufacturing Survey Overview," May 2004, http://www .ota.com/pics/documents/2004SurveyOverview.pdf. Supermarket sales figures from Food Marketing Institute, http://www.fmi.org/facts_figs/superfact.htm.

xx **But for an industry accounting** . . . For figures on organic acreage and farms, see Helga Willer and Minou Yussefi, editors, "The

World of Organic Agriculture Statistics and Emerging Trends 2005," International Federation of Organic Agriculture Movements, p. 11, and Jane Sooby, introduction to "State of the States 2nd Edition: Organic Farming Systems Research at Land Grant Institutions 2001–2003," Organic Farming Research Foundation, Santa Cruz, Calif., 2003, xii.

1. Humus Worshippers: The Origins of Organic Food

1 ***organophosphates, a class of chemicals*** . . . See Environmental Protection Agency, "Organophosphate Pesticides in Food—A Primer on Reassessment of Residue Limits," May 1999, http://www.epa.gov/oppsrrd1/op/primer.htm. See also John Wargo, *Our Children's Toxic Legacy: How Science and Law Fail to Protect Us From Pesticides* (New Haven, Conn: Yale University Press, 1998), 236–238.

2 ***But the 110*** . . . See Chensheng Lu, and others. "Biological Monitoring Survey of Organophosphate Pesticide Exposure among Preschool Children in the Seattle Metropolitan Area," *Environmental Health Perspectives* 109, no. 3 (March 2001). The researchers theorized that urban children had higher metabolites because the rural children were not tested during days of pesticide spraying and because the urban children consumed more fruit and fruit juices. See Richard A. Fenske and others. "Biologic Monitoring to Characterize Organophosphorus Pesticide Exposure among Children and Workers: An Analysis of Recent Studies in Washington State," *Environmental Health Perspectives* 113, no. 11 (November 2005).

Another study . . . See Brian P. Baker, and others. "Pesticide Residues in Conventional, IPM-Grown and Organic foods: Insights from Three U.S. Data Sets," *Food Additives and Contaminants* 19, no. 5 (May 2002).

The study only concluded . . . See Cynthia L. Curl, and others. "Organophosphorus Pesticide Exposure of Urban and Suburban Preschool Children with Organic and Conventional Diets," *Environmental Health Perspectives* 111, no. 3 (March 2003). EPA sets a tolerance, or maximum residue limit for pesticides, which is the amount of pesticide residue that may lawfully remain in each food commodity that has been treated with a pesticide.

3 **When a research team** . . . See Chensheng Lu, and others. "Organic Diets Significantly Lower Children's Dietary Exposure to Organophosphorus Pesticides," *Environmental Health Perspectives*, published online, September 1, 2005, http://ehp.niehs.nih.gov/members/2005/8418/8418.pdf.

Chemicals are up to ten times . . . See National Academy of Sciences, *Pesticides in the Diets of Infants and Children* (Washington, D.C.: National Academy Press, 1993), 3. See also Wargo, *Our Children's Toxic Legacy*, 206. Infants also eat ten times more peaches and seven times more apples than the U.S. average—both of which rank high in pesticide residues. See also, Center for Children's Health and the Environment, "Regulating Pesticides in Food," Mount Sinai School of Medicine, http://www.childenvironment.org/factsheets/pesticides_in_food.htm.

4 **largely women** . . . For the primacy of female purchasing decisions, see Paco Underhill, *Why We Buy: The Science of Shopping* (New York: Touchstone, 1999), chap. 9.

This became apparent in 1989 . . . Alar also became for industry-backed groups an oft-cited example of unsubstantiated fear mongering, though its risks have been established. See Elliott Negin, "The Alar Scare Was for Real," *Columbia Journalism Review*, September/October 1996.

5 **In late 2003** . . . See Shankar Vedantam, "Ban on Meat from 'Downers' Grows," *The Washington Post*, January 27, 2004; Joseph Hallinan, "Cattle Feed Comes Under Scrutiny," *Wall Street Journal*, December 31, 2003.

organic meat sales jumped 78 percent . . . See Organic Trade Association, "The OTA 2004 Survey."

a third of American women . . . See Roper Public Affairs, "Farming and Food 2004," survey for Organic Valley Family of Farms, April 30, 2004, http://organicvalley.coop/pdf/roper_survey.pdf.

6 **"Consumers don't just** . . ."* William Lockeretz and Kathleen Merrigan, "Selling to the Eco-conscious Food Shopper," *Nutrition Today* 40, no. 1 (January/February 2005).

a third of the $29 billion . . . Food Advertising expenditures from

USDA ERS agricultural economist Howard Elitzak, e-mail communication, June 13, 2005.

7 *As British historian* . . . Philip Conford, *The Origins of the Organic Movement* (Edinburgh: Floris Books, 2002), 20.

"Organic matters . . ." Steven Stoll, *Larding the Lean Earth: Soil and Society in Nineteenth-Century America* (New York: Hill and Wang, 2002), 152.

8 *the predominant method* . . . See ibid., chap. 2; also colonial readings in Carolyn Merchant, *Major Problems in American Environmental History* (Lexington, Mass.: D. C. Heath & Co., 1993).

9 *"The maintenance of soil fertility* . . ." Albert Howard, *An Agricultural Testament* (London: Oxford University Press, 1943); chapter 4 provides a detailed description of the Indore method of composting.

11 *Biodynamic farmers* . . . See Biodynamic Farming and Gardening Association, http://www.biodynamics.com/products.html. The biodynamic preparations are described in Peter Tompkins and Christopher Bird, *Secrets of the Soil* (Anchorage: Earthpulse Press, 1998), chap. 1.

12 *by the time he left India* . . . see Conford, *Origins,* 82–87.

13 *the Hunza* . . . See Conford, *Origins,* 50–53, also J. I. Rodale, *The Healthy Hunzas* (Emmaus, Pa.: Rodale Press, 1948); Guy Theodore Wrench, *The Wheel of Health* (New York: Schocken Books, 1972); Homayun Sidky, *Hunza, an Ethnographic Outline* (Jaipur: Illustrated Book Publishers, 1995).

14 *McCarrison decided to compare* . . . Sir Robert McCarrison, "The Cantor Lectures," *Nutrition and Health,* published by the McCarrison Society at http://www.nutritionhealth.org/book.htm.

15 *Such mythical views* . . . See Donald S. Lopez, *Prisoners of Shangri-La: Tibetan Buddhism and the West* (Chicago: University of Chicago Press, 1998), 6.

Agatston came upon his diet . . . See Arthur Agatston, *The South Beach Diet* (New York: Rodale Press, 2003), 61–68.

16 *A diet of high-fiber foods* . . . See Harvard School of Public Health, http://www.hsph.harvard.edu/nutritionsource/index.html, also Bonnie Liebman, "The Whole Grain Guide," *Nutrition Action Health Letter,* March 1997, http://www.cspinet.org/nah/wwheat.html.

Reinvigorating the small farmer . . . See Conford, *Origins,* chap. 7.

17 *In the 1930s . . . a virulent fascist right* . . . See ibid., chap. 8.

Terry Nichols . . . See David Jackson, "Portrait Of A Federal Foe," *Chicago Tribune,* May 11, 1995, and Michael Moore, director, *Bowling for Columbine,* 2002.

18 *"salubrious living . . ."* For the doctrine of salubrious living, see http://www.Rahowa.com.

Southern Poverty Law Center . . . See Mark Potok, "Neither Left Nor Right," *Intelligence Report* 97 (Winter 2000), Southern Poverty Law Center, http://www.splcenter.org/intel/intelreport/article .jsp?pid=516.

19 *"I had been mildly health-conscious . . ."* See J. I. Rodale, *The Healthy Hunzas* (Emmaus, Pa.: Rodale Press, 1948), 31.

His predecessors included . . . See Jane Potter Gates, "Tracing the Evolution of Organic/Sustainable Agriculture," National Agricultural Library, November 1988. This bibliography also notes the origins of the phrase "organic" farming. See http://www.nal.usda .gov/afsic/AFSIC_pubs/tracing.htm.

20 *Rodale likened chemical fertilizers* . . . For biographic details, see J. I. Rodale, *Autobiography* (Emmaus, Pa.: Rodale Press, 1965); Carlton Jackson, *J. I. Rodale: Apostle of Nonconformity* (New York: Pyramid Books, 1974); and Wade Greene, "Guru of the Organic Food Cult," *New York Times Magazine,* June 6, 1971.

21 *"Sounds From the Seed-Power Sitar . . ."* See Warren J. Belasco, *Appetite for Change: How the Counter-Culture Took on the Food Industry* (Ithaca: Cornell University Press, 1993), chap. 1.

22 *"Rising concern . . ."* See Gladwin Hill, "Environment May Eclipse Vietnam as Campus Issue," *New York Times,* November 30, 1969.

"The more we strive . . ." See Garrett De Bell, editor, *The Environmental Handbook: Prepared for the First National Environmental Teach-In* (New York: Ballantine Books, 1977), 153.

avoid "anything complex . . ." Belasco, *Appetite for Change,* 57.

The Whole Earth Catalog . . . See Greene, "Guru of the Organic Food Cult."

23 *Food co-ops had* . . . Daniel Zwerdling, "The Uncertain Revival of Food Co-Ops," in *Co-ops, Communes & Collectives: Experiments in Social Change in the 1960s and 1970s,* edited by John Case and Rosemary C. R. Taylor (New York: Pantheon, 1979).

"Massive scale and centralization . . ." Amanda Griscom, "Pauling Around: A Wide Ranging Interview with Environmental Visionary Paul Hawken," *Grist,* February 18, 2004, http://www.grist.org/news/maindish/2004/02/18/pauling.

"food additives are like friends . . ." See Belasco, *Appetite for Change,* chap. 5.

24 **Earl Butz** . . . Ibid., chap. 5. Butz more famously said, in 1976: "I'll tell you what the coloreds want. It's three things: first, a tight pussy; second, loose shoes; and third, a warm place to shit." He was forced to resign his cabinet post.

claim that manure and compost . . . John Stossel, co-anchor of ABC's *20/20,* in August 2000 issued an on-air apology for misrepresenting evidence in a report that claimed organic produce was more dangerous than conventional produce, and was suspended by ABC for one month without pay. Yet these claims still appear, primarily from Dennis Avery of the Hudson Institute's Center for Global Food Issues; see http://www.cgfi.org. See Jim Rutenberg, "ABC Reprimands Reporter Over Organic Food Report," *New York Times,* August 10, 2000; Jim Rutenberg and Felicity Barringer, "Apology Highlights ABC Reporter's Contrarian Image," *New York Times,* August 14, 2000; Brian Halweil, "Cultivating the Truth about Organics and John Stossel's Lies," *San Francisco Chronicle,* August 21, 2000.

350 million tons . . . See Marc Ribaudo et al., "Manure Management for Water Quality: Costs to Animal Feeding Operations of Applying Manure Nutrients to Land," USDA Economic Research Service, iii and 5, for the increase in animal density.

an eight-acre manure lagoon . . . Manure-spill information from EPA, Office of Inspector General, "Animal Waste Disposal Issues," chap. 1, http://www.epa.gov/oig/reports/1997/hogchp1.htm.

the subject of new EPA regulations . . . See EPA National Pollutant Discharge Elimination System, "CAFO Final Rule," December 15, 2002, http://cfpub.epa.gov/npdes/afo/cafofinalrule.cfm.

Under organic rules, raw manure . . . See USDA Organic Regulations manure standards, section 205.203, "Soil fertility and crop nutrient management practice standard," http://www.ams.usda.gov/nop/NOP/standards/ProdHandReg.html.

Municipal sewage sludge . . . See Jennifer 8. Lee, "Sludge Spread on Fields is Fodder for Lawsuits," *New York Times,* June 26, 2003.

25 *compost is safe* . . . See Sharon Durham, "Composting: Improving On a Time-Tested Technique," *Agricultural Research,* USDA Agricultural Research Service, August 2003; for the University of Minnesota study, see A. Mukherjee, and others. "Preharvest Evaluation of Coliforms, *Escherichia coli, Salmonella, and Escherichia coli* O157:H7 in Organic and Conventional Produce Grown by Minnesota Farmers," *Journal of Food Protection* 67, no. 5 (May 1, 2004): 894–900.

NAS . . . See National Research Council, *Alternative Agriculture* (Washington, D.C.: National Academy Press, 1989), chap. 2; for another discussion of fertilizer runoff see, EPA, "Mississippi River Basin Callenges: Hypoxia," http://www.epa.gov/msbasin/hyp1.htm

associated with bladder and ovarian cancers . . . See P. J. Weyer, and others. "Municipal Drinking Water Nitrate Level and Cancer Risk in Older Women: The Iowa Women's Health Study," *Epidemiology* 11, no. 3 (May 2001): 327–338. For a report on the colon-cancer study, see Amy Norton, "Nitrate in Water Tied to Colon Cancer Risk in Some," *Reuters Health,* November 27, 2003.

26 *may result in lower yields* . . . A 1990 analysis of 205 farm studies found organic farming yields were on average 10 percent below conventional methods. See G. Stanhill, "The Comparative Productivity of Organic Agriculture," *Agriculture, Ecosystems and Environment* 20 (1990): 1–26. Several U.S. university field trials of organic corn and soybeans have reached 94 to 97 percent of conventional yields. See Bill Liebhardt, "Get the Facts Straight: Organic Agriculture Yields Are Good," *Organic Farming Research Foundation Information Bulletin,* no. 10, Summer 2001. A study of twenty-two years of field comparisons at the Rodale Institute found no difference in organic and conventional yields for corn and soybeans but did find that organic yields were 22 percent higher during droughts. See David Pimentel, and others. "Environmental, Energetic, and Economic Comparisons of Organic and Conventional Farming Systems," *BioScience* 55, no. 7 (July 2005): 573–582.

a Swiss study . . . See Paul Mäder, and others. "Soil Fertility and

Biodiversity in Organic Farming," *Science* 296, no. 5573 (May 31, 2002): 1694–1697. Energy data from Danielle Murray, "Oil and Food: A Rising Security Challenge," Earth Policy Institute, May 9, 2005. For Robertson's remarks, see Erik Stokstad, "Organic Farms Reap Many Benefits," *Science* 296, no. 5573 (May 31, 2002): 3–4.

"Guru . . ." See Greene, "Guru of the Organic Food Cult."

27 *Britain's Soil Association* . . . Shane Heaton, "Organic Farming, Food Quality and Human Health: A Review of the Evidence," Soil Association, 2001.

30 *To hold a similar view today* . . . See Marion Nestle, "In Praise of the Organic Environment," *Global Agenda*, World Economic Forum, Davos, 2005, http://www.globalagendamagazine.com/2005/marionnestle.asp.

2. The Organic Method: Strawberries in Two Versions

32 *An organic farm* . . . Berry, Wendell, *The Gift of Good Land: Further Essays Cultural and Agricultural* (New York: North Point Press, 1982), 143–144.

33 *When the USDA tested* . . . USDA, "Pesticide Data Program: Annual Summary Calendar Year 2000," Agriculture Marketing Service, Science and Technology, 14, table 2, and appendixes J and L, http://www.ams.usda.gov/science/pdp/download.htm.

ranking fifth . . . California Department of Pesticide Regulation (DPR), "Pesticide Use Report," October 2003. See also Environmental Working Group analysis of pesticide residues at http://www.foodnews.org.

about 15 to 20 percent . . . Based on author interviews with several farmers who have grown both conventional and organic strawberries.

38 *Over several years* . . . See Steven T. Koike and Krishna V. Subbarao, "Broccoli Residues Can Control Verticillium Wilt of Cauliflower," *California Agriculture* 54, no. 3; also Krishna V. Subbarao and J. C. Hubbard, "Interactive Effects of Broccoli Residue and Temperature on Verticillium dahliae Microsclerotia in Soil and on Wilt in Cauliflower," *Phytopathology* 86, no. 12 (1996).

a single gram of soil . . . See University of Michigan, Center for Microbial Ecology, http://commtechlab.msu.edu/sites/dlc-me/zoo/zdmain.html.

39 *A 1997–1998 survey* . . . Erica Walz, "Third Biennial National Organic Farmers' Survey Results," Organic Farming Research Foundation, 1999, 77–80. For a discussion of organic insecticides, see also Brian Baker, and others. "Organic Farming Compliance Handbook: A Resource Guide for Western Region Agricultural Professionals," "Materials Used in Organic Farming," http://www.sarep.ucdavis.edu/organic/complianceguide/.

40 *Even humans who ingested* . . . For toxicology background on these substances, see National Pesticide Telecommunications Network fact sheets, http://npic.orst.edu/npicfact.htm.

A study published in 2003 . . . Danny K. Asami, and others. "Comparison of the total phenolic and ascorbic acid content of freeze-dried and air-dried marionberry, strawberry, and corn grown using conventional, organic, and sustainable agricultural practices," *Journal of Agricultural and Food Chemistry* 51, no. 5 (2003): 1237–1241. See also Alyson E. Mitchell and Alexander W. Chassy, "Antioxidants and the Nutritional Quality of Organic Agriculture," FAQ at http://mitchell.ucdavis.edu; see also Charles Benbrook, "Elevating Antioxidant Levels in Food through Organic Farming and Food Processing," The Organic Center for Education and Promotion, January 2005.

41 *"Some of the soil* . . ." Mary-Howell Martens, "Letter from New York: Why We Certify," NewFarm.org, Oct. 24, 2003.

As Gliessman writes . . . Stephen R. Gliessman, *Agroecology: Ecological Processes in Sustainable Agriculture* (Chelsea, Mich.: Ann Arbor Press, 1998), preface and chap. 1.

43 *The team reported* . . . Stephen R. Gliessman, and others. "Strawberry Production Systems During Conversion to Organic Management," *California Agriculture* 44, no. 4 (July–August 1990).

44 *"Growers face an urgent* . . ." See James M. Lyons and Frank G. Zalom, "Progress Report: Vice President's Task Force on Pest Control Alternatives"; Michael W. Stimmann and Mary P. Ferguson, "Potential Pesticide Use Cancellations in California"; Mary Louise Flint, "The Research Imperatives: Knowledge to Reduce

the Use of Broadly Toxic Pesticides," *California Agriculture* 44, no. 4 (July–August 1990).

Gliessman's next article . . . Stephen R. Gliessman, and others. "Conversion to Organic Strawberry Management Changes Ecological Processes," *California Agriculture* 50, no. 1 (January–February 1996).

45 *it took until 2004* . . . For Gliessman grant information, see UC Santa Cruz Currents Online, http://currents.ucsc.edu/04-05/09-06/usda.html.

While land used for organic research . . . Jane Sooby, "State of the States 2nd Edition: Organic Farming Systems Research at Land Grant Institutions 2001–2003," Organic Farming Research Foundation, Santa Cruz, California, 2003, Executive Summary.

The roughly $8.5 million . . . Estimated by Brise Tencer, Legislative Coordinator, Organic Farming Research Foundation, e-mail communication, July 5, 2005.

46 *First appearing in* . . . Historical material from George M. Darrow, *The Strawberry: History, Breeding, and Physiology* (New York: Holt, Rinehart and Winston, 1966). History of the California strawberry industry from Stephen Wilhelm and James E. Sagen, *A History of the Strawberry: From Ancient Gardens to Modern Markets*, University of California, Berkeley, Division of Agricultural Sciences, 1974, appendix, "The California Strawberry Industry."

"The strawberry grows . . ." William Shakespeare, *King Henry V*, act 1, scene 1.

48 *From 1810 to 1942, close to 570 species* . . . See Steven Stoll, *The Fruits of Natural Advantage: Making the Industrial Countryside in California* (Berkeley: University of California Press, 1998), 99.

Today, entomologists estimate . . . See Janet White, "Exotic Pest Research Goes High-Tech," *California Agriculture*, 55, no. 2 (March–April 2001).

Globally, pests . . . Wargo, *Our Children's Toxic Legacy*, 6.

49 *annual use of 5.6 billion pounds* . . . For pesticide-use data, see EPA, "Pesticide Market Estimates: Usage, 1998–1999," http://www.epa.gov/oppbead1/pestsales.

Stoll tells a prophetic story . . . Stoll, *Fruits of Natural Advantage*, 105–107.

50 *The nation's first pesticide law* . . . Ibid., 107–112.
    Lead arsenate . . . Wargo, *Our Children's Toxic Legacy*, 68.
    For much of the last century . . . See ibid., chap. 2.
    For humans, DDT . . . See Agency for Toxic Substances and Disease Registry, *Toxicological Profile for DDT, DDE, and DDD*, chap. 2, "Relevance to Public Health," September 2002, http://www.atsdr.cdc.gov/toxprofiles/tp35.html.

51 *Between 1993 and 2003* . . . John S. Punzi, Martha Lamont, Diana Haynes, and Robert L. Epstein, "USDA Pesticide Data Program: Pesticide Residues on Fresh and Processed Fruit and Vegetables, Grains, Meats, Milk and Drinking Water," USDA Agricultural Marketing Service, Science and Technology Programs, Monitoring Programs Office, *Outlooks on Pest Management*, June 2005, 135.
    Cornell University entomologist . . . David Pimentel, "Environment and Economic Costs of Pesticide Use," *BioScience*, November 1992, 750–760, and e-mail communication with Dr. Pimentel.
    The NAS counted . . . NRC, *Alternative Agriculture*, 121–127.
    An international survey . . . International Survey of Herbicide Resistant Weeds, http://www.weedscience.org.
    The adoption of genetically engineered . . . See Charles M. Benbrook, "Genetically Engineered Crops and Pesticide Use in the United States: The First Nine Years," BioTech InfoNet, technical paper no. 7, October 2004, http://www.biotech-info.net/technicalpaper7.html.

52 *The strawberry industry* . . . Historical background from Stephen Wilhelm and Albert O. Paulus, "How Soil Fumigation Benefits the California Strawberry Industry," *Plant Disease* 64 (1980), 264–270, and from Wilhelm and Sagen, *History of the Strawberry*, appendix, "The California Strawberry Industry."

53 *Before fumigation* . . . See Wilhelm and Paulus, "How Soil Fumigation Benefits."

54 *It hit thirty-nine* . . . See USDA Economic Research Service, "The U.S. Strawberry Industry, 1970–2004," data files, February 2004, http://www.ers.usda.gov/Data/sdp/view.asp?f=specialty/95003/. See also Miriam J. Wells, *Strawberry Fields: Politics, Class and Work in California Agriculture* (Ithaca, NY: Cornell University Press, 1996), 29.
    A University of California Cooperative Extension report . . . See

Karen M. Klonsky and Richard L. De Moura, "Sample Costs to Produce Fresh Market Strawberries, Central Coast, Monterey— Santa Cruz Counties," University of California Cooperative Extension, table 6, "Ranging Analysis."

In 2002, growers . . . See DPR, "Summary of Pesticide Use Report Data, 2002, Indexed by Commodity," California Environmental Protection Agency, 77, 324–329. For this and other DPR pesticide-use data, see http://www.cdpr.ca.gov/docs/pur/pur02rep/02_pur.htm.

In Monterey County . . . DPR, "Table of top five pesticides used in each county in 2002," California Environmental Protection Agency, 17.

55 *People have died* . . . See Lori O. Lim, *Methyl Bromide Risk Characterization Document,* vol. 1, *Inhalation Exposure,* Medical Toxicology, Worker Health and Safety, and Environmental Monitoring and Pest Management Branches, Department of Pesticide Regulation, California Environmental Protection Agency, February 14, 2002, 24, http://www.cdpr.ca.gov/docs/dprdocs/methbrom/riskasses_fum.htm.

Farmworkers have been hospitalized . . . Ibid., appendix F, "Estimation of Exposure of Persons to Methyl Bromide," 16–19.

It does not cling to food . . . Ibid., 29. While ground fumigation does not pose a risk, postharvest treatments of foods can leave detectable methyl bromide residues. These dietary exposures have been highest for children one through six years old. However, DPR estimates their exposures would have to increase nearly a thousandfold to be of concern. See also Lori O. Lim, *Methyl Bromide Risk Characterization Document,* vol. 2, *Dietary Exposure,* Medical Toxicology, Worker Health and Safety, and Environmental Monitoring and Pest Management Branches, Department of Pesticide Regulation, California Environmental Protection Agency, February 21, 2002, 22–23, http://www.cdpr.ca.gov/docs/dprdocs/methbrom/riskasses_fum.htm.

as methyl bromide rises . . . See Center for International Earth Science Information Network, Columbia University, http://sedac.ciesin.columbia.edu/ozone/UNEP/chap2.html.

Since the bromine atoms . . . See James H. Butler, "Methyl Bromide Under Scrutiny," *Nature* 376, August 10, 1995.

56 *the opening page* . . . Lim, *Methyl Bromide Risk,* vol. 1, 1.
the concentration . . . Ibid., 19.
By 2004, the DPR had mandated . . . DPR, regulation 03-004, *Text of Final Regulations,* chap. 2, "Pesticides"; subchap. 4, "Restricted Materials"; article 4, "Use Requirements," November 3, 2004, http://www.cdpr.ca.gov/docs/dprdocs/methbrom/seas_expos.htm.

57 *Drifting pesticides* . . . Susan Kegley, Anne Katten, and Marion Moses, *Secondhand Pesticides: Airborne Pesticide Drift in California,* Californians for Pesticide Reform, 2003, 8, http://www.panna.org/resources/documents/secondhandDriftAvail.dv.html.

58 *the DPR relied on* . . . See Lim, *Methyl Bromide,* vol. 1, 4–10; DPR, "DPR Plans More Restrictions on Methyl Bromide Use," press release, September 18, 2003, http://www.cdpr.ca.gov/docs/pressrls/september18.htm.
the school had an average . . . DPR, "Methyl Bromide Subchronic Exposure: Analysis of Data and Risk Management Options," table 2, "Monitored average air concentration and weekly reported methyl bromide use in Kern, Monterey and Santa Cruz," May 21, 2001, http://www.cdpr.ca.gov/docs/dprdocs/methbrom/sub_exp.pdf.
When the test results . . . See Noam Levey, "Pesticide Near Schools Raises Concern," *San Jose Mercury News,* October 14, 2002; Trina Kleist, "Pesticide Fears Fanned After School Tests Find Unacceptable Levels of Methyl Bromide," *Santa Cruz Sentinel,* February 16, 2001.
The Pajaro Valley Unified School District . . . Governing Board of the Pajaro Valley Unified School District, "Resolution in Support of Prompt Analysis and Final Reporting of Methyl Bromide Study," resolution no. 20-01-29, March 28, 2001.

59 *"methyl bromide use should not exceed* . . .*"* DPR, "Methyl Bromide Sub-Chronic Exposure: Analysis of Data and Risk Management Options," May 21, 2001; see also Kegley, Katten, and Moses, *Secondhand Pesticides,* 27; Levey, "Pesticide Near Schools"; DPR, "DPR Plans More Restrictions on Methyl Bromide," press release, September 18, 2003.
Working with a farmworker advocacy group . . . Kegley et al., *Secondhand Pesticides,* 49.

60 *The industry-backed scientists predictably* . . . For the discussions of this assessment, see Lori O. Lim, "Methyl Bromide Risk Char-

acterization Document, Inhalation Exposure, Addendum to Volume 1," February 3, 2003; and its "Appendix E: Selection of Critical NOEL for Methyl Bromide Subchronic Inhalation Toxicity," September 30, 2002, 75–79, http://www.cdpr.ca.gov/docs/dprdocs/methbrom/rafnl/addendum.pdf; and for outside reviewer's opinions and DPR response, see Lori O. Lim, "Response to Comments from Methyl Bromide Subchronic Regulatory Level Workshop on February 26, 2003," memo to Gary Petterson, Supervising Toxicologist, Medical Toxicology Branch, DPR, May 1, 2003, http://www.cdpr.ca.gov/docs/dprdocs/methbrom/docs/wrkshp0203.pdf.

fifty-one other townships . . . Forty-five of these townships . . . One township in Ventura County . . . See Lin Ying Li, associate environmental research scientist, "Evaluation of Ambient Air Monitoring Conducted by the Alliance of the Methyl Bromide Industry in Ventura and Monterey/Santa Cruz Counties in 2002," memo to Randy Segawa, senior environmental research scientist, Environmental Monitoring Branch, DPR, February 19, 2004, http://www.cdpr.ca.gov/docs/dprdocs/methbrom/04_subseas/040219mbr.pdf. Bruce Johnson and Lin Ying Li, "Calculation of a Tolerance Interval for a Township Limit on Methyl Bromide Use to Control Subchronic Exposure," memo to Randy Segawa, senior environmental research scientist, environmental monitoring branch, DPR, July 11, 2003 http://www.cdpr.ca.gov/docs/dprdocs/methbrom/docs/mebr_tolerance_cap.pdf; DPR, "More Restrictions," press release, September 18, 2003.

61 *an epidemiological study of fifty-five thousand farmers* . . . National Cancer Institute, "Agricultural Pesticide Use May Be Associated with Increased Risk of Prostate Cancer," press release, May 1, 2003, http://www.cancer.gov/newscenter/pressreleases/AgricultureHealthStudy. See also, Agricultural Health Study, "Prostate Cancer and Agricultural Pesticides: Risk of Prostate Cancer Increases with Frequent Use of Methyl Bromide," 2003, http://www.aghealth.org.

62 *the state ended the ban* . . . Paul Jacobs, "Regulators OK Use of 2 Banned Pesticides," *Los Angeles Times,* January 16, 1995.

63 *including an incident in 1999* . . . *Secondhand Pesticides,* 15. *Methyl iodide* . . . Ibid., 33–34.

The United States ranked . . . USDA Economic Research Service, "The U.S. Strawberry Industry," data files, February 2004.

64 *the Netherlands had banned* . . . Adolf L. Braun and David M. Supkoff, "Options to Methyl Bromide for the Control of Soil-Borne Diseases and Pests in California with Reference to the Netherlands," Pest Management Analysis and Planning Program, California Department of Environmental Protection, July 1994.

"Many farmers . . ." Margot Wallstrom quoted in Andrew C. Revkin, "At Meetings, U.S. to Seek Support for Broad Ozone Exemptions," *New York Times,* November 10, 2003.

Washington fought hard . . . Environmental News Service, "Global Methyl Bromide Exemptions Over 13,000 tons," March 29, 2004, http://www.ens-newswire.com/ens/mar2004/2004-03-29-04.asp.

65 *Four-fifths of U.S. farmworkers* . . . See Alicia Burgarin and Elias Lopez, "Farmworkers in California," California Research Bureau, California State Library, July 1998, 3. For a detailed look at migrant conditions in the California strawberry industry, see Eric Schlosser, *Reefer Madness: Sex, Drugs, and Cheap Labor in the American Black Market* (New York: Houghton Mifflin Books, 2004).

66 *Unlike disenfranchised farmworkers* . . . John Ritter, "Pesticide Battles on the Rise in USA," *USA Today,* April 12, 2005.

By 2003, 1,290 acres . . . California Department of Food and Agriculture, 2003 State Organic Crop and Acreage Report. The 1,290 organic acres were of a total 28,230 acres, http://www.cdfa.ca.gov/is/fveqc/2003report/2003state.pdf.

3. A Local Initiative: From Farm to Market

70 *worth more than $4.3 billion* . . . Organic Trade Association, "The OTA 2004 Manufacturer Survey Overview," 2.

71 *the 1,500 to 2,500 miles* . . . See Brian Halweil, *Eat Here: Reclaiming Homegrown Pleasures in a Global Supermarket* (New York: W. W. Norton, 2004), chap. 2.

A survey of 3,500 people . . . Elaine Lipson, "La Vida Local: Support Regional Foods," *Natural Grocery Buyer,* Summer 2005, cites survey carried out by Ohio State University.

Another survey of 1,500 people . . . Leopold Center for Sustainable Agriculture and the Iowa State University Business Analysis Laboratory, "Ecolabel Value Assessment: Consumer and Food Business Perceptions of Local Foods," Iowa State University, November 2003, http://www.leopold.iastate.edu/pubs/staff/ecolabels/.

One percent . . . U.S. Census Bureau, "Statistical Abstract of the United States," 2002, found 3.054 million farmers in a total U.S. population of 291 million, http://www.census.gov/statab/www/.

compared with 23 percent . . . peak of seven million . . . From Northeast Sustainable Agriculture Working Group (NESAWG), "Northeast Farms to Food: Understanding Our Region's Food System" (Belchertown, Mass., 2002), 5, 8.

The largest 2 percent . . . Robert A. Hoppe and Penni Korb, "Farm Numbers: Largest Growing Fastest," UDSA Economic Research Service, *Agricultural Outlook,* October 2002, 27.

72 *found that 2 percent of California's* . . . Michael Sligh and Carolyn Christman, "Who Owns Organic: The Global Status, Prospects, and Challenges of a Changing Organic Market," Rural Advancement Foundation International-USA, 2003, 15, citing figures from Karen Klonsky, and others. *Statistical Picture of California's Organic Agriculture 1995–1998* (Oakland: University of California, Division of Agriculture and Natural Resources, 2003).

Pennsylvania still has . . . NESAWG, "Northeast Farms," 1.

Lancaster County . . . USDA Economic Research Service, 2002 Census of Agriculture, county data.

76 *"had rejected . . ."* Helen Nearing and Scott Nearing, *Living the Good Life* (New York: Schocken Books, 1989), 3 and chap. 1.

77 *"We yearned for . . ."* Eleanor Agnew, *Back From the Land: How Young Americans Went to Nature in the 1970s and Why They Came Back* (Chicago: Ivan R. Dee, 2004), 4–9.

78 *"The objective is not dogmatically . . ."* Duane Elgin, *Voluntary Simplicity: Toward a Life That Is Outwardly, Inwardly Rich, Revised Edition* (New York: William Morrow, 1993), 25.

84 *The USDA counted 3,706* . . . See USDA Agricultural Marketing Service, http://www.ams.usda.gov/farmersmarkets;

340 in 1970 . . . Cited in Lydia Oberholtzer and Shelly Grow, "Producer-Only Farmers' Markets in the Mid-Atlantic Region,"

Henry A. Wallace Center for Agricultural & Environmental Policy at Winrock International, October 2003, 2, and in Halweil, *Eat Here,* chap. 6.

San Francisco's bustling *...* Kim Severson, "Tourists at Market to Look Crowd Those Who Cook," *New York Times,* April 27, 2005. Background on San Francisco market at http://www .ferryplazafarmersmarket.com.

Madison, Wisconsin, boasts *...* See Madison Farmer's Market at http://www.madfarmmkt.org.

New York City alone *...* See figures of New York farmers' markets at http://www.cenyc.org/HTMLGM/maingm.htm.

less than 2 percent *...* Amy Kremen, and others. "Organic Produce, Eco-Labeling and U.S. Farmers' Markets," USDA Economic Research Service, April 2004, 2.

About 80 percent *...* Erica Walz, "Fourth National Organic Farmers Survey: Sustaining Organic Farms in a Changing Organic Marketplace," Organic Farming Research Foundation, 2004, 42.

A USDA survey *...* Kremen, and others. "Organic Produce," 4.

compared with less than 1 percent *...* It is my estimate that organic farms make up less than 1 percent of all farms, with 15,000 to 20,000 certified and noncertified organic farms nationwide.

85 ***prices farmers receive*** *...* Oberholtzer and Grow, "Producers-Only Farmers' Markets," 2.

While they still make up about half *...* Hoppe and Penni, "Farm Numbers," 24.

86 ***worries about this trend*** *...* See Rick Schnieders, CEO, Sysco Corp., Presentation to the Eighth Annual Corporate Counsel Institute, Georgetown University Law School, March 12, 2004, http://www.agofthemiddle.org.

threatens to "hollow out... *"* Fred Kirschenmann, and others. "Why Worry About Agriculture of the Middle?" http://www .agofthemiddle.org.

87 ***bigger than 96 percent*** *...* Data from Economic Research Service, table 56, "Summary by Market Value of Agricultural Products Sold: 2002," 2002 Census of Agriculture, USDA.

A 2002 survey *...* Walz, "Organic Farmers Survey," 42.

91 ***Inspectors visit*** *...* Details of certification explained by James Riddle, National Organic Standards Board, in phone interview.

92 *the fifty-six* . . . USDA National Organic Program accredited certifiers as of August 19, 2005.

93 **Only half of all organic farmers** . . . Kreman, Greene, and Hanson, "Organic Produce," 8.

100 **now number more than 1,700** . . . See Ron Strochlic and Crispin Shelley, "Community Supported Agriculture in California, Washington and Oregon: Challenges and Opportunities," California Institute for Rural Studies, May 2004, 2, http://www.cirsinc.org/news.html.

   But a 1999 survey reported . . . Daniel Lass, and others. "CSA Across the Nation: Findings from the 1999 CSA Survey," Center for Integrated Agricultural Systems, College of Agricultural and Life Sciences, University of Wisconsin–Madison, October 2003, 13, http://www.cias.wisc.edu/pdf/csaacross.pdf.

101 **promising when it opened a new store** . . . Florence Fabricant, "Wary Greenmarket Greets New Neighbor," *New York Times,* March 16, 2005.

105 **only 10 percent of all U.S. farms** . . . USDA, 2002 Census of Agriculture, "Net Cash Farm Income of the Operations and Operators: 2002."

106 *from three thousand in 1993 to seven thousand in 2001* . . . Figures cited by USDA Economic Research Service, at http://www.ers.usda.gov/Data/organic.

   nine thousand in 2004 . . . From an unpublished certifier survey conducted by Erica Walz, Organic Farming Research Foundation. The estimate of 15,000 to 20,000 farms is based upon USDA findings that only half of all organic farms at farmers' markets are certified, and on estimates of Walz at OFRF in a telephone interview.

4. A Spring Mix: Growing Organic Salad

110 **third-largest organic food brand** . . . Based on data gathered by SPINS, a San Francisco market research firm. Fifty-two week sales for Horizon Organic were $330.7 million; Silk, $324.8 million; and Earthbound, $264.7 million, through September 11, 2005. These figures do not include sales at warehouse stores like

Costco and Wal-Mart, which might propel Earthbound to the number-two spot.

111 *The Jeffersonian ideal* . . . For historical background, I relied upon Cletus Daniel, *Bitter Harvest: A History of California Farmworkers 1870–1941* (Berkeley: University of California Press, 1982), chap. 1; Stoll, *Fruits of Natural Advantage,* preface and chap. 1; also Julie Guthman, *Agrarian Dreams: The Paradox of Organic Farming in California* (Berkeley: University of California Press, 2004), chap. 4.

113 *Monterey County* . . . Monterey County Agricultural Commissioner's Office, "Monterey County 2003 Crop Report."

114 *This practice continued until* . . . Guthman, *Agrarian Dreams,* 79. *The Tanimura family* . . . Historical background at http://www.taproduce.com/About/familyhistory.html.

115 *Steinbeck thought* . . . From a compilation of his dispatches for the *San Francisco News* in 1936: John Steinbeck, *The Harvest Gypsies: On the Road to the Grapes of Wrath* (Berkeley: Heyday Books, 1988), chap. 1; also introduction by Charles Wollenberg.

116 *"It was the first time* . . ." Alice Waters, *Chez Panisse Menu Cookbook* (New York: Random House, 1982), introduction.

117 *Derived from the Provençal word* . . . See Georgeanne Brennan, *Great Greens* (San Francisco: Chronicle Books, 2003), 34. *"How well I remember* . . ." Waters, *Chez Panisse,* 164; also see Isaac Cronin, "Todd Koons and the Evolution of Salad in America," Epic Roots press material.

118 *The pair introduced* . . . Brennan, 15, and author interview with Brennan.

119 *Ultimately, the Berkeley gardens* . . . Sibella Kraus, "The Farm Restaurant Project: Regional Self-Reliance and High Quality Produce," October 1983, and author interview with Kraus.

121 *Under a contract* . . . Ibid., appendix F, an undated contract signed by Weber and Waters.

126 *What he didn't do* . . . Burkhard Bilger, "Salad Days: How a Lowly Leaf Became a High-End Delicacy," *New Yorker,* September 6, 2004.

127 *the product has a long and illustrious history* . . . See J. C. Brock, 'Pushing the Rope' With Salads, *Packer/Shipper,* May 1993; Ken Hodge, "Salt Lake Processor Is 63 and Still Growing," Interna-

tional Fresh-Cut Produce Association, Washington, D.C., 2001, and "Ready Pac Produce: Beyond the First Try," *Fresh Cut,* March/April 1994.

A company known as TransFresh . . . Sources for this history are Fresh Express corporate communications material; Dave Fusaro, "Lettuce for the '90s," *Prepared Foods,* October 1995; Brian Gaylord, "Taylor to retire at Fresh Express," *The Californian,* September 23, 2003; John Nolan, "Chiquita to Buy Bagged Salad Maker Fresh Express for $855 Million in Cash," *Associated Press,* February 23, 2005; and author interview with Steve Taylor, CEO Fresh Express.

132 *When an industry trade journal* . . . David Eddy, "Out of this World," *American Vegetable Grower,* October 2003.

137 *While organic produce* . . . Lydia Oberholtzer, and others. "Price Premiums Hold on as U.S. Organic Produce Market Expands," USDA Economic Research Service, May 2005.

139 *One was the use of Chilean nitrate* . . . Guthman, *Agrarian Dreams,* 124–125. For debates on Chilean nitrate, see minutes of National Organic Standards Board, October 31–November 4, 1995; September 17, 2002; October 19, 2002.

growers monocropped . . . Guthman, *Agrarian Dreams,* 159.

growers "were known" to have fumigated . . . Ibid., 152.

140 *As Guthman points out* . . . Ibid., chap. 8. Gutman writes, "The problem with agribusiness is its legacy of social and ecological exploitation rather than its scale of production per se," 61.

143 *"The pundits will say* . . ." See Neil Buckley, "Interview with McDonald's CEO Jim Cantalupo," *Financial Times,* August 28, 2003.

5. Mythic Manufacturing: Health, Spirituality, and Breakfast

147 *Whole grains have* . . . For background on Graham, See Stephen Nissenbaum, *Sex Diet and Debility in Jacksonian America: Sylvester Graham and Health Reform* (Westport, Conn.: Greenwood Press, 1980), and Scott Bruce and Bill Crawford, *Cerealizing America: The Unsweetened Story of American Breakfast Cereal* (Boston: Faber and Faber, 1995).

150 *Fruitlands, a transcendentalist community* . . . See Frederick C. Dahlstrand, *Amos Bronson Alcott: An Intellectual Biography* (Rutherford, N.J.: Fairleigh Dickinson University Press, 1982), and Robert D. Richardson, *Emerson: The Mind on Fire* (Berkeley: University of California Press, 1995).

151 **Dr. John Harvey Kellogg, who was raised** . . . For background on Kellogg, see Bruce and Crawford, *Cerealizing America,* chap. 1. Also Horace B. Powell, *The Original Has This Signature—W. K. Kellogg* (Englewood Cliffs, N.J.: Prentice-Hall, 1956).

152 *"salt baths, steam baths . . ."* Bruce and Crawford, *Cerealizing America,* 15.

154 *"Never had anyone . . ."* Ibid., 30.

Battle Creek turned into . . . For a brief history, see Paul Lukas, "Kellogg: Champion of Breakfast," and Maggie Overfelt, "The Flaky Cereal Rush," *Fortune Small Business,* April 2003.

155 **the marketing of health** . . . See Marion Nestle, *Food Politics: How the Food Industry Influences Nutrition and Health* (Berkeley and Los Angeles: University of California Press, 2002), 239–242.

By 2000, seven-billion-dollar Kellogg . . . Scott C. Yates, "Kellogg Gobbles Up Kashi, More to Come?" *Natural Foods Merchandiser,* August 2000.

161 **right livelihood can be understood** . . . See Lewis Richmond, *Work as a Spiritual Practice* (New York: Broadway Books, 1999); Steve Hagen, *Buddhism: Plain and Simple* (New York: Broadway Books, 1997); Bernard Glassman, *Instructions to the Cook: A Zen Master's Lessons in Living a Life that Matters* (New York: Bell Tower, 1996), 58.

162 **The Book of Tofu** . . . William Shurtleff and Akiko Aoyagi, *The Book of Tofu* (New York: Ballantine Books, 1979), first published 1975.

163 *"If all this protein . . ."* Ibid., 4.

Lappé's argument . . . Frances Moore Lappé, *Diet for a Small Planet* (New York: Ballantine Books, 1991), first published in 1971.

"These losses . . ." Shurtleff and Aoyagi, *Book of Tofu,* 5.

164 *"By rediscovering . . ."* Ibid., 10.

The book also presented . . . Ibid., 13.

The International Soy Program . . . See the Intsoy program at http://web.aces.uiuc.edu/intsoy/index.html.

165 **But the starting point** . . . Soy manufacturing process, based on interview with Peter Golbitz, president of Soyatech Inc. See also, Walter O. Scott and Samuel R. Aldrich, *Modern Soybean Production* (Champaign, Ill.: S&A Publications Inc., 1983).

creating twenty million pounds of oil . . . Consumption data from Institute of Shortening and Edible Oils, http://www.iseo.org/statistics.htm.

The soybean industry . . . United Soybean Board, "Soy Industry to Launch a Healthier Future with QUALISOY," press release, October 14, 2004, http://www.qualisoy.com/.

These oils contain . . . Agency for Toxic Substances and Disease Registry, "Toxicological Profile for n-Hexane," July 1999, http://www.atsdr.cdc.gov/toxprofiles/tp113.html.

166 **One petroleum research facility** . . . American Cancer Society, "BP Amoco Cancer Cluster," September 24, 1999, ACS News Center, http://www.cancer.org.

But the EPA . . . For EPA background on hexane, see http://www.epa.gov/ttn/atw/hlthef/hexane.html and http://www.epa.gov/iris/subst/0486.htm.

167 **With three decades' hindsight** . . . For a brief discussion of these issues, see Food and Agriculture Organization, *The State of Food Insecurity in the World 2004*, Rome, 2004, and FAO, *World Agriculture: Towards 2015/2030*, Rome, 2002.

These crops have lowered . . . See Fred Gale, Bryan Lohmar, and Francis Tuan, "China's Demand for Commodities Outpacing Supply," *Amber Waves*, U.S. Department of Agriculture, November 2004; FAO, *World Agriculture: Towards 2015/2030*, Rome, 2002; Halweil, *Eat Here*, 23–26.

169 **soybeans contain sugars** . . . See Harold McGee, *On Food and Cooking* (New York: Scribner, 2004), 493–494.

174 **Vitasoy, the top brand** . . . Shurtleff and Aoyagi, *Book of Tofu*, 294; USDA Foreign Agricultural Service, "Hong Kong Retail Foods Sector Report, 2003," Global Agricultural Information Network, November 12, 2003, 6; Shurtleff and Aoyagi, "K. S. Lo and Vitasoy in Hong Kong and North America: Work with Soyfoods," posted at http://www.thesoydailyclub.com/SFC/Vitasoy83.asp.

lactose intolerance . . . See National Digestive Diseases Information Clearinghouse, National Institutes of Health, http://digestive

.niddk.nih.gov/ddiseases/pubs/lactoseintolerance/; also McGee, *On Food and Cooking,* 14.

179 *In 1995, the* **New England Journal of Medicine** . . . See J. W. Anderson, and others. "Meta-analysis of the effects of soy protein intake on serum lipids," *New England Journal of Medicine* 333, no. 5 (August 3, 1995): 276–82.

Many of the studies were funded . . . For funding of soy studies see Center for Science in the Public Interest, Integrity in Science Project, http://cspinet.org/integrity/index.html.

180 *more than 300 soy foods* . . . Grant Ferrier and Joe Lewandowski, "No End Seen to Soy Sales Trend," *Natural Food Merchandiser,* April 1, 2002; for soy industry see Nestle, *Food Politics,* 328–330.

By 2004, there were 5,137 products . . . Based on market data from Soyatech Inc., Bar Harbor, Maine.

The hype around soy . . . For a litany of criticisms on soy, see the Weston A. Price Foundation, http://www.westonaprice.org/soy/index.html. For a counterargument, see John Robbins, "What About Soy," http://www.foodrevolution.org/what_about_soy.htm.

Since the early studies . . . See Janet Walzer, "The Soy Puzzle," *Tufts Nutrition,* Spring 2002.

There are also questions . . . For phytoestrogens and cancer, see, "You've Survived the Cancer—Now What?" *Tufts Health and Nutrition Letter,* February 2003; also see Laurie Tarken, "As a Hormone Substitute, Soy Is Ever More Popular, but Is It Safe?" *New York Times,* August 24, 2004.

181 *The Okinawa Centenarian Study* . . . For the Okinawan study, see http://www.okinawaprogram.com.

It takes about a pound and a half . . . A hundred-weight of milk (11.63 gallons) costs about $22 or $1.89 a gallon; a bushel of soybeans (60 pounds) costs about $18.00 or $0.30 a pound. Author interviews with Golbitz, Demos, Nordquist.

183 *As for Engles* . . . Janet Adamy, "Behind a Food Giant's Success: An Unlikely Soy-Milk Alliance," *Wall Street Journal,* February 1, 2005.

split the $192.8 million . . . See Dean Foods Company, *2004 Annual Report,* Dallas, Texas, 59.

185 *"The fact that* . . ." For a discussion of Hirshberg's deal, see David

Goodman, "Culture Change," *Mother Jones,* January/February 2003, and Julie Rose, "Selling His Soul To Dannon?" *Fortune Small Business,* December 2001.

6. Backlash: The Meaning of Organic

188 ***Hard as I try*** . . . From September 1992 to September 1996, the National Organic Program only kept minutes of National Organic Standards Board meetings, then has no minutes of meetings held after September 1996 through February 1999. NOP began keeping minutes once again in February 1999 and in June 2001 began recording meetings and offering public transcripts. Meeting minutes are posted at http://www.ams.usda.gov/nosb/archives/archive .html and transcripts at http://www.ams.usda.gov/nosb/transcripts/ transcripts.html. Pierce's comment appears in the transcript of the NOSB meeting on May 14, 2003.

*"**Who SHOULD Own Organic?** . . ."* Elizabeth Henderson's speech can be found at http://www.newfarm.org/depts/talking_shop/ 0304/moseshenderson.shtml.

190 ***Her talk was similar*** . . . Wendell Berry's address at the "Agriculture for a Small Planet" conference can be seen at http://www .tilthproducers.org/berry 1974.htm. See also Wendell Berry, *The Unsettling of America: Culture and Agriculture* (San Francisco: Sierra Club Books, 1977).

191 *"**money with a great deal of suspicion** . . ."* Charles Frazier, *Cold Mountain* (New York: Vintage Books, 1997), 95.

192 ***Writer Michael Pollan*** . . . See Michael Pollan, "Naturally: Behind the Organic-Industrial Complex," *New York Times Magazine,* May 13, 2001.

193 *"**An ecological-based system** . . ."* See Vicky Uhland, "The Path of Kahn," *Natural Foods Merchandiser,* March 1, 2004.

*"**I've always been a scale freak** . . ."* Ibid.

196 ***The "Great Carrot Caper*** . . ." See Elliot Diringer, "Carrot Bombshell Hits Organic Industry," *San Francisco Chronicle,* May 12, 1988.

Nine years later, a food wholesaler . . . For a discussion of fraud cases, see USDA, "U.S. National Standards on Organic Agricultural

Production and Handling, Appendixes to Preamble: Appendix A. Regulatory Impact Assessment for Final Rule Implementing the Organic Foods Production Act of 1990," National Organic Program, http://www.ams.usda.gov/nop/NOP/standards/FullText.pdf

"Clearly, some organic samples . . ." See Charles M. Benbrook, "Minimizing Pesticide Dietary Exposure Through the Consumption of Organic Food," an Organic Center State of Science Review, May 2004, 23, http://www.organic-center.org/science.htm?groupid=4.

New York City food retailers . . . See Marrion Burros, "Stores Say Wild Salmon, But Tests Say Farm Raised," *New York Times,* April 10, 2005.

"If a labeling concept . . ." See Mark Lipson, "The First 'Ecolabel': Lesson from the Organic Experience," OFRF, February 1998. Also see Elaine Lipson, "A Brief History of the National Organic Standards," *California Certified Organic Farmers Newsletter,* Spring 1998, for the early history of organic regulations, CCOF, Santa Cruz, California.

197 *As early as 1994 . . .* See minutes of NOSB, October 10, 1994, 12–13, also Lipson, "Brief History," see minutes at http://www.ams.usda.gov/nosb/archives/archive.html.

198 *the Clinton administration . . .* See Leora Broydo, "Organic Engineering," *Mother Jones,* May/June 1998, and accompanying memo at http://www.motherjones.com/news/outfront/1998/05/usda_doc1.html.

199 *a record 275,603 comments . . .* Figures from author interview with Merrigan.

Working Assets . . . See this and other form letters at http://www.ams.usda.gov/nop/archive/1997comments/1997FormLetters.html.

200 *the Organic Trade Association's . . .* See "A Proposed Clarification of 'Origin of Livestock' Comments of the Organic Trade Association to the National Organic Standards Board," Organic Trade Association, October 19, 2002, http://www.ota.com/standards/nosb/otacomments/20021019com.html.

201 *But limited antibiotic use . . .* The regulations also allowed organic dairy farmers to bring conventionally raised "replacement heifers," or young cows, onto the organic farm, if they converted to organic

production before 2002 or with 100 percent organic feed for a year, an approach followed by well-capitalized farms. Conventional heifers are routinely treated with medicines and antibiotics from birth, though are drug-free once on the organic farm. Other farms transitioning with only 80 percent organic feed and 20 percent conventional grain in the first nine months of a year-long dairy-herd conversion had to rely on only organically reared heifers. The NOSB voted to close this inconsistency and require all organic farms to rely upon organically reared calves, but the NOP never acted on this recommendation. Although Congress modified the transition for organic dairy farms in 2005, by easing the organic feed requirements, the law change did not address replacement heifers, meaning conventionally raised calves treated with antibiotics could still enter an organic farm.

At the semiannual meeting . . . See NOSB transcript, April 28, 2004, 168–260, http://www.ams.usda.gov/nosb/transcripts/transcripts .html.

203 *Appearing before the NOSB* . . . See NOSB transcript, May 8, 2002, http://www.ams.usda.gov/nosb/transcripts/transcripts.html; see also "Who is Arthur Harvey and Why Did He Sue the USDA?" *Organic Business News,* vol. 16, no. 12, December 2004, posted at http:// www.organicconsumers.org/organic/morelawsuit010505.cfm.

205 *"Organic foods in the form* . . ." See Soil Association, "Processed Food and the Soil Association—Some Common Questions Answered," information sheet, October 8, 2003.

206 *By 2004, multi-ingredient* . . . OTA, "The OTA 2004 Overview," May 2004, http://www.ota.com/pics/documents/ 2004SurveyOverview.pdf.

207 *In an internal poll* . . . Author interview with Katherine DiMatteo, OTA.

California's first organic law . . . See Lisa Hamilton, "Mainstreaming America to Organic Processed Food," *CCOF Magazine* (Summer 2004).

208 *As late as 1993* . . . See NOSB minutes, July 9, 1993, http://www .ams.usda.gov/nosb/archives/archive.html.

209 *USDA staffers* . . . See NOSB minutes, July 10, 1993, http://www .ams.usda.gov/nosb/archives/archive.html.

210 **Only one NOSB member** . . . For votes and debates on the synthetics issue, see NOSB minutes, May 18, 1993; July 10, 1993; April 24, 1995; April 26, 1995; October 31–November 4, 1995, http://www.ams.usda.gov/nosb/archives/archive.html.

211 **As Sligh later stated** . . . See Michael Sligh, "Toward Organic Integrity: A Guide to the Development of U.S. Organic Standards," Rural Advancement Foundation International—USA, July 1997. **Joan Dye Gussow** . . . See Joan Dye Gussow, "Can an Organic Twinkie Be Certified?" *For All Generations: Making World Agriculture More Sustainable* (WSAA Publications, 1997), 143–153. **organic chocolate truffles** . . . One serving (3 pieces) contains 11 grams of saturated fat or 55 percent of the daily recommended amount, according to the nutrition label data. **In another essay** . . . Kate Clancy and Frederick Kirschenmann, "Keeping it 'Organic': Making Sense Out of the Processing of Organic Food," June 4, 1999, posted at http://www.biotech-info.net.

212 **In a reply, Kahn** . . . Gene Kahn, Craig Weakley, and Steven Harper, "A Response to 'Keeping it Organic': Making Sense Out of the Processing of Organic Food," June 12, 1999, posted at http://www.pmac.net/spf.html.

213 **On this vote, the board** . . . NOSB minutes, February 9–11, 1999, http://www.ams.usda.gov/nosb/archives/archive.html. Also based on author interviews with DiMatteo, Kirschenmann, and Gussow.

214 **issued a statement in late 2002** . . . See National Organic Program, "Synthetic Substances Subject to Review and Recommendation by the National Organic Standards Board When Such Substances Are Used as Ingredients in Processed Food Products," USDA, December 12, 2002, http://www.ams.usda.gov/nop/NOP/PolicyStatements/SyntheticSubstances.html. **styrene-divinylbenzene** . . . Author interview with Urvashi Rangan, Consumer Union. **"Just as the use** . . ." Yvonne Frost, Brian Baker, and Emily Rosen, Organic Materials Review Institute, "Ion Exchange Resins," memo to the USDA NOP, October 16, 2002; OMRI, "The National Organic Program Policy on Synthetic Substances Used in Food Processing, A Background Paper," May 7, 2003; Emily

Brown Rosen, Policy Director Organic Materials Review Institute, NOSB testimony, May 13, 2003; author interviews with Urvashi Rangan, Consumers Union, and Emily Brown Rosen, OMRI.

215 *Still they worried about the impact* . . . See "Statement from Organizations Concerning the Outcome of Harvey v. Veneman, Docket No. 04-1379 (1st Cir.)," March 17, 2005, at http://www .organicconsumers.org/organic/statement031805.cfm.

216 *"We now find ourselves . . ."* James Riddle, e-mail, September 25, 2005.

218 *Organic milk had grown 20 percent a year* . . . OTA, "The OTA 2004 Overview," May 2004, http://www.ota.com/pics/documents/ 2004SurveyOverview.pdf.

"When people look for organic food . . ." Horizon executive quoted in Aaron Dalton, "Organic Milk: The Cream of the Crop," *Natural Grocery Buyer*, Spring 2005; see Rebecca Clarren, "Land of Milk and Money," Salon.com, April 13, 2005; OTA, "The OTA 2004 Overview," May 2004, http://www.ota.com/pics/documents/ 2004SurveyOverview.pdf.

The cows need to be fed . . . In the year-long dairy herd transition, cows may be fed pasture and forages that are in the third year of the dairy farm's transition. This change to the OFPA adopted in 2005 meant that a dairy farm could transition its entire operation—fields, pasture, and cows—in a total of three years.

220 *grazing operations have tripled* . . . Grazing farms rose from 7.3 percent of Wisconsin dairy farms in 1993 to nearly 22 percent in 1999. See Matthew J. Mariola, Kaelyn Stiles, and Sarah Lloyd, "The Social Implications of Management Intensive Rotational Grazing: An Annotated Bibliography," Center for Integrated Agricultural Systems University of Wisconsin (Madison), January 2005, http://www.cias.wisc.edu/bibliog2.php.

44 percent . . . USDA, "2002 Census of Agriculture," http://www .nass.usda.gov/census.

Nationally, only 5 to 15 percent . . . Jonathan R. Winsten and Bryan T. Petrucci, "Seasonal Dairy Grazing: A Viable Alternative for the 21st Century," Henry A. Wallace Center for Agricultural and Environmental Policy at Winrock International and American Farmland Trust, February 2003.

At the extreme . . . For a brief discussion, see Hubert J. Karreman, *Treating Dairy Cows Naturally: Thoughts and Strategies* (Paradise, Pa.: Paradise Publications, 2004); daily manure figures cited by farmers author interviewed; on subacute rumen acidosis, see Tharron Gains, "Guarding Against a Silent Thief," *Western Dairy Business,* September 2000; also based on author interview with Kathy Soder, animal scientist, Pasture Systems and Watershed Management Research Unit, USDA Agricultural Research Service.

221 *In the land-intensive grazing model* . . . For a discussion of the benefits of grazing, see Winsten and Petrucci, "Seasonal Dairy Grazing."

40 pounds of milk a day . . . Figures from author interview with Professor T. R. Dhiman, Utah State University.

A 1999 study . . . T. R. Dhiman, and others. "Conjugated Linoleic Acid Content of Milk from Cows Fed Different Diets," *Journal of Dairy Science* 82, no. 10 (1999): 2146–2156.

A 2004 study . . . Author interview with Jacob Nielsen, director of the Food Science Research Section at the Danish Institute of Agricultural Sciences. See also report at http://www.darcof.dk/enews/sep04/milk.html.

224 *Horizon spent $24 million* . . . Emily Esterson, "How Can I Dominate My Competitors," *Inc.,* September 1999, at http://www.inc.com/articles/1999/09/11805.html.

While the Idaho farm . . . See Rebecca Clarren, "Land of Milk and Money," Salon.com, April 13, 2005.

As early as 1993 . . . See NOSB minutes, May 16, 1993. Retzloff was not alone in this position, as even George Siemon said: "Mandating pasture is a mistake; the issue is what is best ecologically for each farm. Address density instead," according to these minutes. In 1999, Retzloff submitted a statement to the NOSB saying that "We strongly suggest that the NOSB amend the requirement for managed pasture to read 'recommend' or 'encourage' . . . instead of 'shall' or 'require.'" He continued, "the NOSB would limit the organic conversion of conventional dairy farmers by requiring pasture," see attachment to NOSB meeting minutes, February 9–11, 1999, http://www.ams.usda.gov/nosb/archives/archive.html.

225 *critics worried about studies* . . . See Sandra Steingrabber, "The Ecology of Pizza," part 8, for a brief but illuminating discussion

of this issue, http://www.theorganicreport.com/pages/328_the_ ecology_of_pizza_part_8.cfm.

"It is too early . . ." See Cornell University's Program on Breast Cancer and Environmental Risk Factors, fact sheet, at http://envirocancer .cornell.edu/Factsheet/Diet/fs37.hormones.cfm.

227 **If his figures were right** . . . 2,900 acres of irrigated lands would support 290 to 580 cows, at a density of 5 to 10 acres per cow; 12,000 acres of native grasslands would support 300 to 480 cows, at 25 to 40 acres per cow. That means a total of 590 to 1,060 cows. **While its Web site showed** . . . See http://www.auroraorganic.com. *"If we're not the lowest . . ."* Vicky Uhland, "Horizon Founder Launches Private-Label Organic Dairy," *Natural Foods Merchandiser,* February 1, 2004. See also Tom Locke, "Colorado Companies Find Financial Backers, A Real Cash Cow," *Denver Business Journal,* October 31, 2003.

"With consumer demand . . ." See Aurora Organic, "Aurora Dairy Corporation receives growth capital financing," press release, October 21, 2003, http://www.auroraorganic.com/aodweb/site/ itemContent.aspx?iContentID=23&iCategoryID=5&iSubCate goryID=1.

228 **One group, the Northeast Organic** . . . Source for number of organic dairy farms is NODPA; for the article, see Kathie Arnold, "Aurora Dairy Goes Organic In Colorado," *NODPA News,* August 2004, http://www.nodpa.com/newsletter.html.

membership of 179 . . . Source is NODPA, Ed Maltby, e-mail, April 12, 2005.

"Can anyone who really understands . . ." See *NODPA News,* November 2005, 12, http://www.nodpa.com/newsletter.html.

229 *"I will be very surprised . . ."* Joel McNair, "Organic 'Cheese Whiz' Hard to Stomach," *The Milkweed,* June 2004. Reprinted in *NODPA News,* August 2004, http://www.nodpa.com/newsletter .html.

conventional milk prices . . . See Scott Kilman, "Dairy Aisle's Secret: Milk Is a Cash Cow," *Wall Street Journal,* July 28, 2003.

Demand for milk . . . Milk demand figures from USDA Economic Research Service, Food Consumption Data System, http://www .ers.usda.gov/data/foodconsumption.

Dairy farmers who couldn't compete . . . See Kilman, "Dairy Aisle's

Secret"; also author interview with Gary Hirshberg, CEO, Stonyfield Farm, who received correspondence from northeast dairy
farmers short of food.

"The farmers calling me . . ." Brenda Cochran's columns "Dispatches from Dairyland," available at http://www.newfarm.org/
archive/columns.shtml#dairy.

231 *the Cornucopia Institute* . . . See Cornucopia Institute, "Complaint
concerning violation of the NOP pasture rule by the Aurora Organic," January 10, 2005, at http://www.cornucopia.org/aurora_
complaint.html. The complaint was eventually dismissed by the
NOP.

232 *Aurora's officials* . . . See NOSB meeting transcript, March 1,
2005, http://www.ams.usda.gov/nosb/transcripts/transcripts.html.
"The full set of data . . ." For this and other comments see
http://www.ams.usda.gov/nosb/PublicComments/Feb05/
AccessToPasture.html.
"You do have people . . ." NOSB meeting transcript, March 1,
2005, http://www.ams.usda.gov/nosb/transcripts/transcripts.html.

233 *The company later announced* . . . See Horizon Organic, "Land
Stewardship Initiative Announced by Horizon Organic," press
release, December 6, 2005, http://www.horizonorganic.com/
newsreleases/2005/landstewardship.html.
Even the USDA Office of Inspector General . . . See Office of Inspector General Northeast Region, "Audit Report: Agricultural
Market Service's National Organic Program," July 14, 2005, page i,
http://www.usda.gov/oig/rptsauditsams.htm.

7. Consuming Organic: Why We Buy

238 *articulated by William Grimes* . . . See William Grimes, "A Pleasure Palace Without the Guilt," *New York Times,* February 18,
2004.

239 *The restaurant movement* . . . See Frank Bruni, "The Contemporary Dining Scene, Est. 1985," *New York Times,* October 12, 2005.

240 *Fifty-five percent* . . . For these statistics see Food Marketing Institute, "Shopping for Health 2004: Making Sense of Nutrition

News and Health Claims," Food Marketing Institute, and *Prevention*, 2005.

Pesticides, antibiotics, and hormones . . . See Roper Public Affairs, "Food and Farming 2004, Prepared for Organic Valley Family of Farms," April 30, 2004, for a survey on attitudes toward these substances, http://organicvalley.coop/pdf/roper_survey.pdf.

health and nutrition motivate . . . See FMI survey, "Shopping for Health," tables 36 and 37. These findings are supported by many other surveys, too, though percentages differ slightly.

241 *When the cofounder and CEO* . . . See Charles Fishman, "The Anarchist's Cookbook," *Fast Company*, July 2004, about the origins of the company.

"We didn't think . . ." See Amanda Griscom Little, "The Whole Foods Shebang: An Interview With John Mackey," December 17, 2004, http://www.grist.org/news/maindish/2004/12/17/little-mackey.

242 *Selling meat* . . . See Fishman, "Anarchist's Cookbook," also Little, "Whole Foods Shebang."

The company won . . . PETA named Whole Foods the Best Animal-Friendly Retailer, saying, "Whole Foods has consistently done more for animal welfare than any retailer in the industry," http://www.peta.org/feat/proggy/2004/winners.html.

The company's broader success . . . See Fishman, "Anarchist's Cookbook," for a good description of how the business works; also see John Gertner, "The Virtue in $6 Heirloom Tomatoes," *New York Times Magazine*, June 6, 2004.

244 *"the temptation to contract . . ."* John Mackey e-mail to employees, July 17, 2002.

A year later, two organizers . . . See Laurie Apple, "Whole Foods Union Busting?" *Austin Chronicle*, December 20, 2002. For background on the Madison dispute, see http://www.wholeworkersunite.org.

245 *"What if we only sold . . ."* Little, "Whole Foods Shebang."

When the Hartman Group . . . The Hartman Group, "Organic Consumer Evolution 2003," Spring 2003, Hartman Group, Bellevue, Washington.

246 *The Food Marketing Institute* . . . FMI, "Shopping for Health," 55.

In Washington, D.C., a local nonprofit . . . Lindsay Ryan, "Where Gardens Fill a Supermarket Void"; Petula Dvorak, "Ward 8 Is Getting a Supermarket (Yes It's True)"; Petula Dvorak, "Fresh Alternatives in Anacostia," *Washington Post*, August 4, 2005.

247 *Poor diet* . . . See Joann Loviglio, "Initiative aims to bring healthy food to inner city," Associated Press, September 26, 2005.

While Whole Foods . . . "We tend to appeal to higher income, higher education levels, smaller family size," John Mackey said at the company's 2004 annual meeting. Wild Oats described its customer as college educated with a median income over $65,000, at a 2003 investor meeting.

Only 11 percent . . . FMI, "Shopping for Health," 60, table 35.

the shoppers who frequent these stores . . . See Laurie Budgar, "Organic Cereals Snap, Crackle, Pop with Growth," *Natural Foods Merchandiser*, market overview, 2003.

milk, soy milk, baby food . . . Mainstream stores dominate in nondairy organic beverages (86 percent of all sales), organic packaged produce (75 percent), organic baby food (74 percent) and organic dairy (74 percent), cited in ibid.

248 *They call these premium products* . . . Michael J. Silverstein and Neil Fiske, *Trading Up: The New American Luxury* (New York: Portfolio, 2003), see chap. 1.

They sold 81 percent . . . See Janet Adamy, "Grocery Stores Cut Out The Weekly Special," *Wall Street Journal*, July 20, 2005.

"Anyway, I make up . . ." See Melanie Warner, "An Identity Crisis for Supermarkets," *New York Times*, October 6, 2005. Whole Foods makes more money from its pricing too, with gross profit—sales, minus the cost of goods—averaging around 35 percent, compared with 25–30 percent for a traditional grocer.

251 *the underpaid but well-educated shopper* . . . See Athima Chansanchai, "Trader Joe's Shoppers in the Market for Love," *Seattle Post-Intelligencer*, April 2, 2005.

253 *number of consumers* **declined** *in 2004* . . . Natural Marketing Institute, "Organic Food & Beverage Sales Increase 18 percent; Household Penetration Decreases," press release, February 22, 2005, Harleysville, Pennsylvania.

254 *"I feel that it is crucial* . . ." George Siemon, e-mail, September 23, 2005.